THE WOODS

JAMES **TYNION** IV • MICHAEL DIALYNAS

VOL. 1
THE ARROW

BOOM! STUDIOS

THE WOODS Volume One, September 2014. Published by BOOM! Studios, a division of Boom Entertainment, Inc. The Woods is ™ & © 2014 Boom Entertainment, Inc. Originally published in single magazine form as THE WOODS No. 1-4. ™ & © 2014 Boom Entertainment, Inc. All rights reserved. BOOM! Studios™ and the BOOM! Studios logo are trademarks of Boom Entertainment, Inc., registered in various countries and categories. All characters, events, and institutions depicted herein are fictional. Any similarity between any of the names, characters, persons, events, and/or institutions in this publication to actual names, characters, and persons, whether living or dead, events, and/or institutions is unintended and purely coincidental. BOOM! Studios does not read or accept unsolicited submissions of ideas, stories, or artwork.

A catalog record of this book is available from OCLC and from the BOOM! Studios website, www.boom-studios.com, on the Librarians page.

BOOM! Studios, 5670 Wilshire Boulevard, Suite 450, Los Angeles, CA 90036-5679. Printed in Canada. First Printing.

ISBN: 978-1-60886-454-6, eISBN: 978-1-61398-308-9

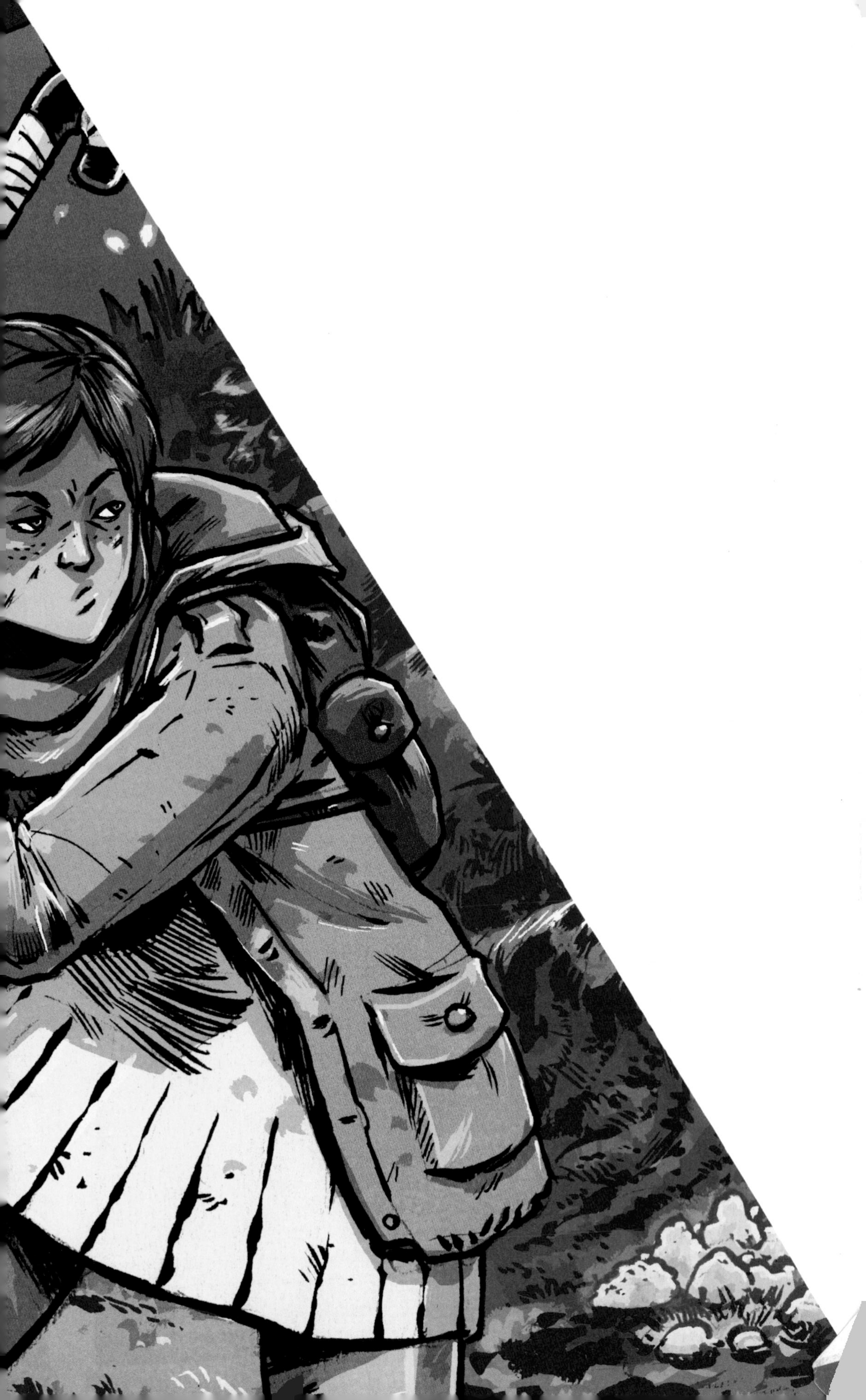

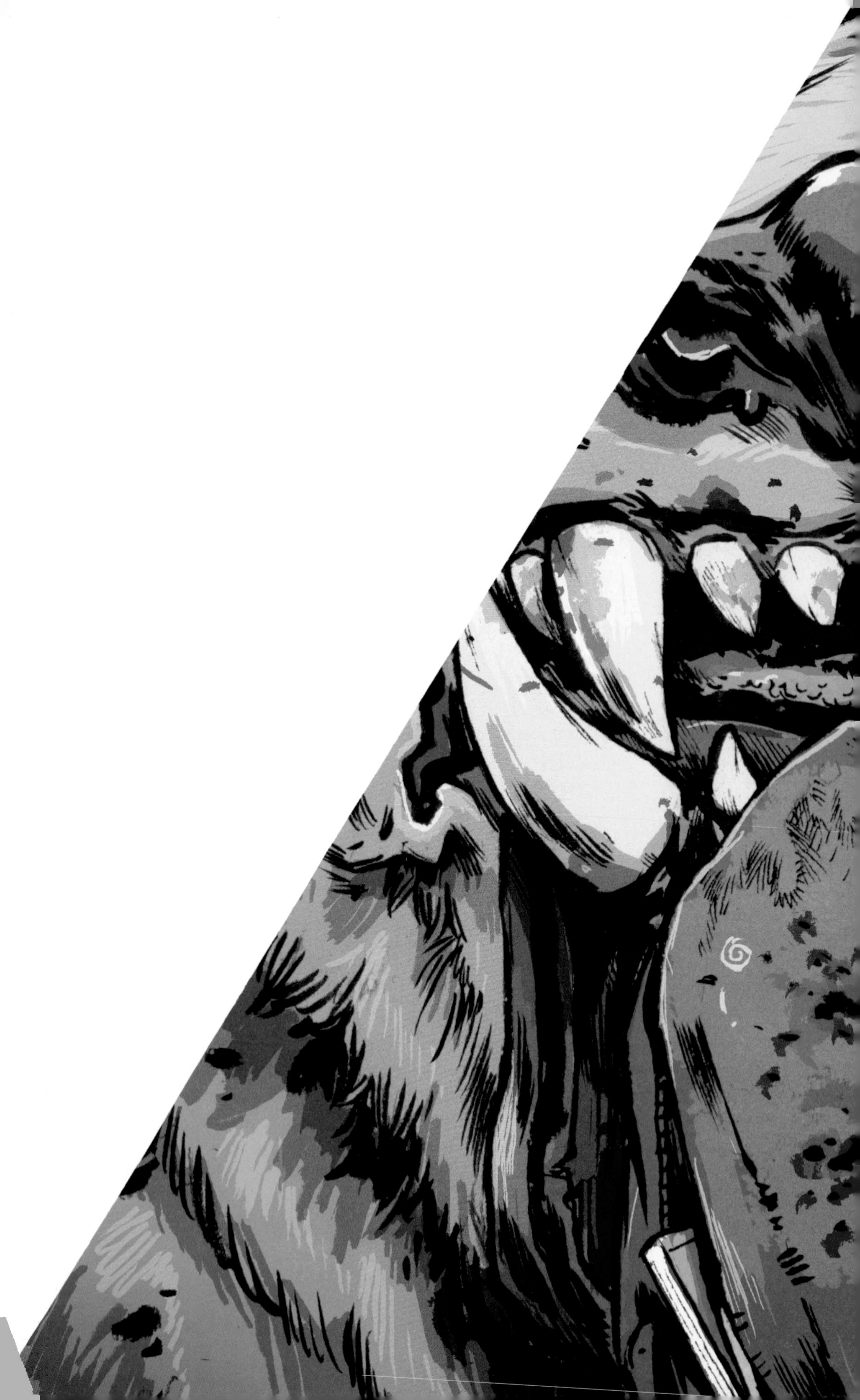

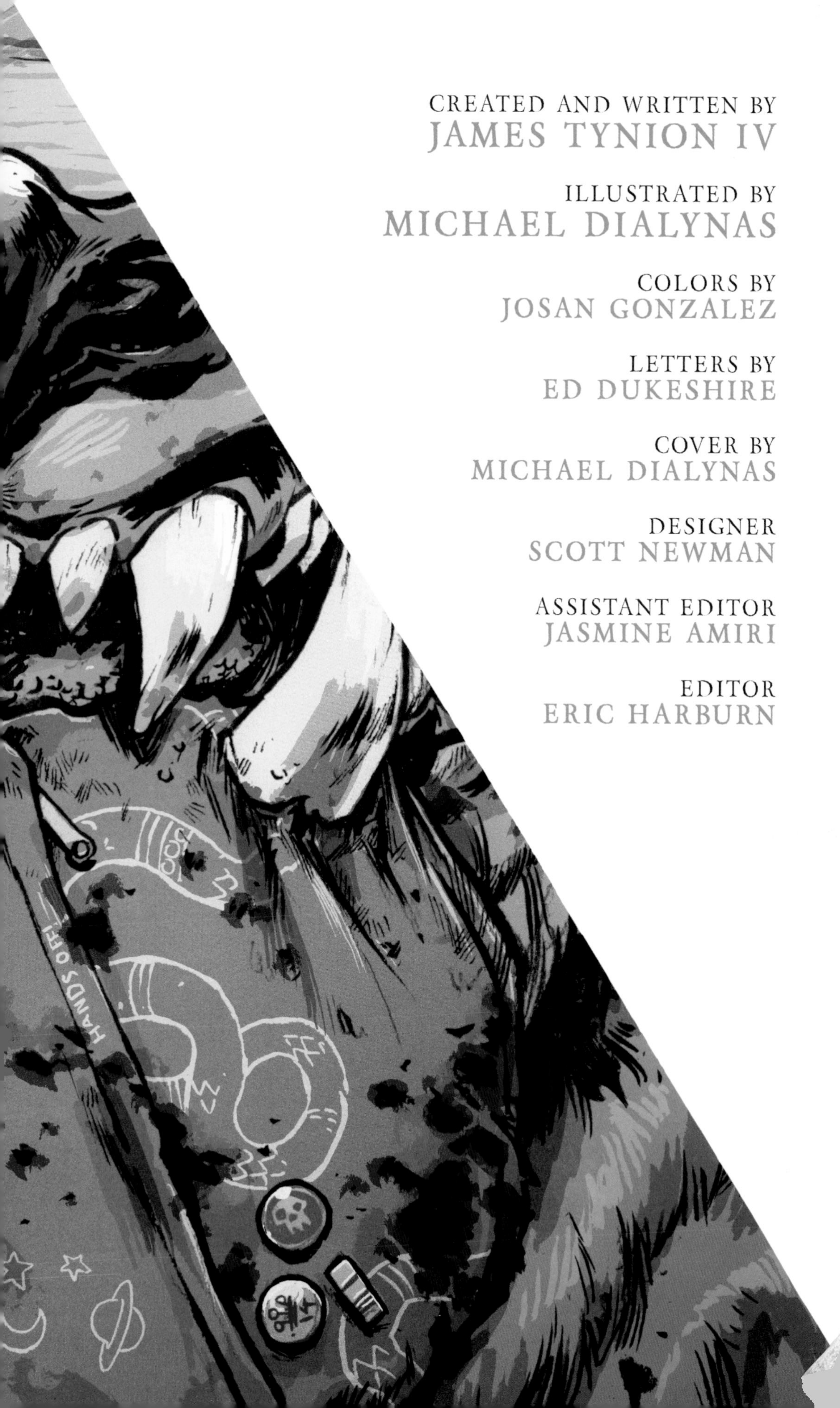
HANDS OFF!

CREATED AND WRITTEN BY
JAMES TYNION IV

ILLUSTRATED BY
MICHAEL DIALYNAS

COLORS BY
JOSAN GONZALEZ

LETTERS BY
ED DUKESHIRE

COVER BY
MICHAEL DIALYNAS

DESIGNER
SCOTT NEWMAN

ASSISTANT EDITOR
JASMINE AMIRI

EDITOR
ERIC HARBURN

CHAPTER
ONE

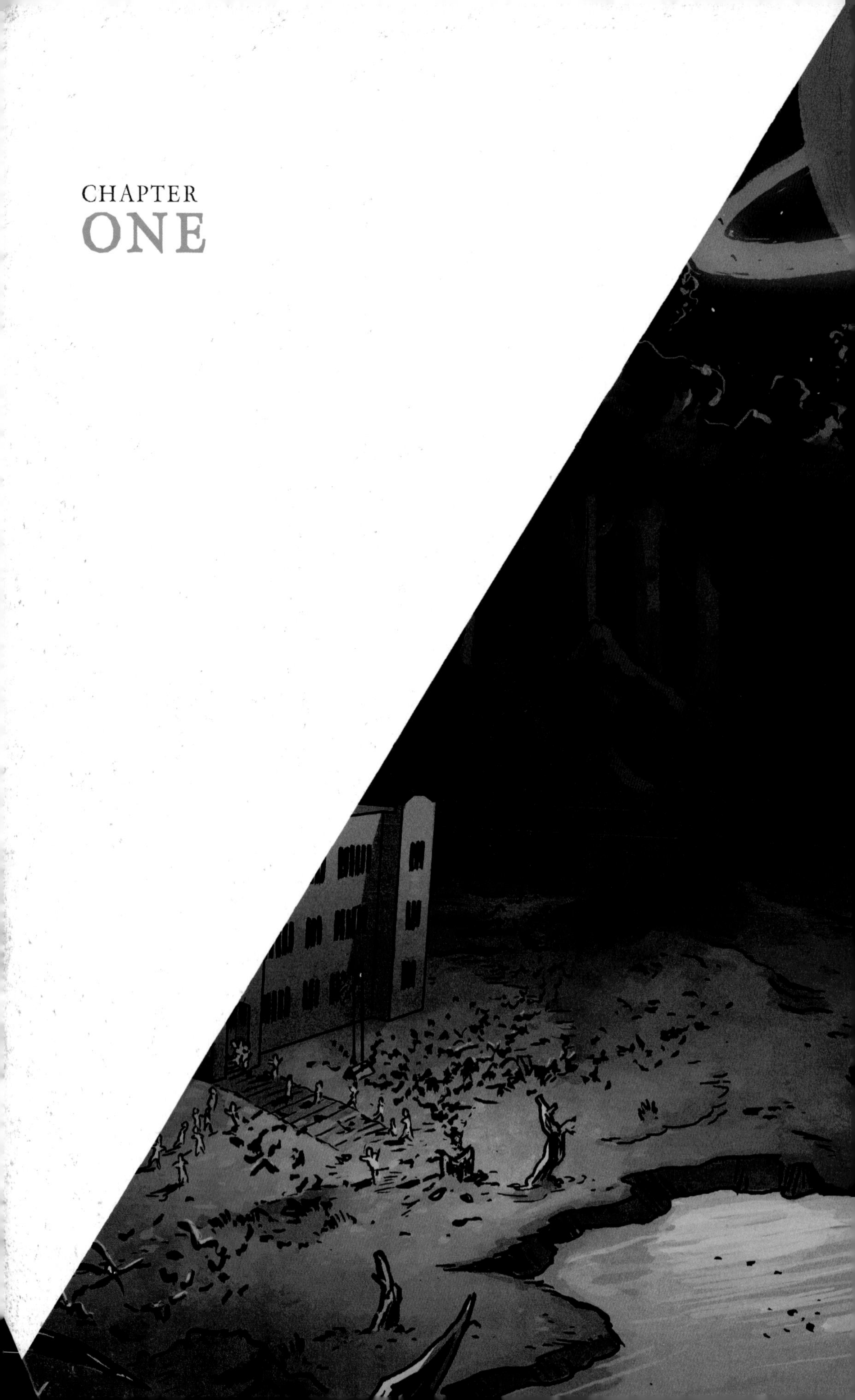

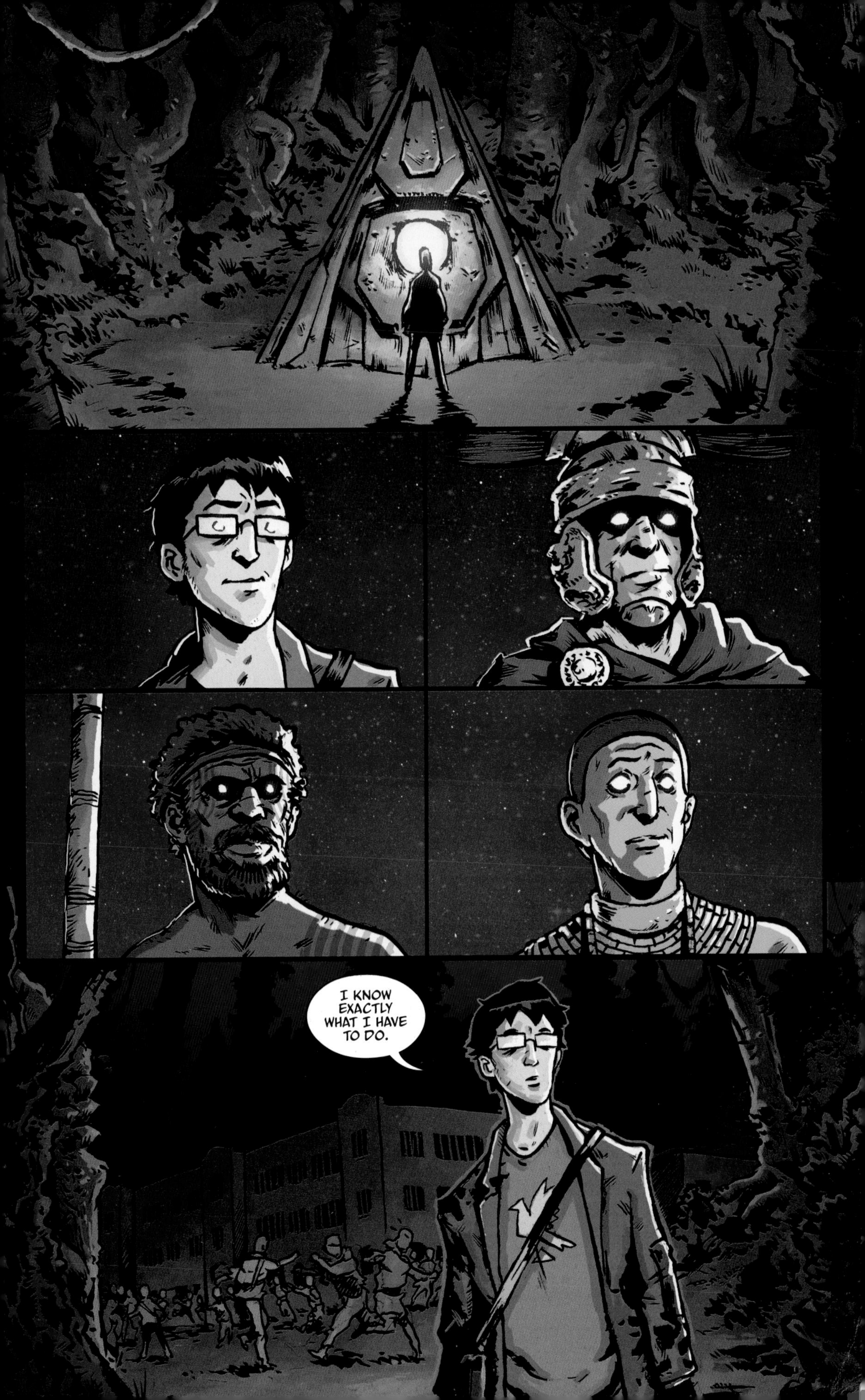
I KNOW EXACTLY WHAT I HAVE TO DO.

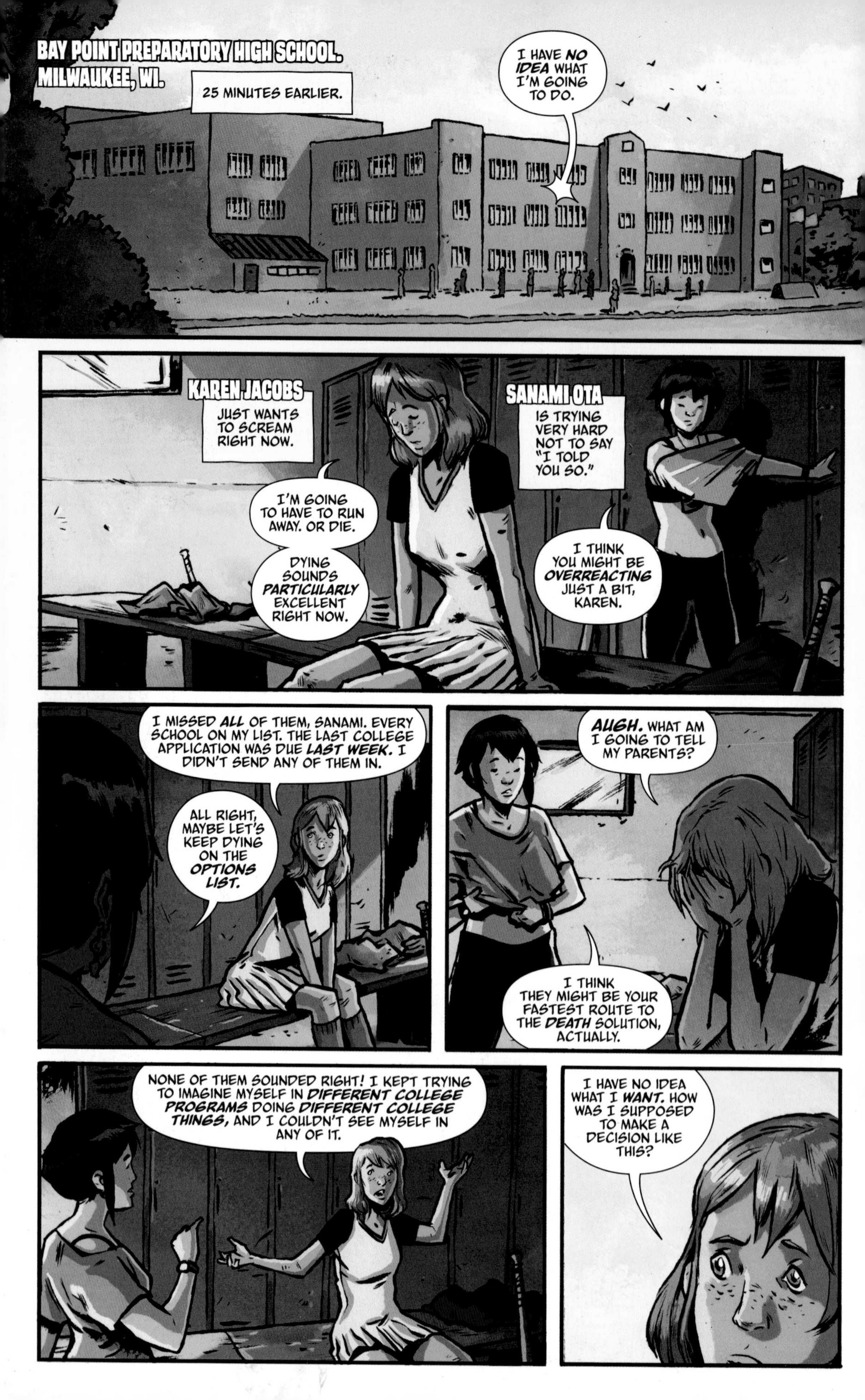
BAY POINT PREPARATORY HIGH SCHOOL.
MILWAUKEE, WI.
25 MINUTES EARLIER.
I HAVE NO IDEA WHAT I'M GOING TO DO.
KAREN JACOBS
JUST WANTS TO SCREAM RIGHT NOW.
I'M GOING TO HAVE TO RUN AWAY. OR DIE.
DYING SOUNDS PARTICULARLY EXCELLENT RIGHT NOW.
SANAMI OTA
IS TRYING VERY HARD NOT TO SAY "I TOLD YOU SO."
I THINK YOU MIGHT BE OVERREACTING JUST A BIT, KAREN.
I MISSED ALL OF THEM, SANAMI. EVERY SCHOOL ON MY LIST. THE LAST COLLEGE APPLICATION WAS DUE LAST WEEK. I DIDN'T SEND ANY OF THEM IN.
ALL RIGHT, MAYBE LET'S KEEP DYING ON THE OPTIONS LIST.
AUGH. WHAT AM I GOING TO TELL MY PARENTS?
I THINK THEY MIGHT BE YOUR FASTEST ROUTE TO THE DEATH SOLUTION, ACTUALLY.
NONE OF THEM SOUNDED RIGHT! I KEPT TRYING TO IMAGINE MYSELF IN DIFFERENT COLLEGE PROGRAMS DOING DIFFERENT COLLEGE THINGS, AND I COULDN'T SEE MYSELF IN ANY OF IT.
I HAVE NO IDEA WHAT I WANT. HOW WAS I SUPPOSED TO MAKE A DECISION LIKE THIS?

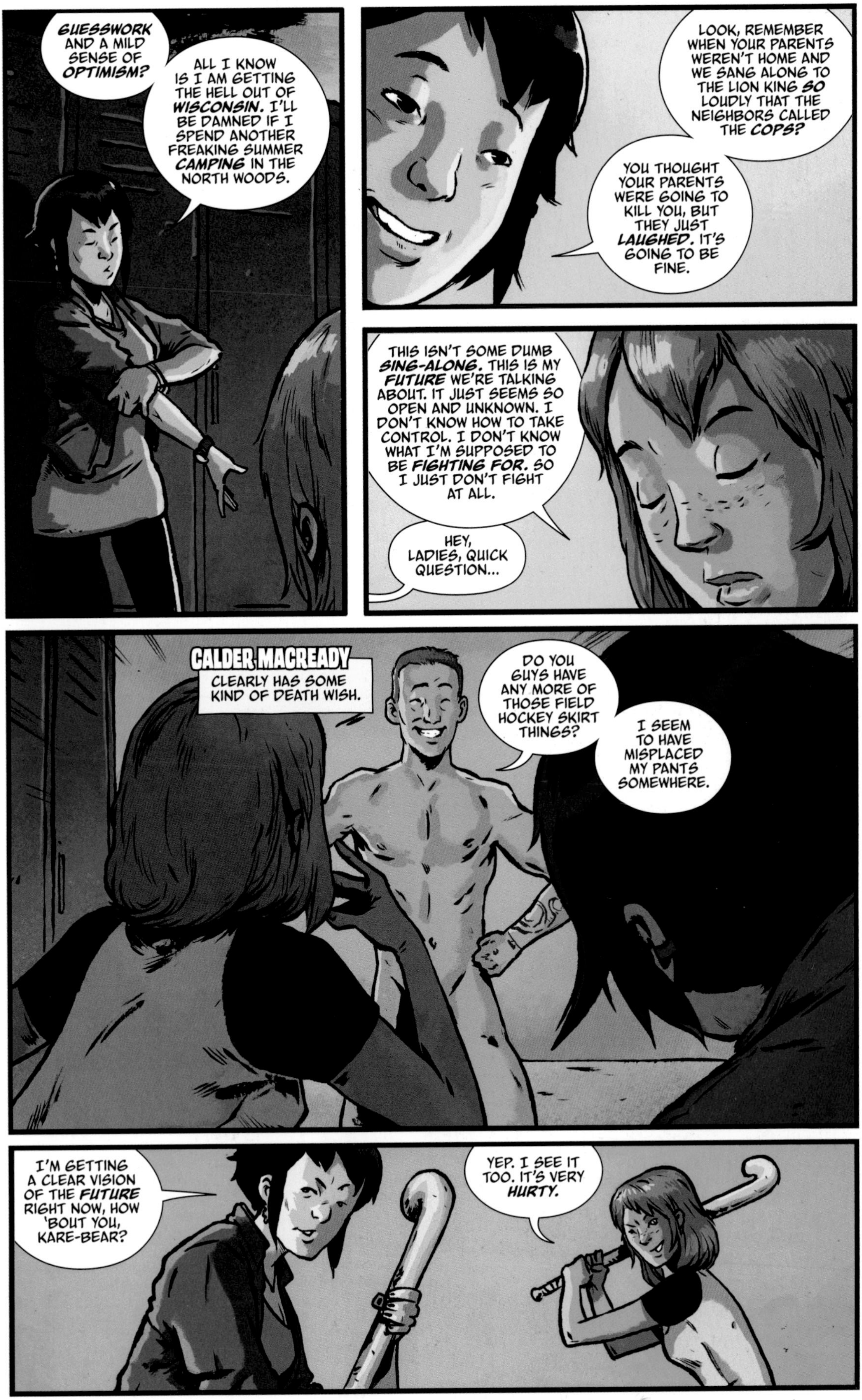
GUESSWORK AND A MILD SENSE OF OPTIMISM?
ALL I KNOW IS I AM GETTING THE HELL OUT OF WISCONSIN. I'LL BE DAMNED IF I SPEND ANOTHER FREAKING SUMMER CAMPING IN THE NORTH WOODS.
LOOK, REMEMBER WHEN YOUR PARENTS WEREN'T HOME AND WE SANG ALONG TO THE LION KING SO LOUDLY THAT THE NEIGHBORS CALLED THE COPS?
YOU THOUGHT YOUR PARENTS WERE GOING TO KILL YOU, BUT THEY JUST LAUGHED. IT'S GOING TO BE FINE.
THIS ISN'T SOME DUMB SING-ALONG. THIS IS MY FUTURE WE'RE TALKING ABOUT. IT JUST SEEMS SO OPEN AND UNKNOWN. I DON'T KNOW HOW TO TAKE CONTROL. I DON'T KNOW WHAT I'M SUPPOSED TO BE FIGHTING FOR. SO I JUST DON'T FIGHT AT ALL.
HEY, LADIES, QUICK QUESTION...
CALDER MACREADY
CLEARLY HAS SOME KIND OF DEATH WISH.
DO YOU GUYS HAVE ANY MORE OF THOSE FIELD HOCKEY SKIRT THINGS?
I SEEM TO HAVE MISPLACED MY PANTS SOMEWHERE.
I'M GETTING A CLEAR VISION OF THE FUTURE RIGHT NOW, HOW 'BOUT YOU, KARE-BEAR?
YEP. I SEE IT TOO. IT'S VERY HURTY.

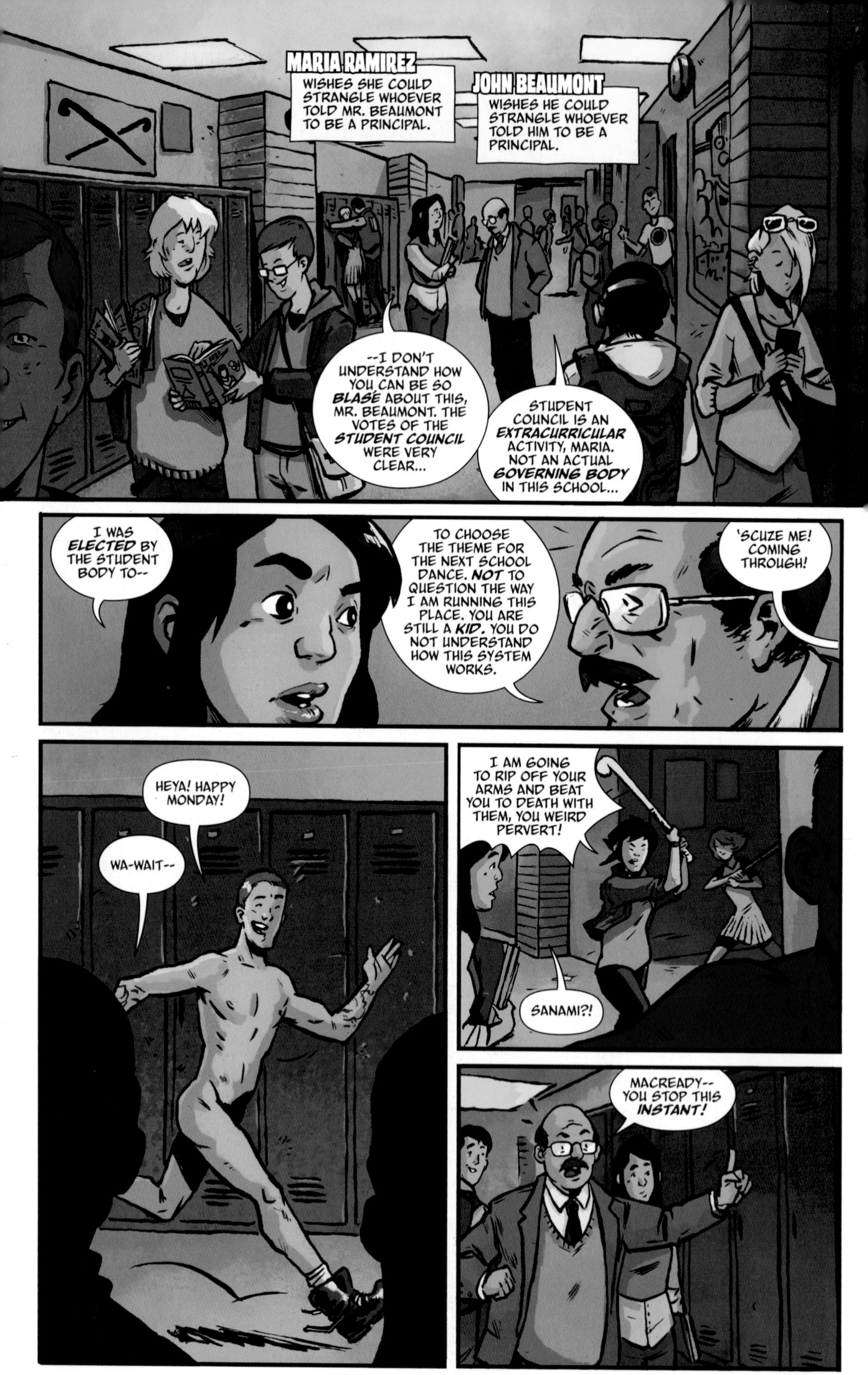

MARIA RAMIREZ
WISHES SHE COULD STRANGLE WHOEVER TOLD MR. BEAUMONT TO BE A PRINCIPAL.
JOHN BEAUMONT
WISHES HE COULD STRANGLE WHOEVER TOLD HIM TO BE A PRINCIPAL.
--I DON'T UNDERSTAND HOW YOU CAN BE SO BLASÉ ABOUT THIS, MR. BEAUMONT. THE VOTES OF THE STUDENT COUNCIL WERE VERY CLEAR...
STUDENT COUNCIL IS AN EXTRACURRICULAR ACTIVITY, MARIA. NOT AN ACTUAL GOVERNING BODY IN THIS SCHOOL...
I WAS ELECTED BY THE STUDENT BODY TO--
TO CHOOSE THE THEME FOR THE NEXT SCHOOL DANCE. NOT TO QUESTION THE WAY I AM RUNNING THIS PLACE. YOU ARE STILL A KID. YOU DO NOT UNDERSTAND HOW THIS SYSTEM WORKS.
'SCUZE ME! COMING THROUGH!
HEYA! HAPPY MONDAY!
WA-WAIT--
I AM GOING TO RIP OFF YOUR ARMS AND BEAT YOU TO DEATH WITH THEM, YOU WEIRD PERVERT!
SANAMI?!
MACREADY-- YOU STOP THIS INSTANT!

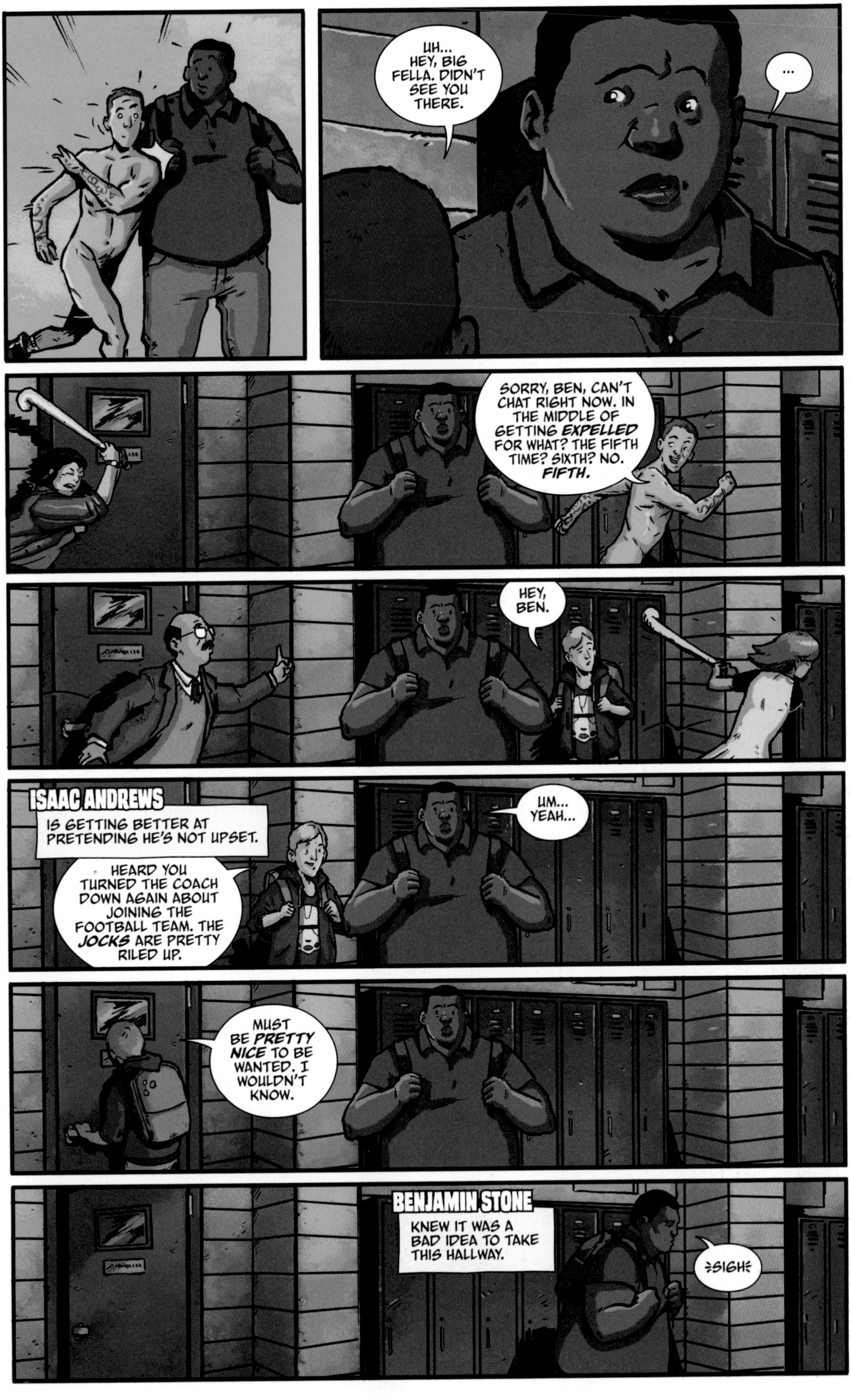
UH... HEY, BIG FELLA. DIDN'T SEE YOU THERE.
...
SORRY, BEN, CAN'T CHAT RIGHT NOW. IN THE MIDDLE OF GETTING EXPELLED FOR WHAT? THE FIFTH TIME? SIXTH? NO. FIFTH.
HEY, BEN.
ISAAC ANDREWS
IS GETTING BETTER AT PRETENDING HE'S NOT UPSET.
UM... YEAH...
HEARD YOU TURNED THE COACH DOWN AGAIN ABOUT JOINING THE FOOTBALL TEAM. THE JOCKS ARE PRETTY RILED UP.
MUST BE PRETTY NICE TO BE WANTED. I WOULDN'T KNOW.
BENJAMIN STONE
KNEW IT WAS A BAD IDEA TO TAKE THIS HALLWAY.
SIGH

KNOWS HE'S SMARTER THAN THE REST OF THESE IDIOTS.

RAWR.

LET ME GUESS. THE *CAST LIST* JUST WENT UP.

I AM A DINOSAUR NOW AND I DON'T CARE ABOUT CAST LISTS, ADRIAN.

RAAAAWR.

YOU DIDN'T GET THE PART.

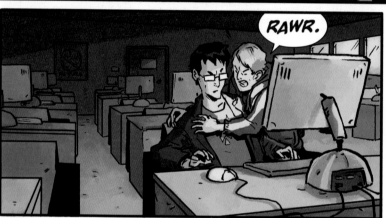

NOPE. *NONE* OF THE PARTS. NOT EVEN *ENSEMBLE.*

THEY *NEVER* CAST ME IN ANYTHING. I'M JUST THE WEIRD STAGE CREW MONKEY. THEY ONLY CARE ABOUT ME WHEN I'M HOLDING *PROP SWORDS* OR *PLASTIC BANANAS.*

YOU'LL COME OUT FOR *STAGE CREW* THIS YEAR, RIGHT? YOU'RE NOT JUST GOING TO LEAVE ME *ALONE* AGAIN?

WE'LL SEE.

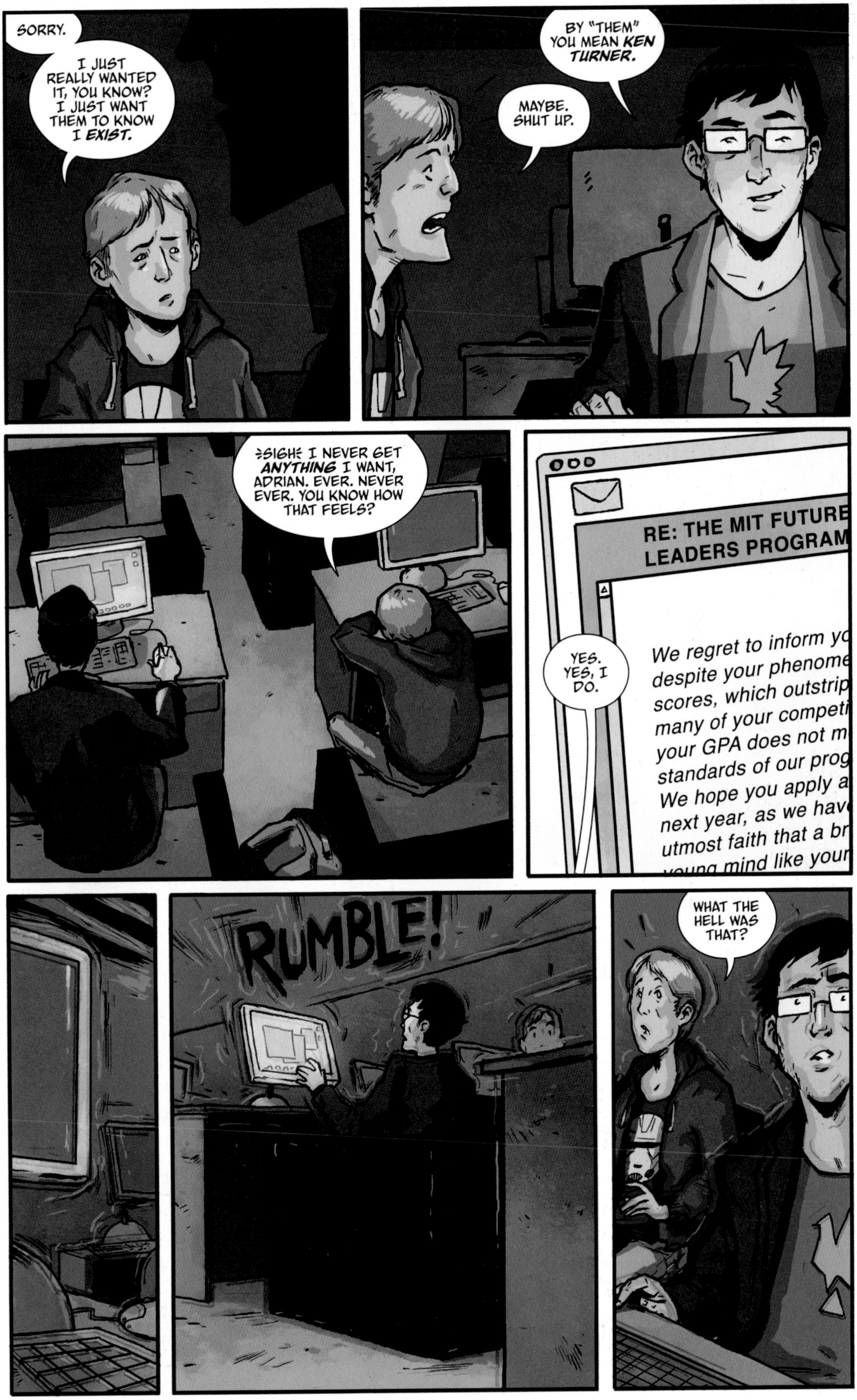
SORRY.
I JUST REALLY WANTED IT, YOU KNOW? I JUST WANT THEM TO KNOW I *EXIST.*
BY "THEM" YOU MEAN *KEN TURNER.*
MAYBE. SHUT UP.
⋟SIGH⋞ I NEVER GET *ANYTHING* I WANT, ADRIAN. EVER. NEVER EVER. YOU KNOW HOW THAT FEELS?
RE: THE MIT FUTURE LEADERS PROGRAM
We regret to inform yo despite your phenome scores, which outstrip many of your competi your GPA does not m standards of our prog We hope you apply a next year, as we hav utmost faith that a br
YES. YES, I DO.
RUMBLE!
WHAT THE HELL WAS THAT?

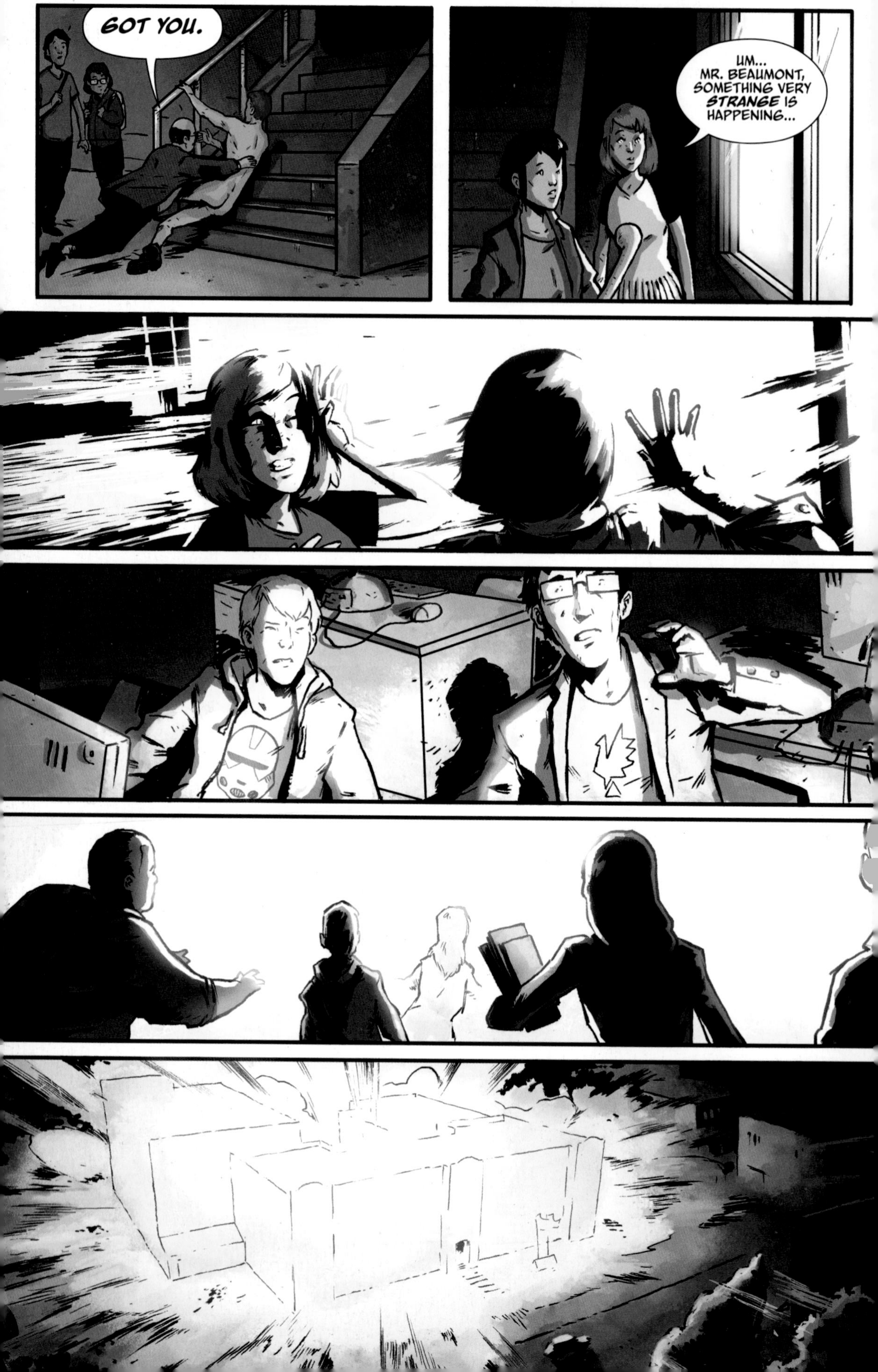
GOT YOU.
UM... MR. BEAUMONT, SOMETHING VERY STRANGE IS HAPPENING...

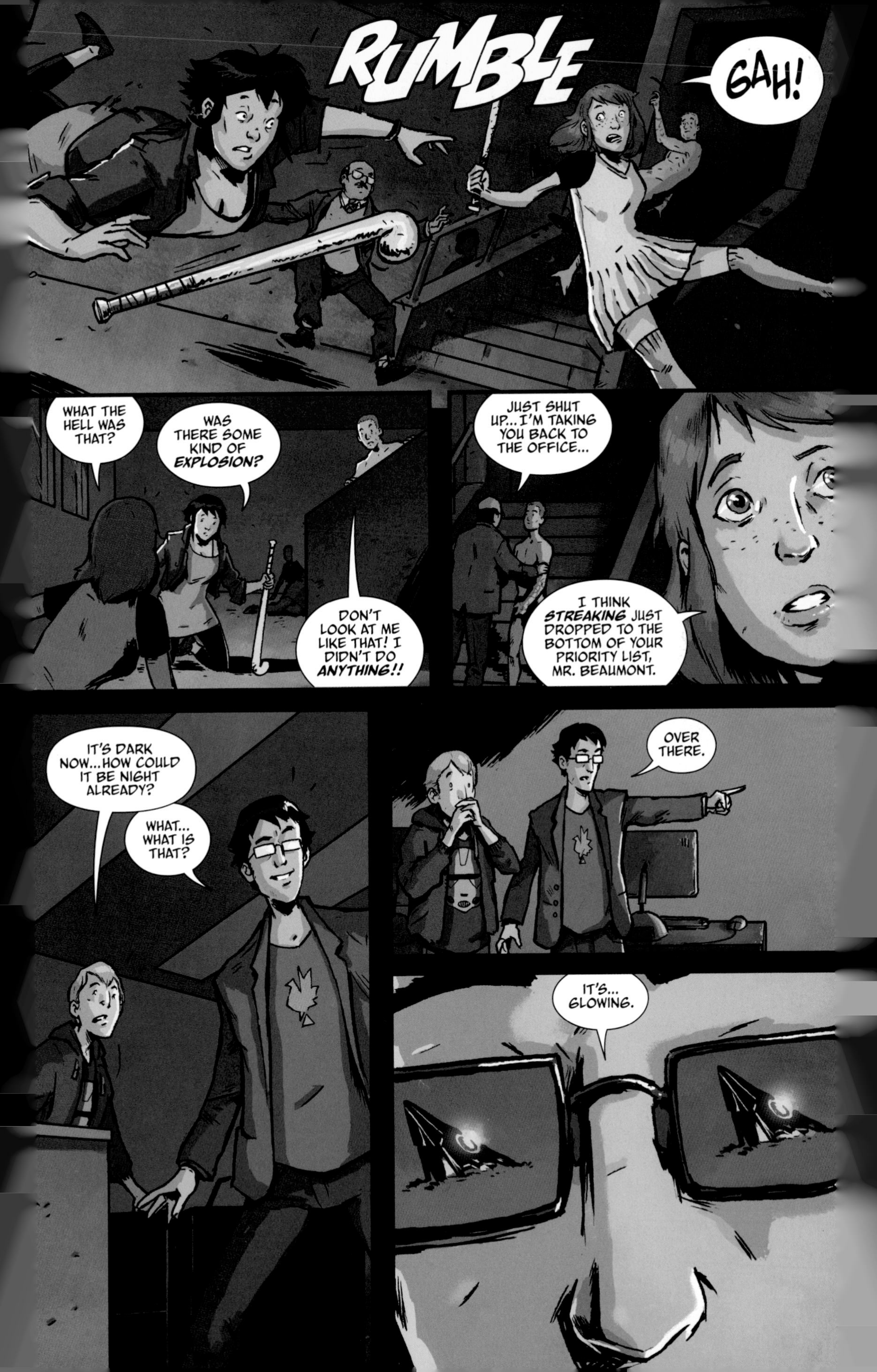
RUMBLE
GAH!
WHAT THE HELL WAS THAT?
WAS THERE SOME KIND OF EXPLOSION?
DON'T LOOK AT ME LIKE THAT! I DIDN'T DO ANYTHING!!
JUST SHUT UP... I'M TAKING YOU BACK TO THE OFFICE...
I THINK STREAKING JUST DROPPED TO THE BOTTOM OF YOUR PRIORITY LIST, MR. BEAUMONT.
IT'S DARK NOW...HOW COULD IT BE NIGHT ALREADY?
WHAT... WHAT IS THAT?
OVER THERE.
IT'S... GLOWING.

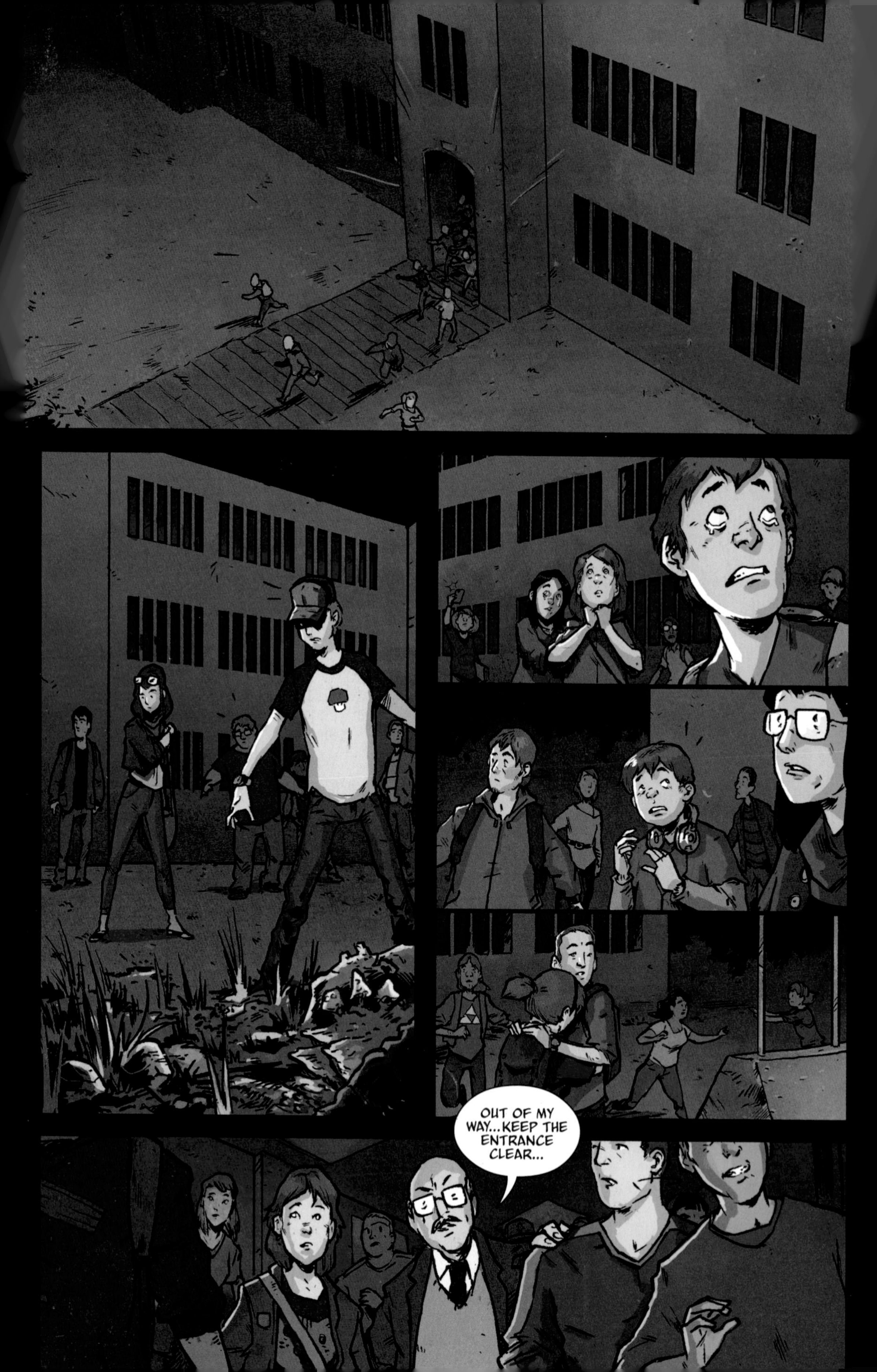
OUT OF MY WAY...KEEP THE ENTRANCE CLEAR...

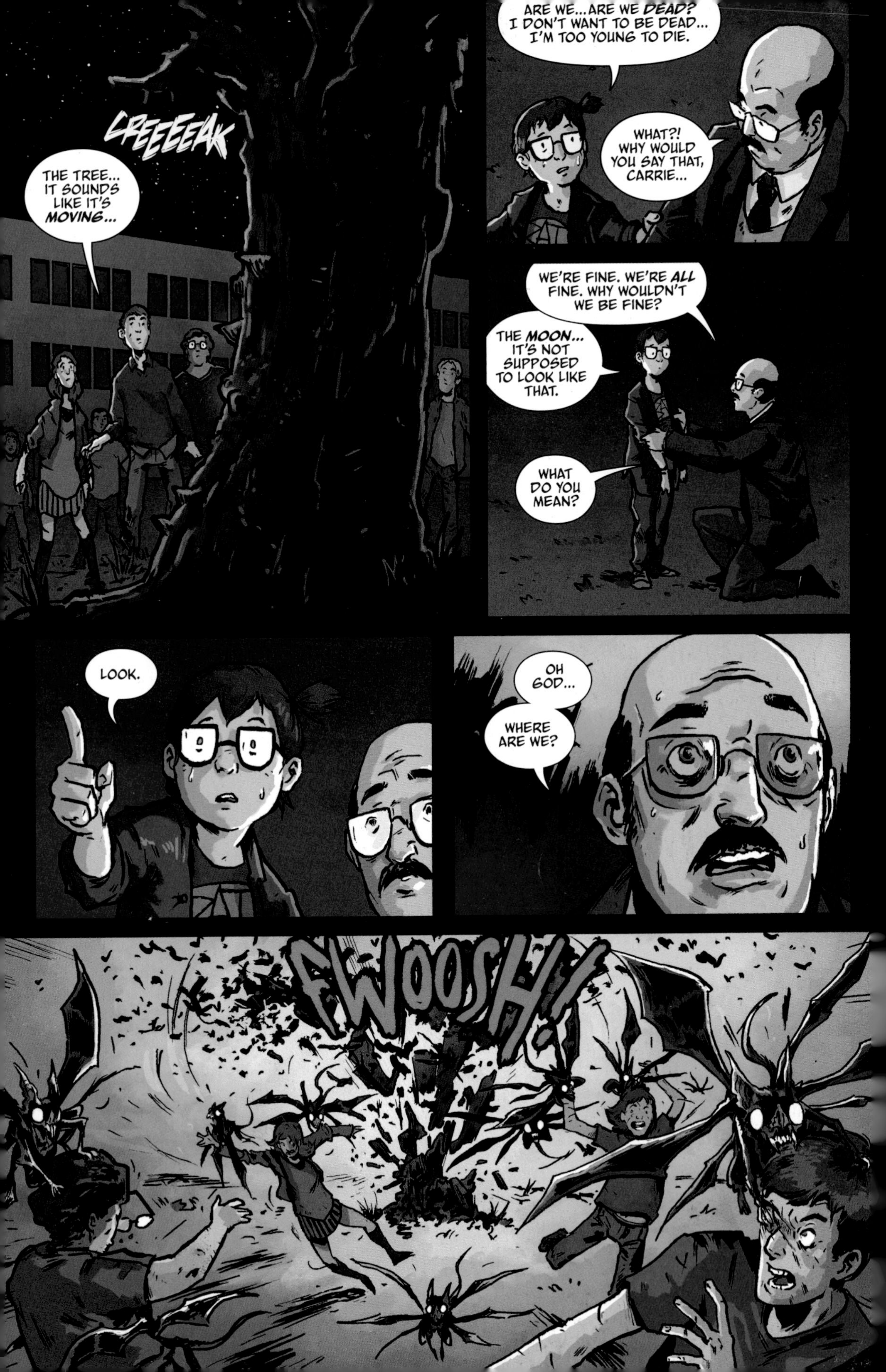
CREEEEAK
THE TREE... IT SOUNDS LIKE IT'S MOVING...
ARE WE...ARE WE DEAD? I DON'T WANT TO BE DEAD... I'M TOO YOUNG TO DIE.
WHAT?! WHY WOULD YOU SAY THAT, CARRIE...
WE'RE FINE. WE'RE ALL FINE. WHY WOULDN'T WE BE FINE?
THE MOON... IT'S NOT SUPPOSED TO LOOK LIKE THAT.
WHAT DO YOU MEAN?
LOOK.
OH GOD...
WHERE ARE WE?
FWOOSH!!

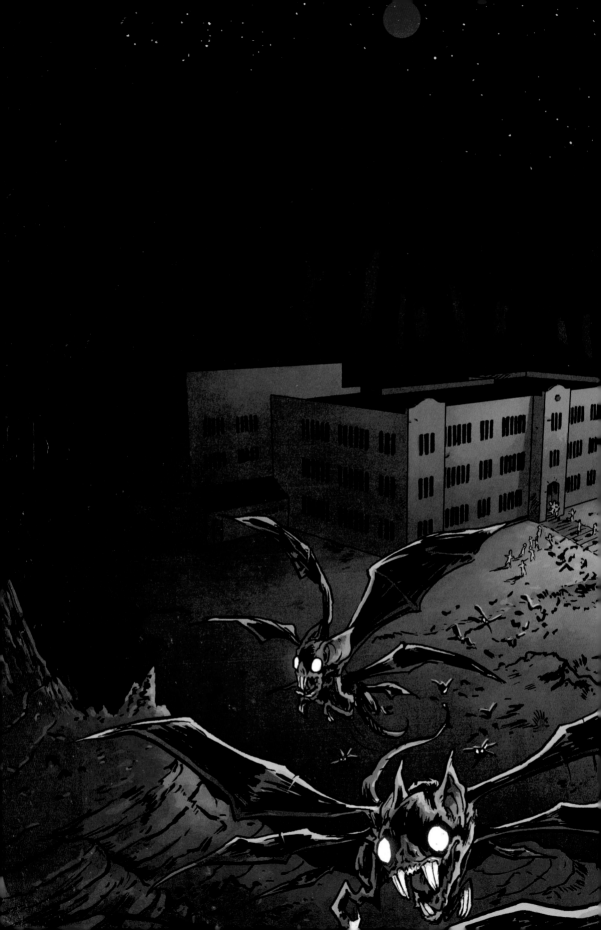

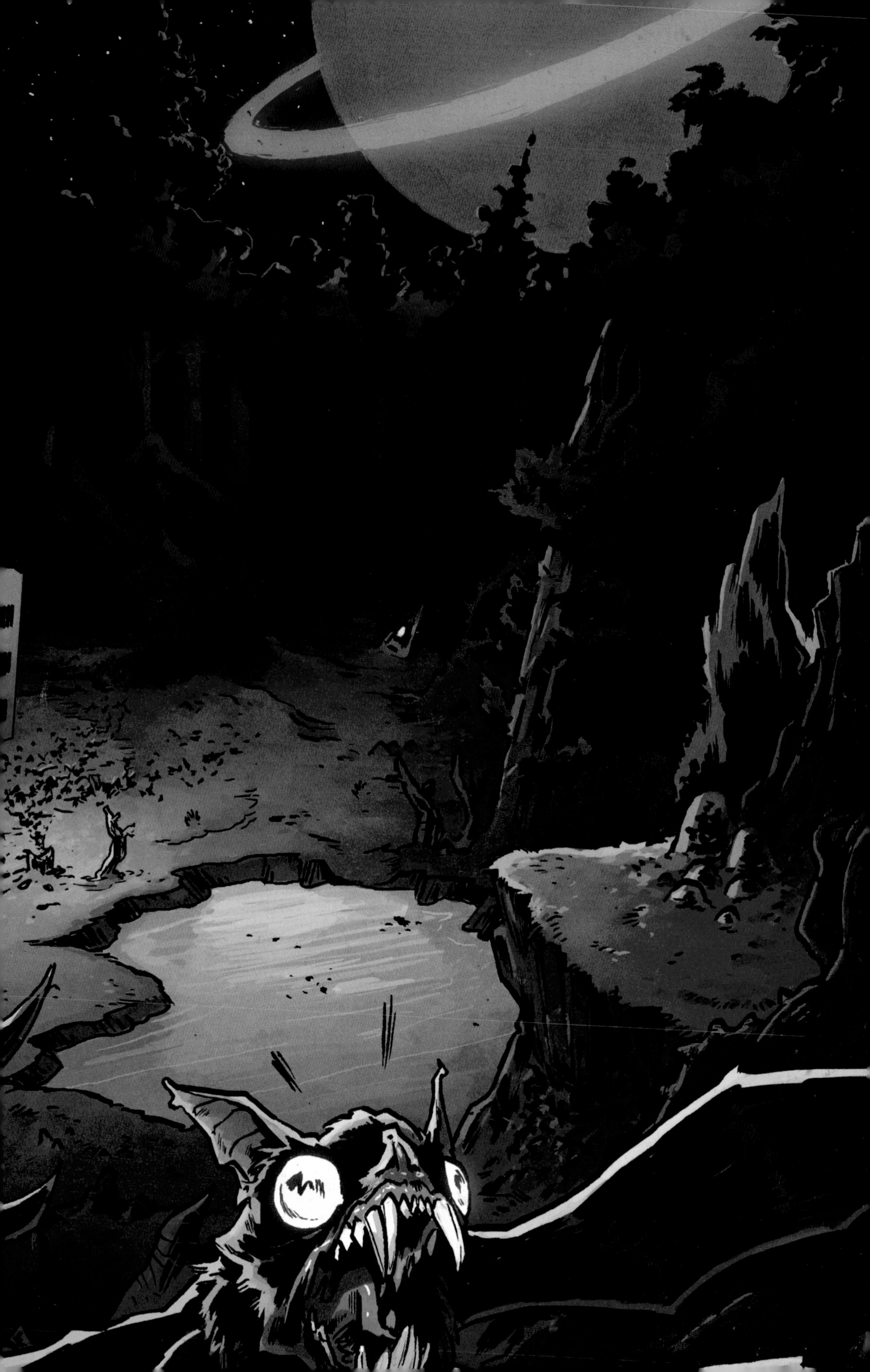

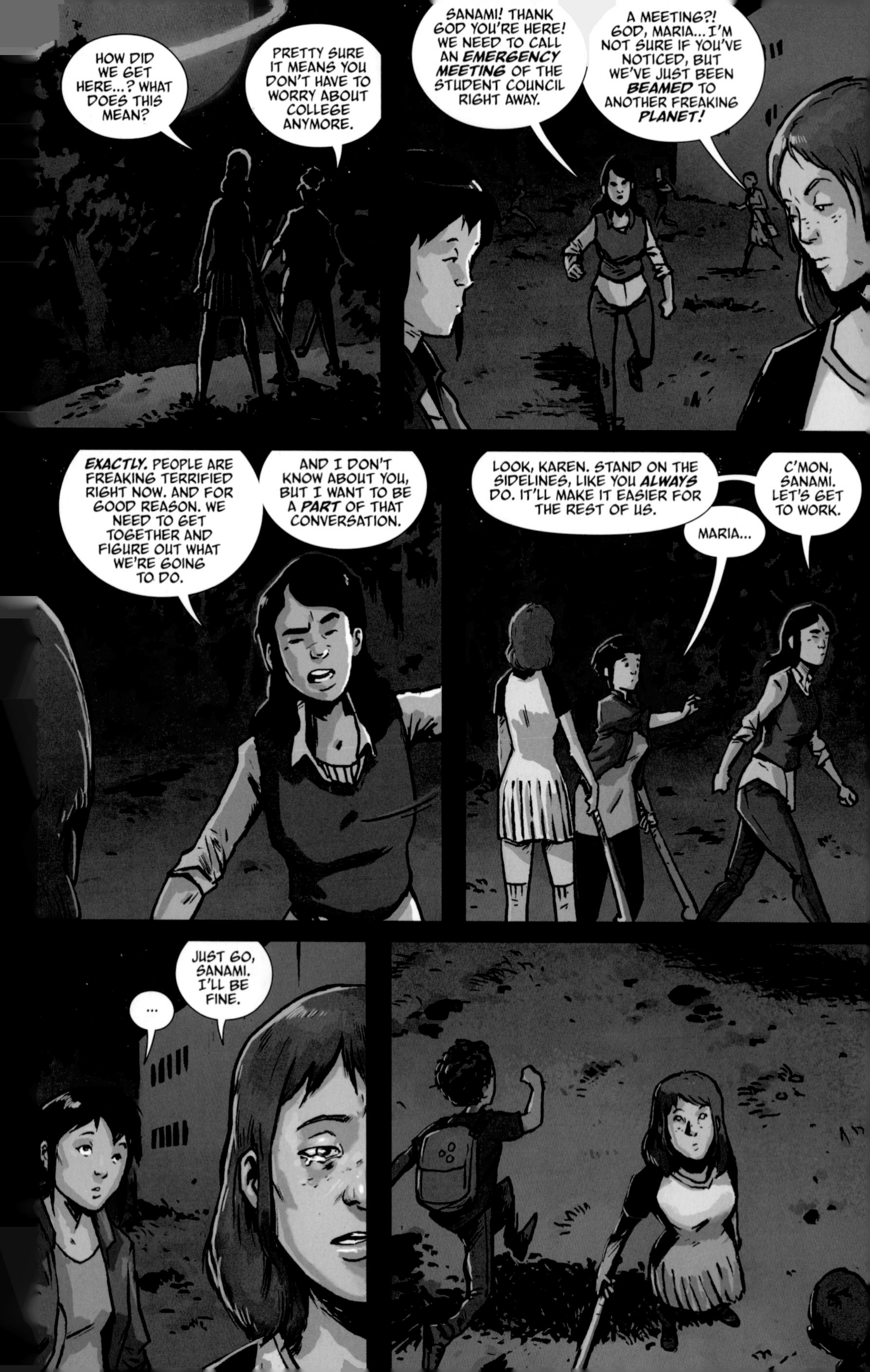
HOW DID WE GET HERE...? WHAT DOES THIS MEAN?
PRETTY SURE IT MEANS YOU DON'T HAVE TO WORRY ABOUT COLLEGE ANYMORE.
SANAMI! THANK GOD YOU'RE HERE! WE NEED TO CALL AN EMERGENCY MEETING OF THE STUDENT COUNCIL RIGHT AWAY.
A MEETING?! GOD, MARIA... I'M NOT SURE IF YOU'VE NOTICED, BUT WE'VE JUST BEEN BEAMED TO ANOTHER FREAKING PLANET!
EXACTLY. PEOPLE ARE FREAKING TERRIFIED RIGHT NOW. AND FOR GOOD REASON. WE NEED TO GET TOGETHER AND FIGURE OUT WHAT WE'RE GOING TO DO.
AND I DON'T KNOW ABOUT YOU, BUT I WANT TO BE A PART OF THAT CONVERSATION.
LOOK, KAREN. STAND ON THE SIDELINES, LIKE YOU ALWAYS DO. IT'LL MAKE IT EASIER FOR THE REST OF US.
C'MON, SANAMI. LET'S GET TO WORK.
MARIA...
...
JUST GO, SANAMI. I'LL BE FINE.

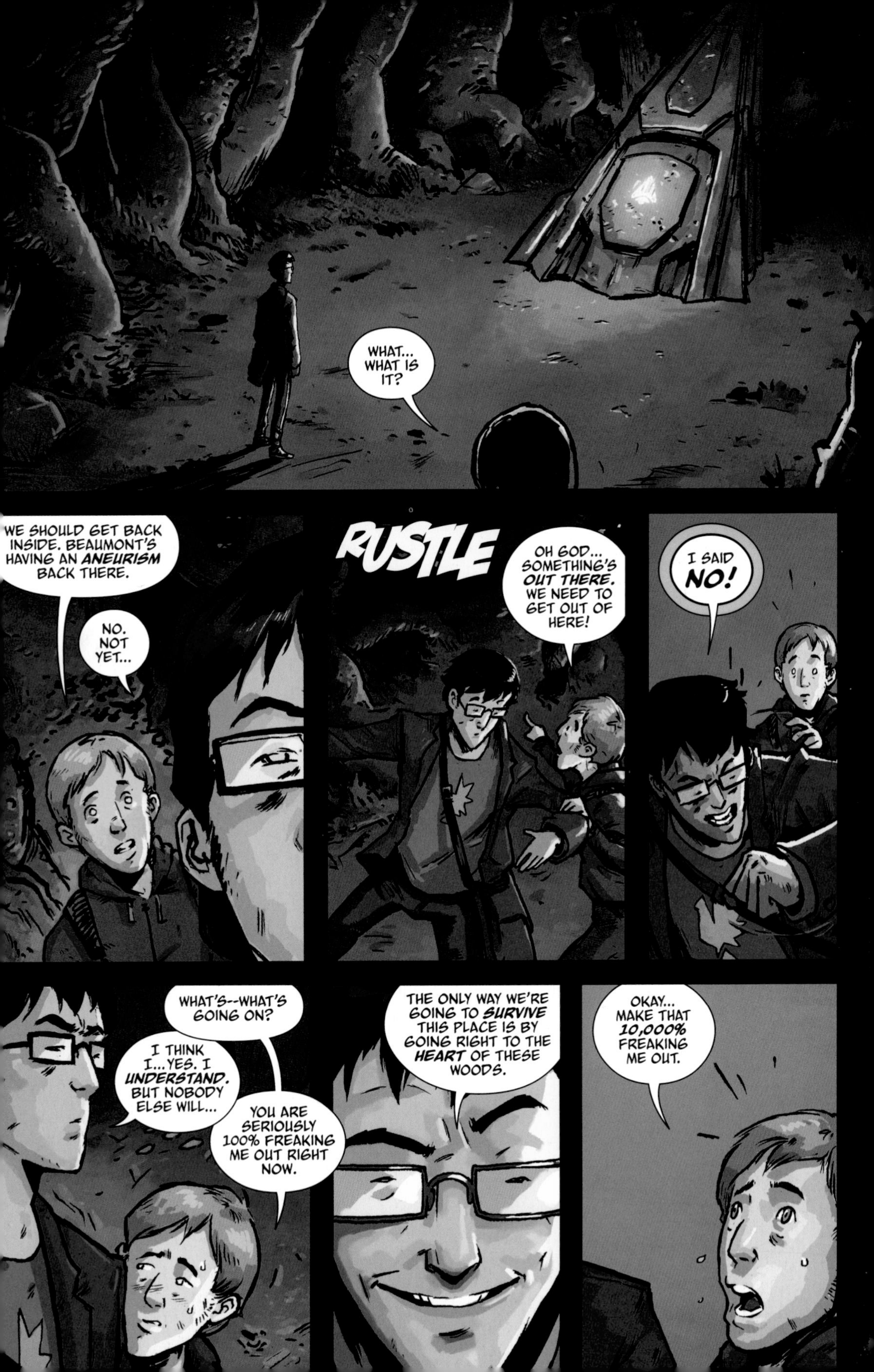
WHAT... WHAT IS IT?
WE SHOULD GET BACK INSIDE. BEAUMONT'S HAVING AN ANEURISM BACK THERE.
NO. NOT YET...
RUSTLE
OH GOD... SOMETHING'S OUT THERE. WE NEED TO GET OUT OF HERE!
I SAID NO!
WHAT'S--WHAT'S GOING ON?
I THINK I...YES. I UNDERSTAND. BUT NOBODY ELSE WILL...
YOU ARE SERIOUSLY 100% FREAKING ME OUT RIGHT NOW.
THE ONLY WAY WE'RE GOING TO SURVIVE THIS PLACE IS BY GOING RIGHT TO THE HEART OF THESE WOODS.
OKAY... MAKE THAT 10,000% FREAKING ME OUT.

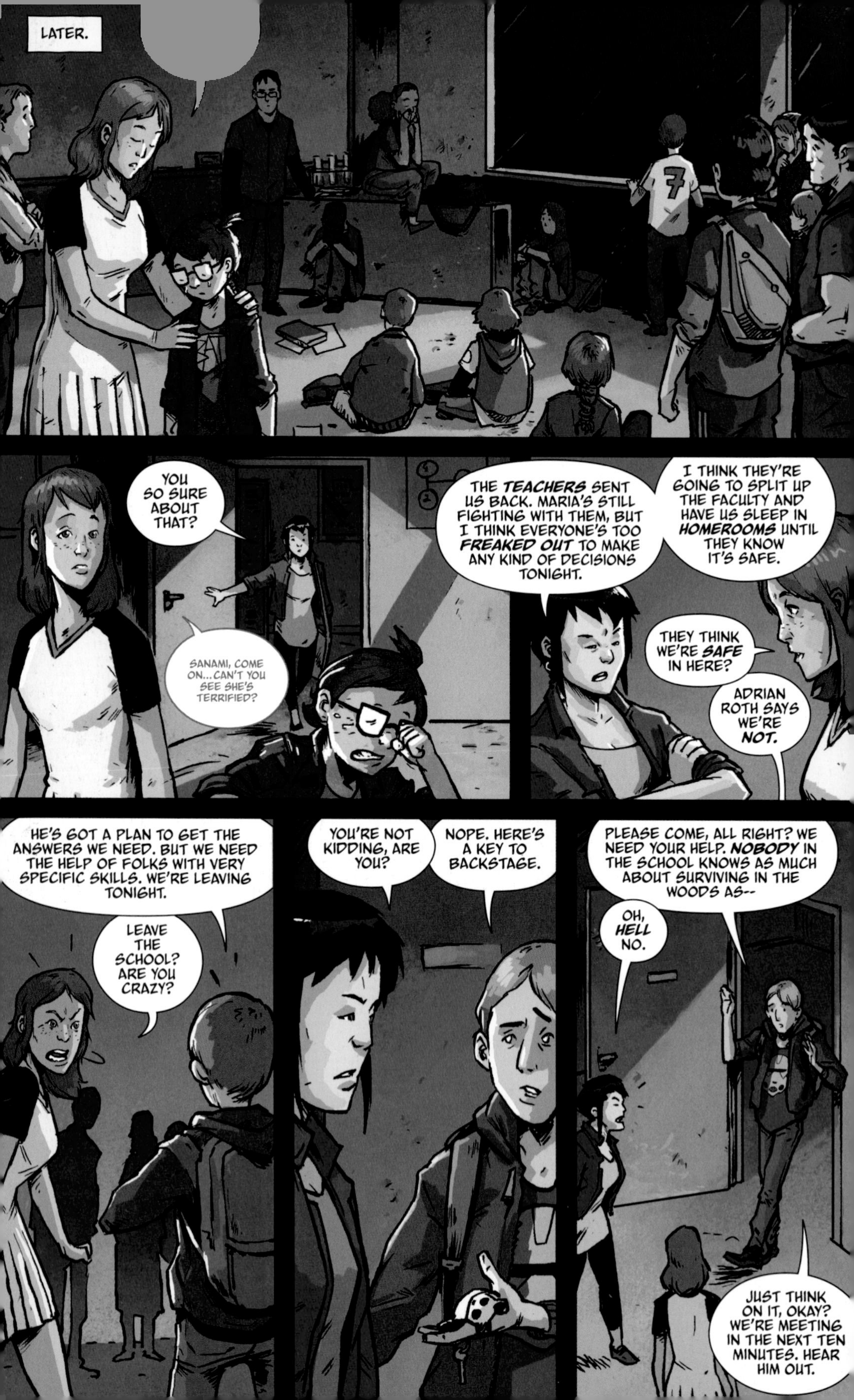
LATER.
YOU SO SURE ABOUT THAT?
SANAMI, COME ON... CAN'T YOU SEE SHE'S TERRIFIED?
THE TEACHERS SENT US BACK. MARIA'S STILL FIGHTING WITH THEM, BUT I THINK EVERYONE'S TOO FREAKED OUT TO MAKE ANY KIND OF DECISIONS TONIGHT.
I THINK THEY'RE GOING TO SPLIT UP THE FACULTY AND HAVE US SLEEP IN HOMEROOMS UNTIL THEY KNOW IT'S SAFE.
THEY THINK WE'RE SAFE IN HERE?
ADRIAN ROTH SAYS WE'RE NOT.
HE'S GOT A PLAN TO GET THE ANSWERS WE NEED. BUT WE NEED THE HELP OF FOLKS WITH VERY SPECIFIC SKILLS. WE'RE LEAVING TONIGHT.
LEAVE THE SCHOOL? ARE YOU CRAZY?
YOU'RE NOT KIDDING, ARE YOU?
NOPE. HERE'S A KEY TO BACKSTAGE.
PLEASE COME, ALL RIGHT? WE NEED YOUR HELP. NOBODY IN THE SCHOOL KNOWS AS MUCH ABOUT SURVIVING IN THE WOODS AS--
OH, HELL NO.
JUST THINK ON IT, OKAY? WE'RE MEETING IN THE NEXT TEN MINUTES. HEAR HIM OUT.

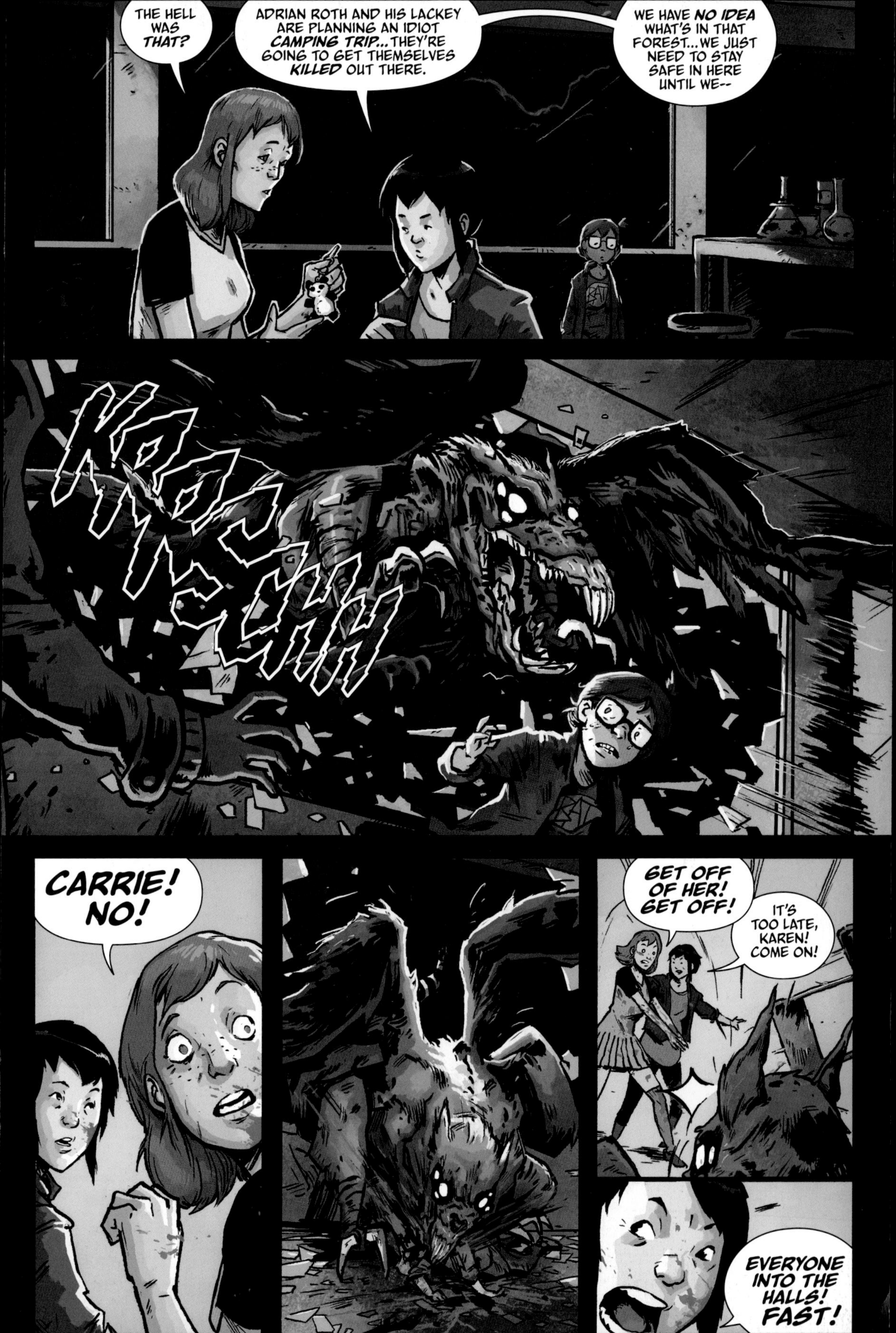
THE HELL WAS THAT?
ADRIAN ROTH AND HIS LACKEY ARE PLANNING AN IDIOT CAMPING TRIP... THEY'RE GOING TO GET THEMSELVES KILLED OUT THERE.
WE HAVE NO IDEA WHAT'S IN THAT FOREST... WE JUST NEED TO STAY SAFE IN HERE UNTIL WE--
KRASSHH
CARRIE! NO!
GET OFF OF HER! GET OFF!
IT'S TOO LATE, KAREN! COME ON!
EVERYONE INTO THE HALLS! FAST!

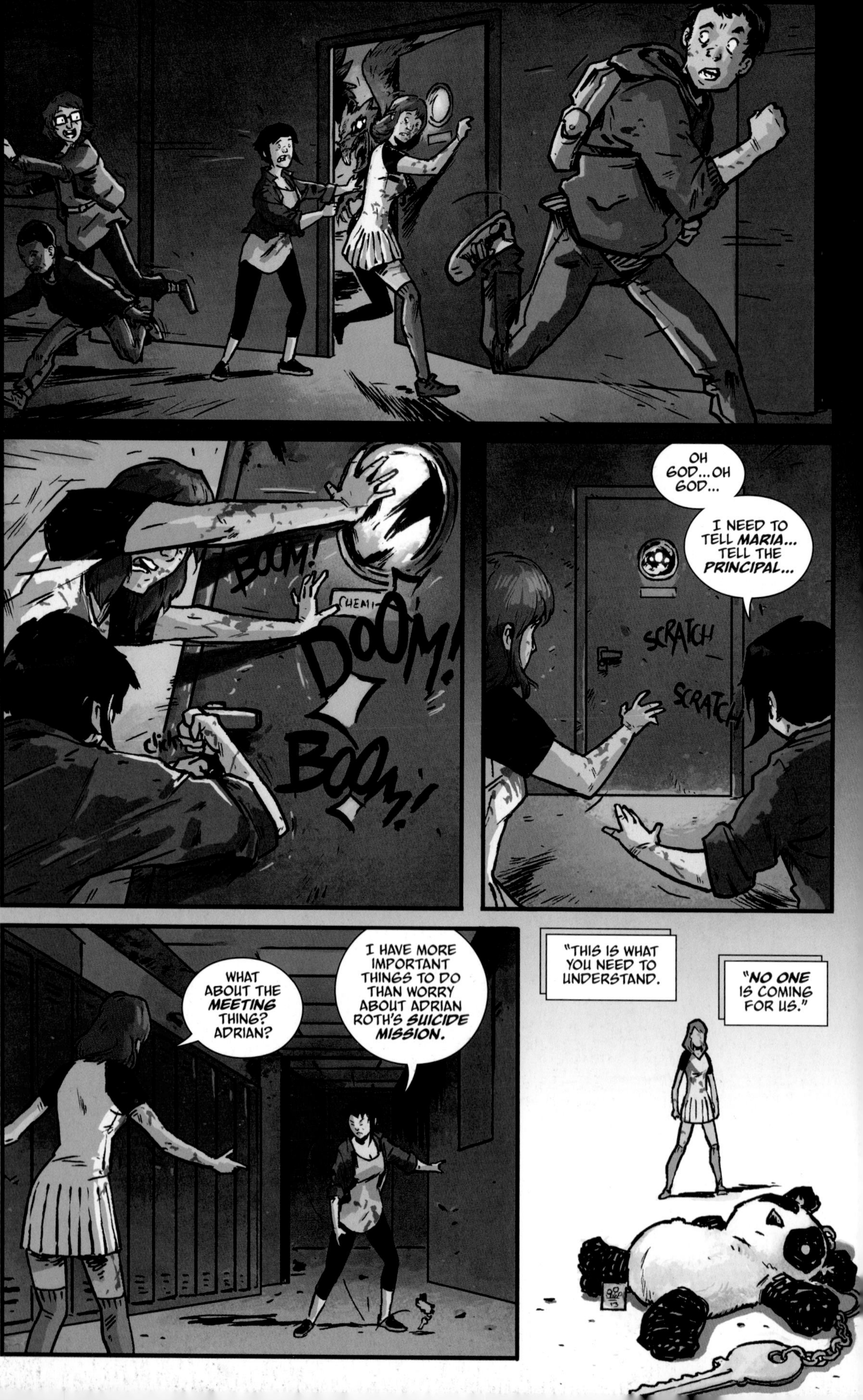
BOOM!
DOOM!
BOOM!
OH GOD...OH GOD...
I NEED TO TELL *MARIA*... TELL THE *PRINCIPAL*...
SCRATCH
SCRATCH
WHAT ABOUT THE *MEETING* THING? ADRIAN?
I HAVE MORE IMPORTANT THINGS TO DO THAN WORRY ABOUT ADRIAN ROTH'S *SUICIDE MISSION*.
"THIS IS WHAT YOU NEED TO UNDERSTAND.
"*NO ONE* IS COMING FOR US."

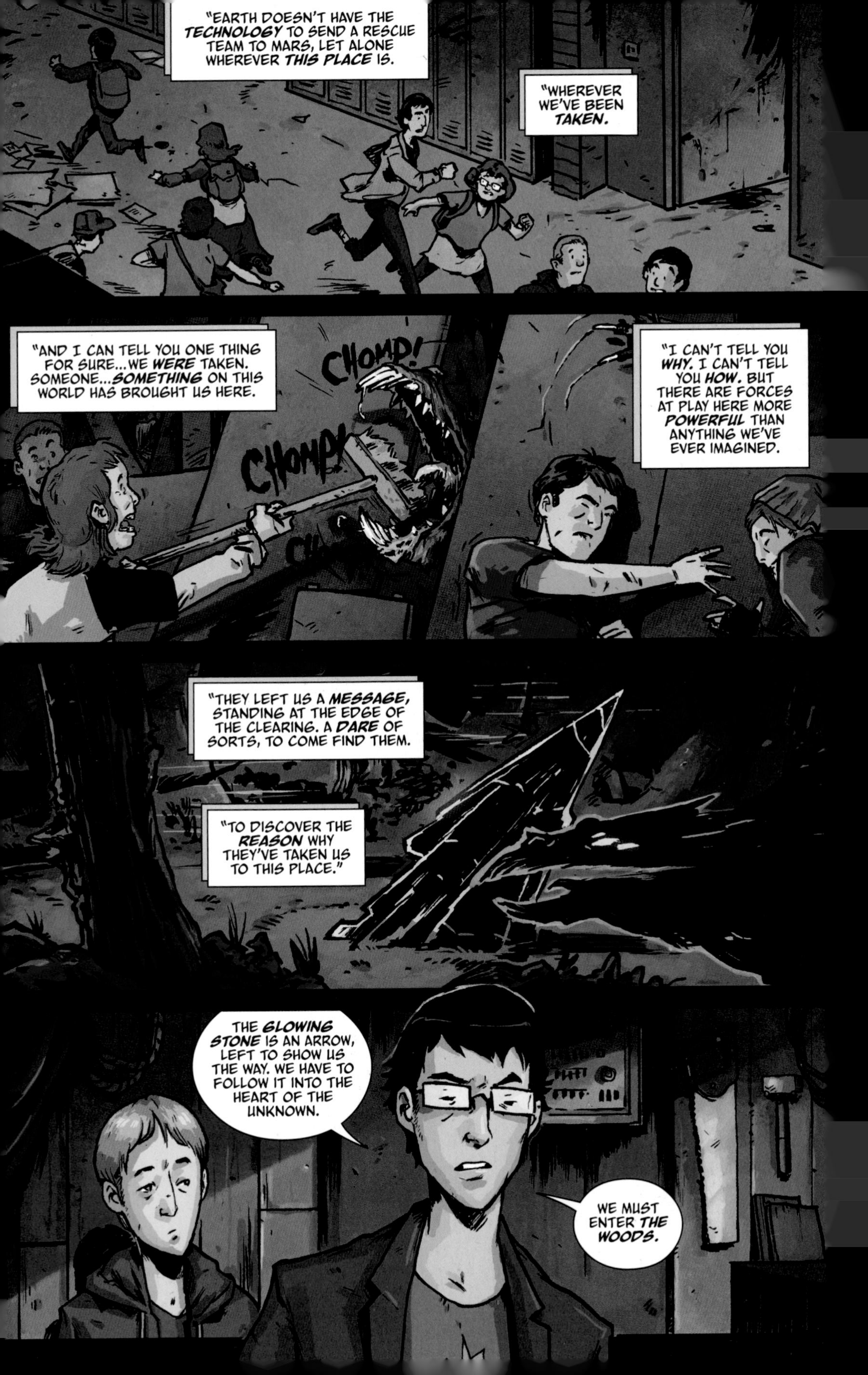
"EARTH DOESN'T HAVE THE TECHNOLOGY TO SEND A RESCUE TEAM TO MARS, LET ALONE WHEREVER THIS PLACE IS.
"WHEREVER WE'VE BEEN TAKEN.
"AND I CAN TELL YOU ONE THING FOR SURE...WE WERE TAKEN. SOMEONE...SOMETHING ON THIS WORLD HAS BROUGHT US HERE.
CHOMP!
CHOMP!
"I CAN'T TELL YOU WHY. I CAN'T TELL YOU HOW. BUT THERE ARE FORCES AT PLAY HERE MORE POWERFUL THAN ANYTHING WE'VE EVER IMAGINED.
"THEY LEFT US A MESSAGE, STANDING AT THE EDGE OF THE CLEARING. A DARE OF SORTS, TO COME FIND THEM.
"TO DISCOVER THE REASON WHY THEY'VE TAKEN US TO THIS PLACE."
THE GLOWING STONE IS AN ARROW, LEFT TO SHOW US THE WAY. WE HAVE TO FOLLOW IT INTO THE HEART OF THE UNKNOWN.
WE MUST ENTER THE WOODS.

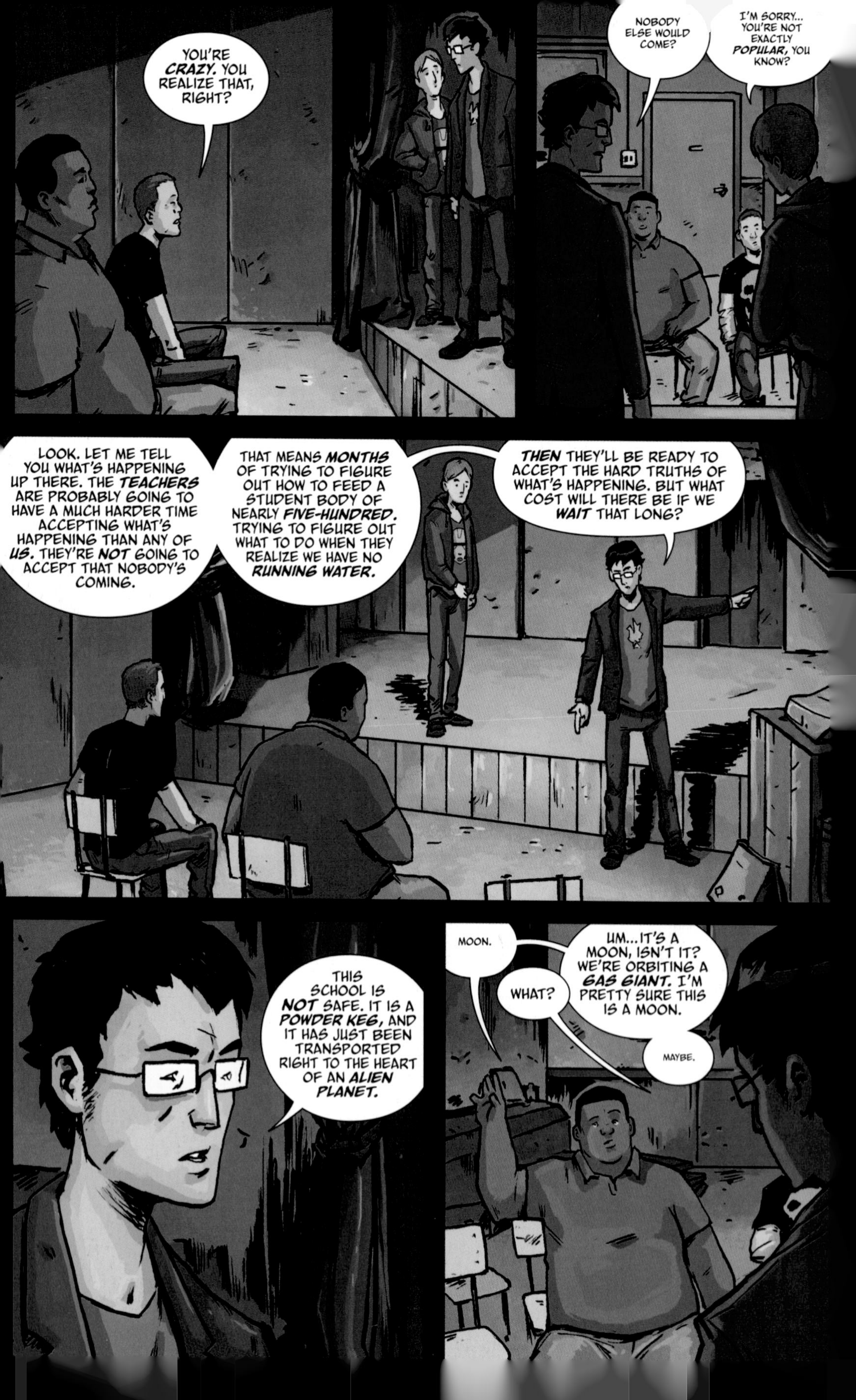
YOU'RE CRAZY. YOU REALIZE THAT, RIGHT?
NOBODY ELSE WOULD COME?
I'M SORRY... YOU'RE NOT EXACTLY POPULAR, YOU KNOW?
LOOK. LET ME TELL YOU WHAT'S HAPPENING UP THERE. THE TEACHERS ARE PROBABLY GOING TO HAVE A MUCH HARDER TIME ACCEPTING WHAT'S HAPPENING THAN ANY OF US. THEY'RE NOT GOING TO ACCEPT THAT NOBODY'S COMING.
THAT MEANS MONTHS OF TRYING TO FIGURE OUT HOW TO FEED A STUDENT BODY OF NEARLY FIVE-HUNDRED. TRYING TO FIGURE OUT WHAT TO DO WHEN THEY REALIZE WE HAVE NO RUNNING WATER.
THEN THEY'LL BE READY TO ACCEPT THE HARD TRUTHS OF WHAT'S HAPPENING. BUT WHAT COST WILL THERE BE IF WE WAIT THAT LONG?
THIS SCHOOL IS NOT SAFE. IT IS A POWDER KEG, AND IT HAS JUST BEEN TRANSPORTED RIGHT TO THE HEART OF AN ALIEN PLANET.
MOON.
UM...IT'S A MOON, ISN'T IT? WE'RE ORBITING A GAS GIANT. I'M PRETTY SURE THIS IS A MOON.
WHAT?
MAYBE.

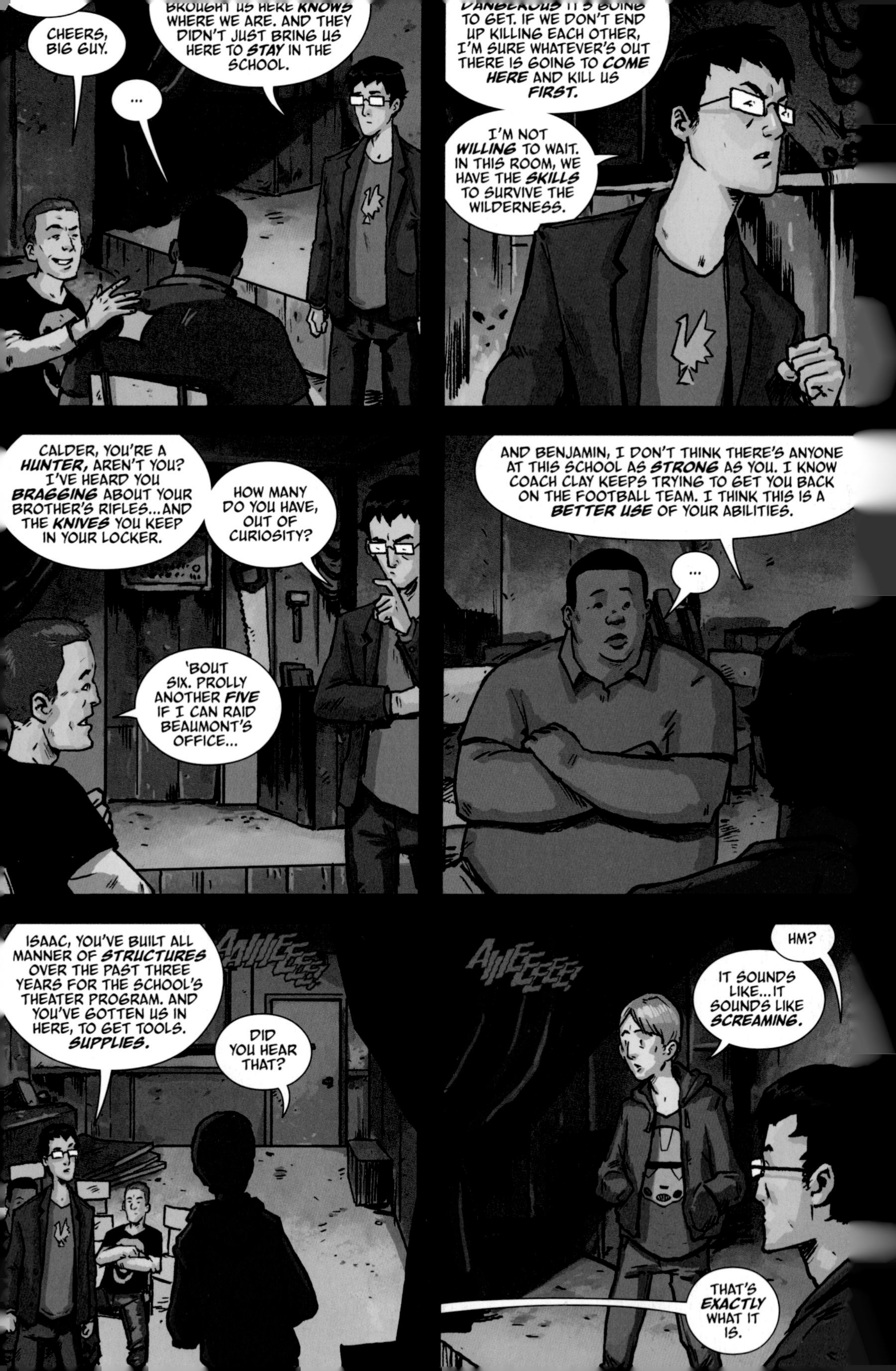

CHEERS, BIG GUY.
...
BROUGHT US HERE KNOWS WHERE WE ARE. AND THEY DIDN'T JUST BRING US HERE TO STAY IN THE SCHOOL.
TO GET. IF WE DON'T END UP KILLING EACH OTHER, I'M SURE WHATEVER'S OUT THERE IS GOING TO COME HERE AND KILL US FIRST.
I'M NOT WILLING TO WAIT. IN THIS ROOM, WE HAVE THE SKILLS TO SURVIVE THE WILDERNESS.
CALDER, YOU'RE A HUNTER, AREN'T YOU? I'VE HEARD YOU BRAGGING ABOUT YOUR BROTHER'S RIFLES...AND THE KNIVES YOU KEEP IN YOUR LOCKER.
HOW MANY DO YOU HAVE, OUT OF CURIOSITY?
'BOUT SIX. PROLLY ANOTHER FIVE IF I CAN RAID BEAUMONT'S OFFICE...
AND BENJAMIN, I DON'T THINK THERE'S ANYONE AT THIS SCHOOL AS STRONG AS YOU. I KNOW COACH CLAY KEEPS TRYING TO GET YOU BACK ON THE FOOTBALL TEAM. I THINK THIS IS A BETTER USE OF YOUR ABILITIES.
...
ISAAC, YOU'VE BUILT ALL MANNER OF STRUCTURES OVER THE PAST THREE YEARS FOR THE SCHOOL'S THEATER PROGRAM. AND YOU'VE GOTTEN US IN HERE, TO GET TOOLS. SUPPLIES.
AIIIEEEE!
DID YOU HEAR THAT?
AIIEEEEE!
HM?
IT SOUNDS LIKE...IT SOUNDS LIKE SCREAMING.
THAT'S EXACTLY WHAT IT IS.

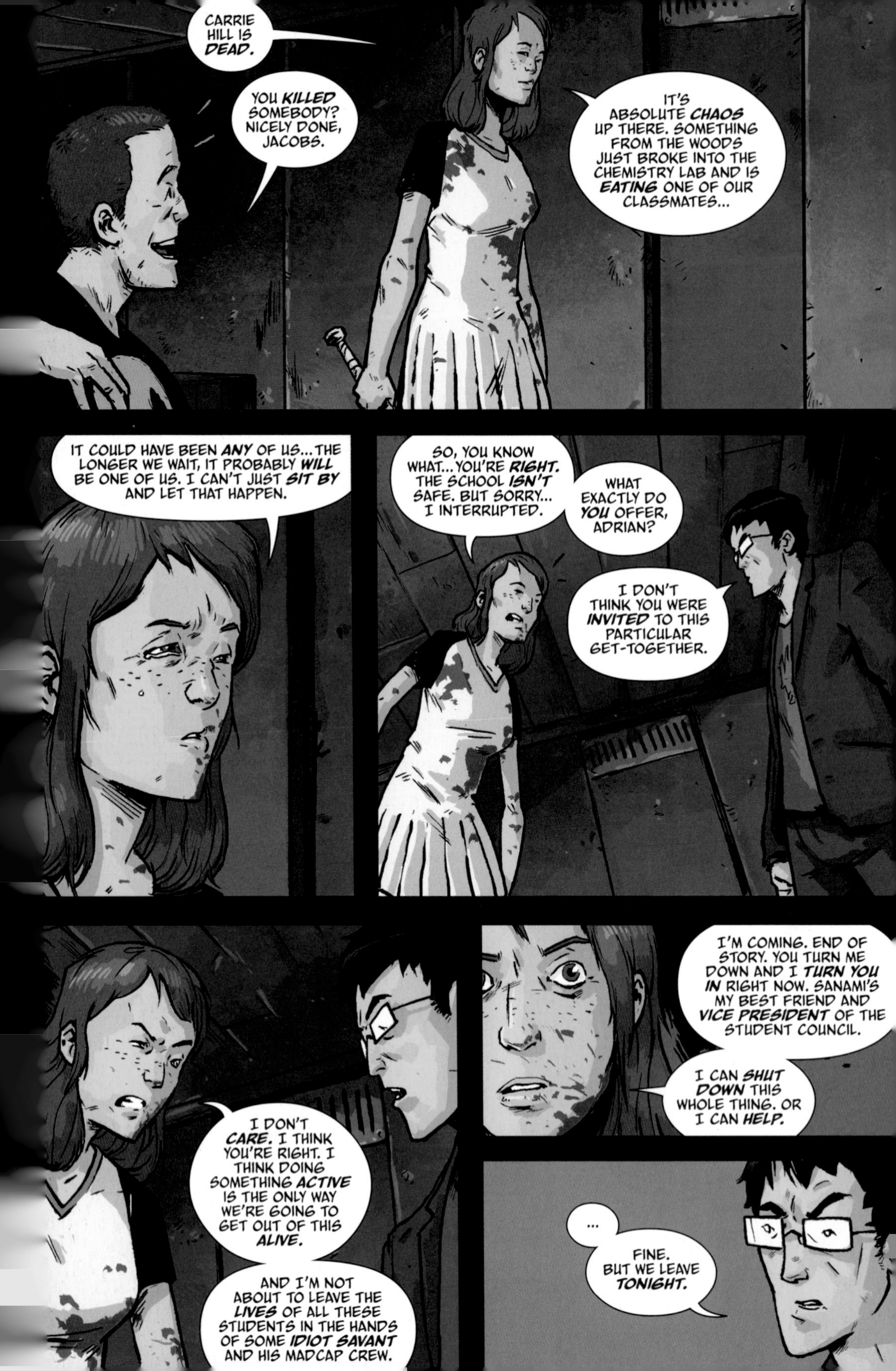
CARRIE HILL IS DEAD.
YOU KILLED SOMEBODY? NICELY DONE, JACOBS.
IT'S ABSOLUTE CHAOS UP THERE. SOMETHING FROM THE WOODS JUST BROKE INTO THE CHEMISTRY LAB AND IS EATING ONE OF OUR CLASSMATES...
IT COULD HAVE BEEN ANY OF US...THE LONGER WE WAIT, IT PROBABLY WILL BE ONE OF US. I CAN'T JUST SIT BY AND LET THAT HAPPEN.
SO, YOU KNOW WHAT...YOU'RE RIGHT. THE SCHOOL ISN'T SAFE. BUT SORRY... I INTERRUPTED.
WHAT EXACTLY DO YOU OFFER, ADRIAN?
I DON'T THINK YOU WERE INVITED TO THIS PARTICULAR GET-TOGETHER.
I DON'T CARE. I THINK YOU'RE RIGHT. I THINK DOING SOMETHING ACTIVE IS THE ONLY WAY WE'RE GOING TO GET OUT OF THIS ALIVE.
AND I'M NOT ABOUT TO LEAVE THE LIVES OF ALL THESE STUDENTS IN THE HANDS OF SOME IDIOT SAVANT AND HIS MADCAP CREW.
I'M COMING. END OF STORY. YOU TURN ME DOWN AND I TURN YOU IN RIGHT NOW. SANAMI'S MY BEST FRIEND AND VICE PRESIDENT OF THE STUDENT COUNCIL.
I CAN SHUT DOWN THIS WHOLE THING. OR I CAN HELP.
...
FINE. BUT WE LEAVE TONIGHT.

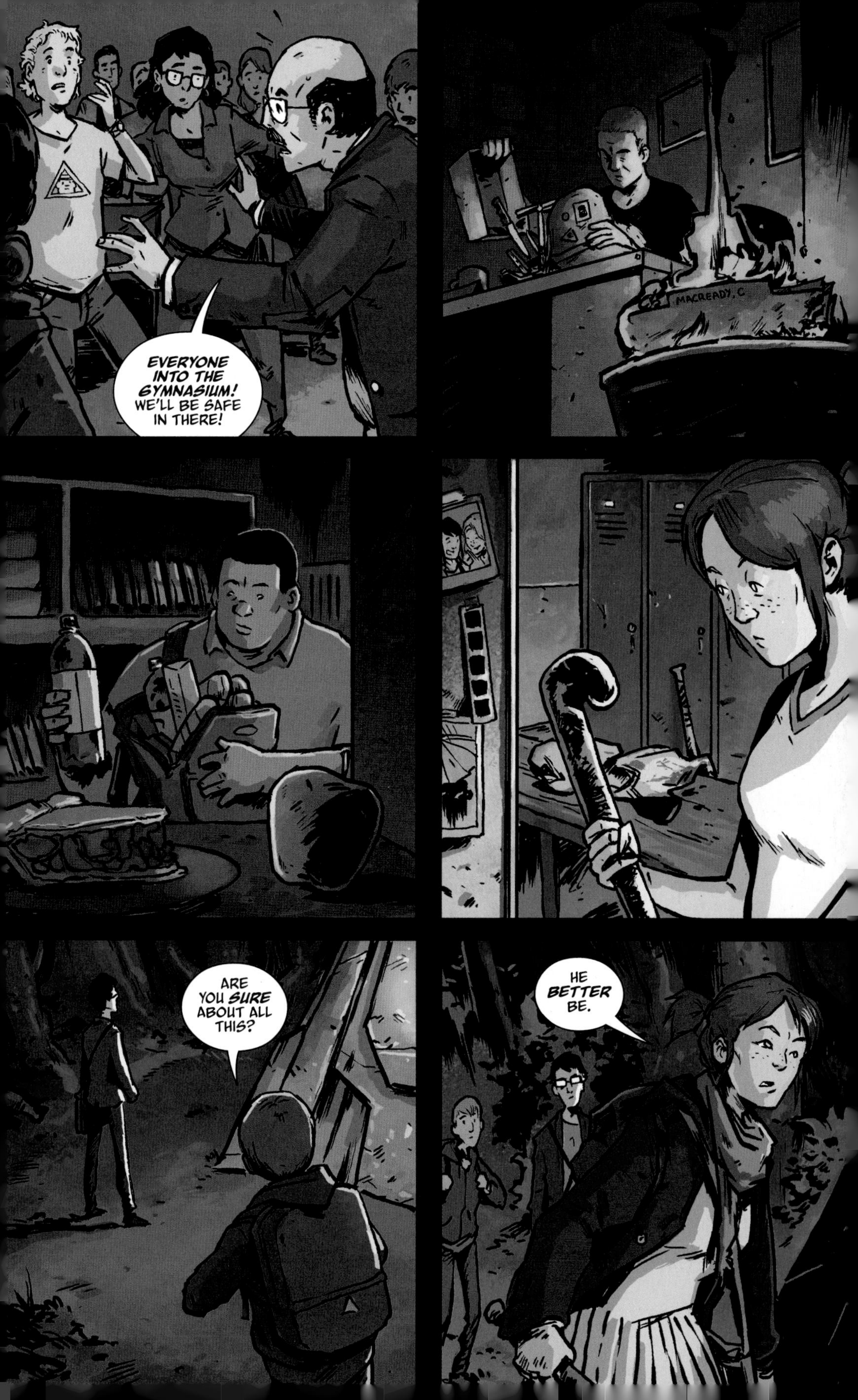
EVERYONE INTO THE GYMNASIUM! WE'LL BE SAFE IN THERE!
MACREADY, C
ARE YOU SURE ABOUT ALL THIS?
HE BETTER BE.

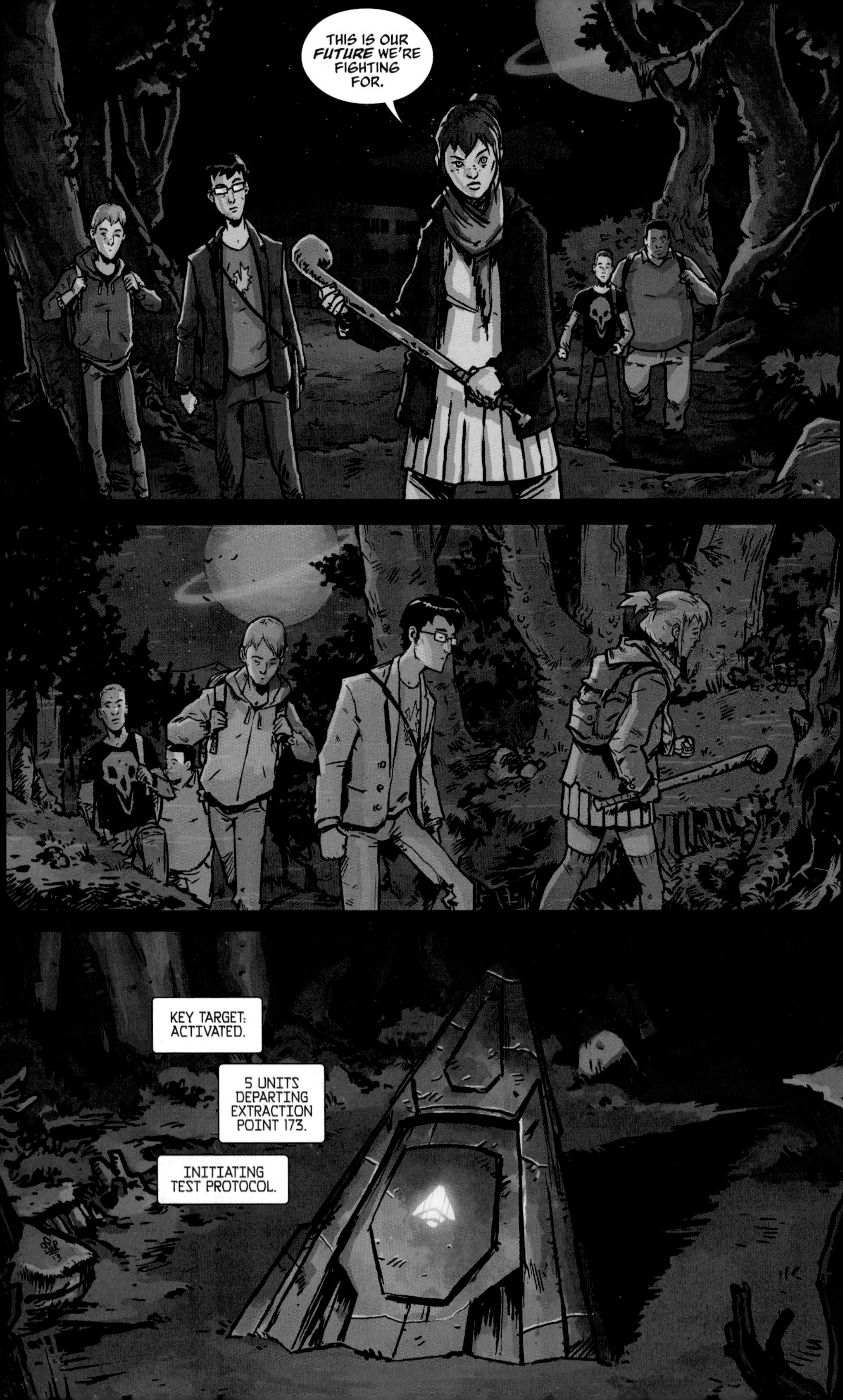
THIS IS OUR FUTURE WE'RE FIGHTING FOR.
KEY TARGET: ACTIVATED.
5 UNITS DEPARTING EXTRACTION POINT 173.
INITIATING TEST PROTOCOL.

ISSUE ONE COVER **RAMÓN K. PÉREZ**

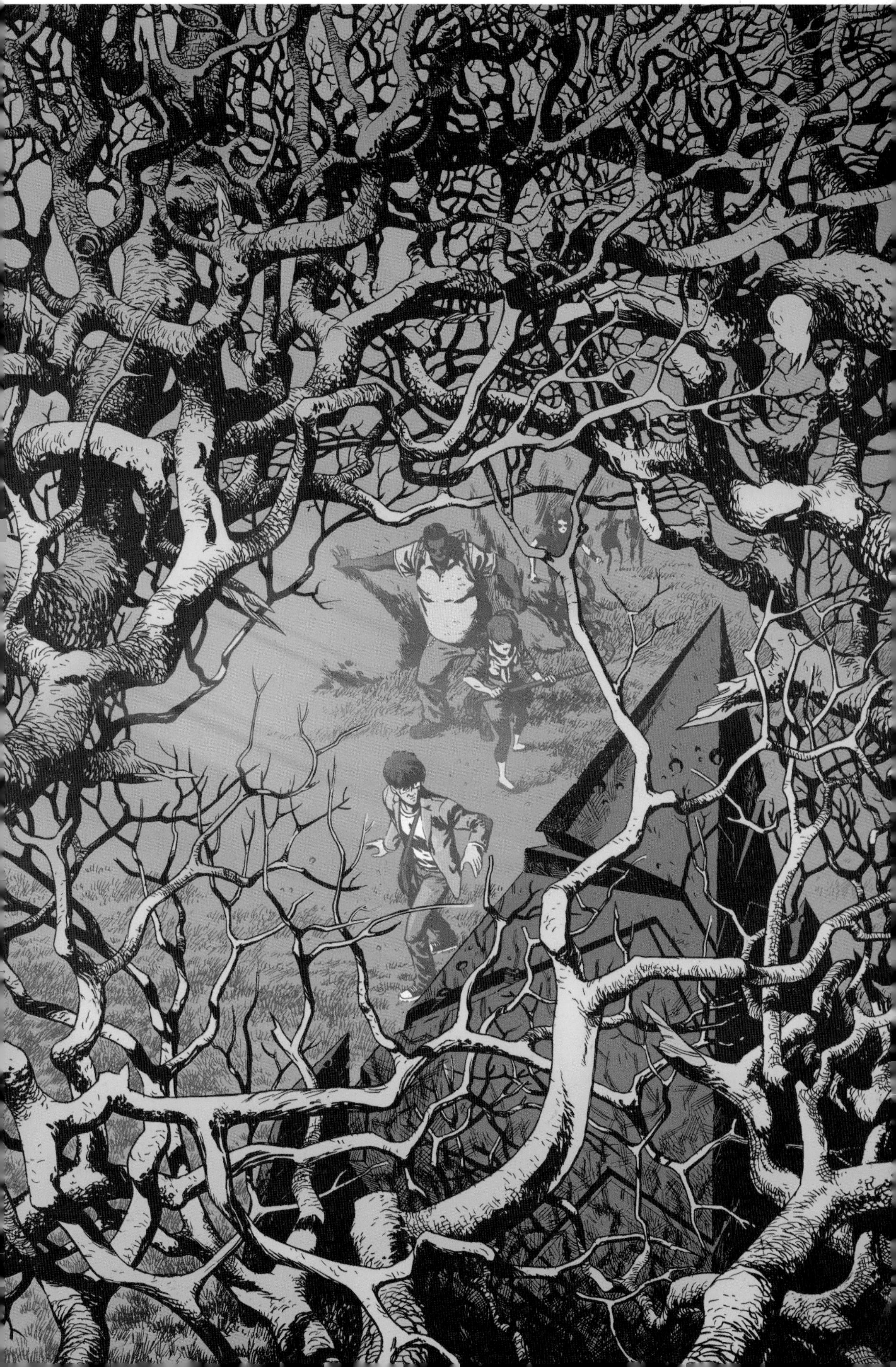

CHAPTER TWO

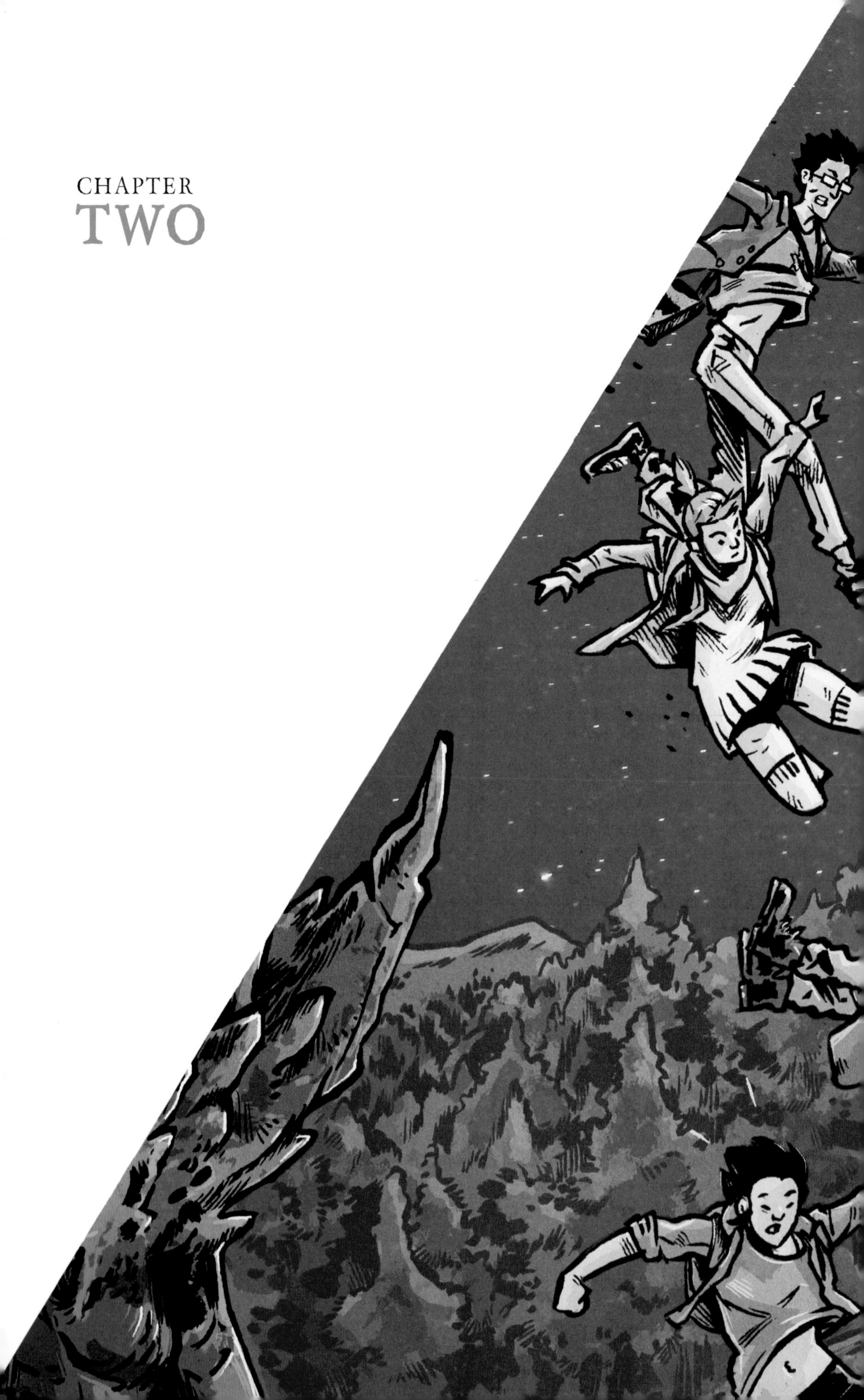

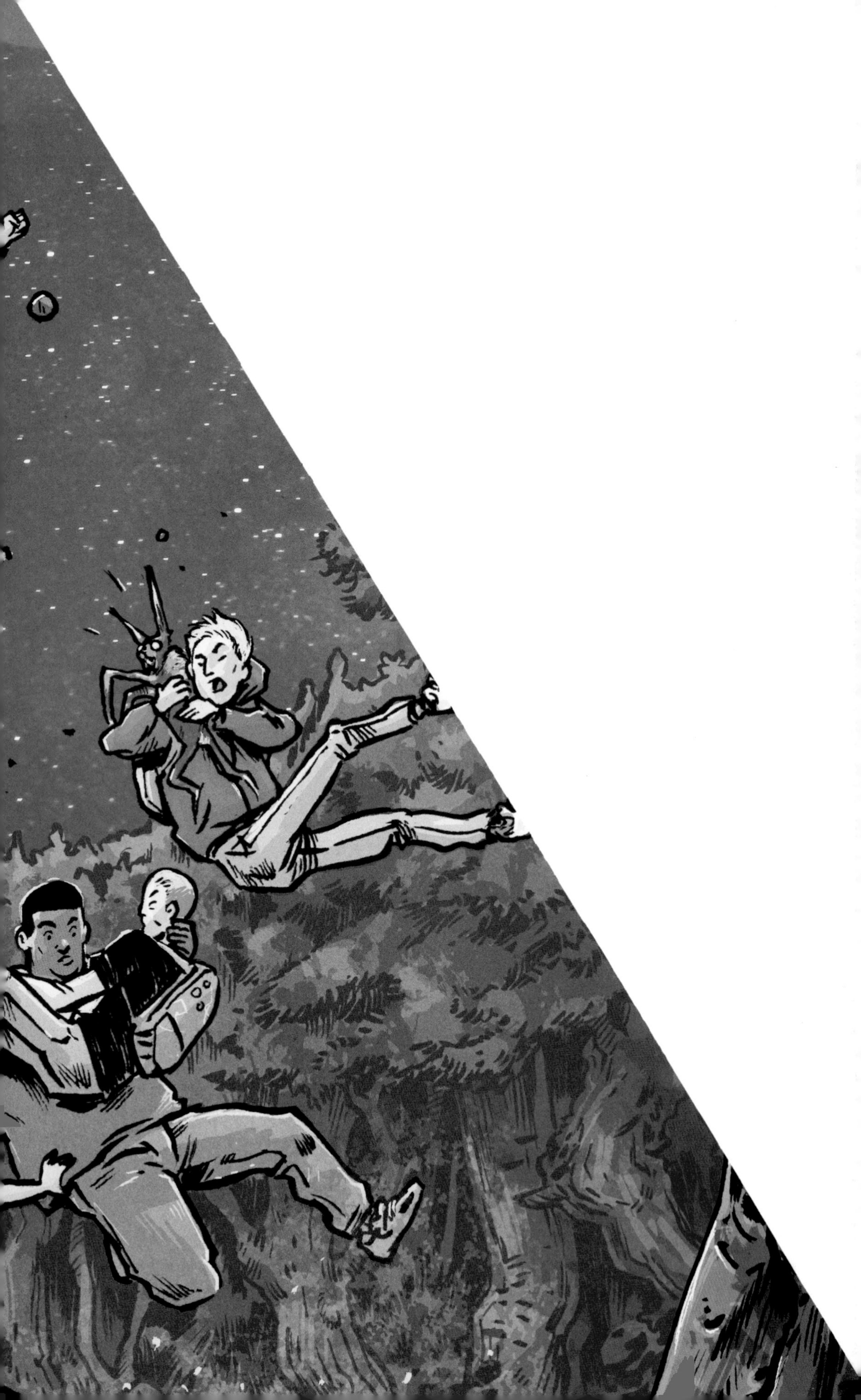

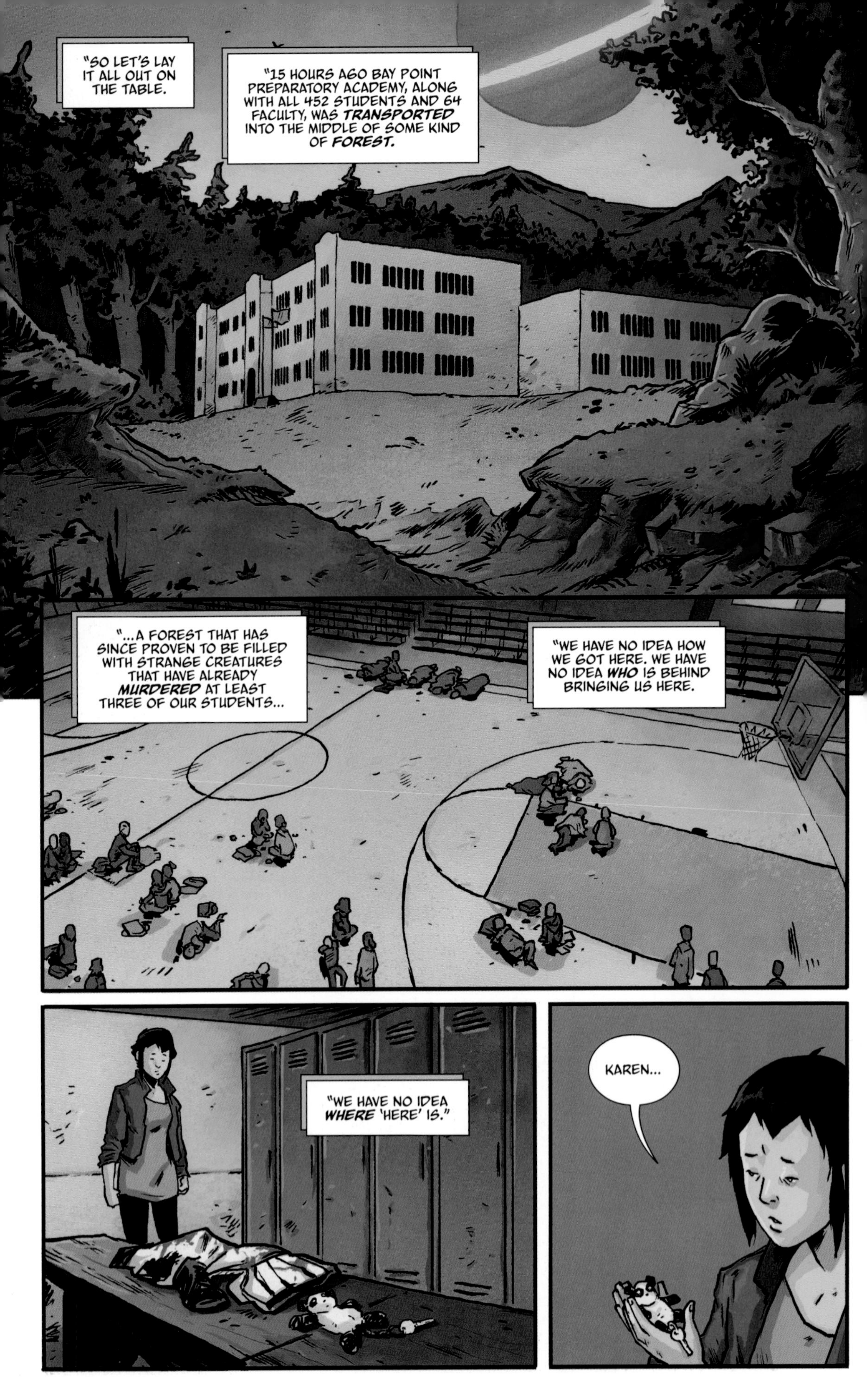
"SO LET'S LAY IT ALL OUT ON THE TABLE.
"15 HOURS AGO BAY POINT PREPARATORY ACADEMY, ALONG WITH ALL 452 STUDENTS AND 64 FACULTY, WAS TRANSPORTED INTO THE MIDDLE OF SOME KIND OF FOREST.
"...A FOREST THAT HAS SINCE PROVEN TO BE FILLED WITH STRANGE CREATURES THAT HAVE ALREADY MURDERED AT LEAST THREE OF OUR STUDENTS...
"WE HAVE NO IDEA HOW WE GOT HERE. WE HAVE NO IDEA WHO IS BEHIND BRINGING US HERE.
"WE HAVE NO IDEA WHERE 'HERE' IS."
KAREN...

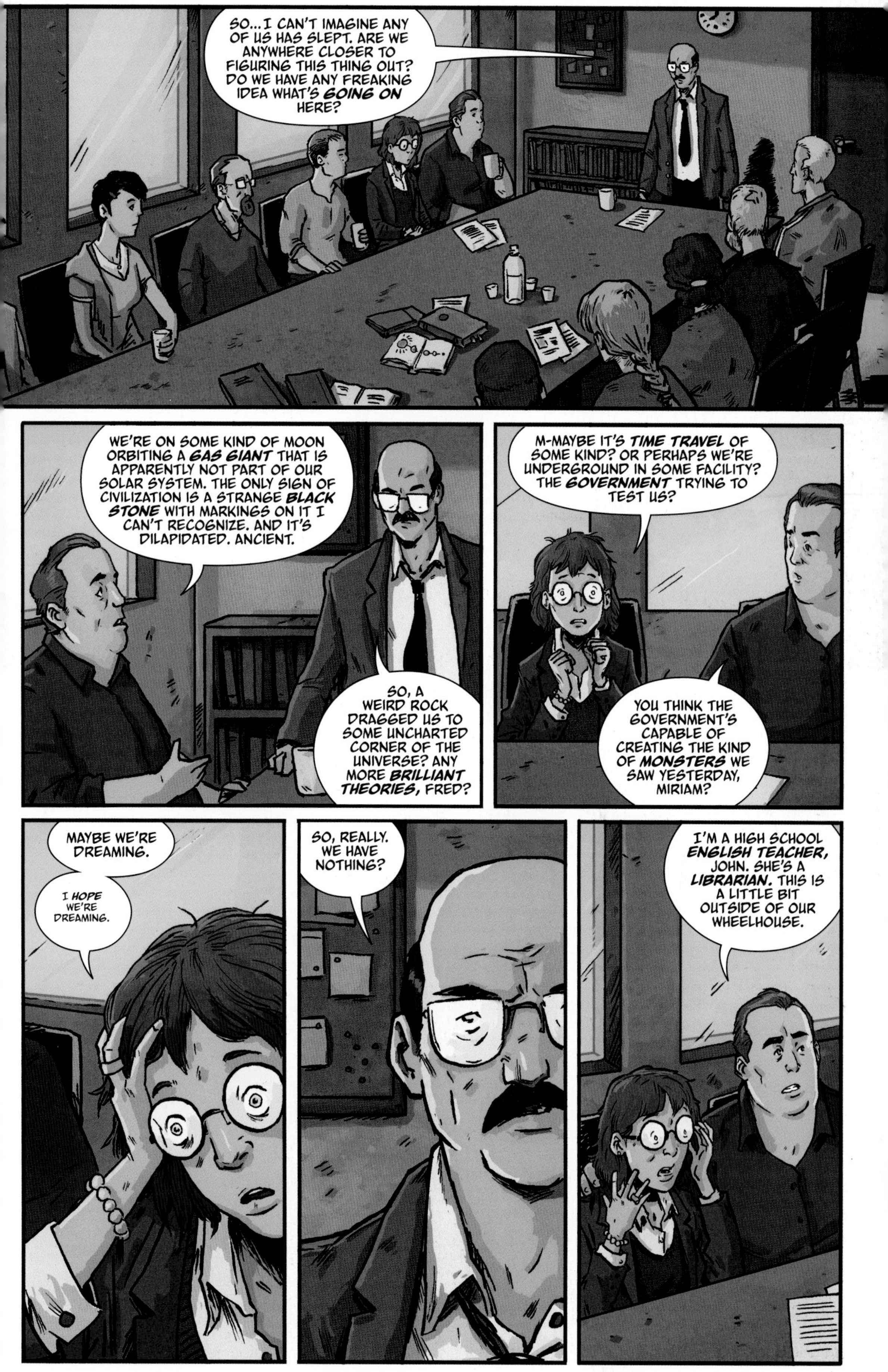

SO... I CAN'T IMAGINE ANY OF US HAS SLEPT. ARE WE ANYWHERE CLOSER TO FIGURING THIS THING OUT? DO WE HAVE ANY FREAKING IDEA WHAT'S GOING ON HERE?
WE'RE ON SOME KIND OF MOON ORBITING A GAS GIANT THAT IS APPARENTLY NOT PART OF OUR SOLAR SYSTEM. THE ONLY SIGN OF CIVILIZATION IS A STRANGE BLACK STONE WITH MARKINGS ON IT I CAN'T RECOGNIZE. AND IT'S DILAPIDATED. ANCIENT.
SO, A WEIRD ROCK DRAGGED US TO SOME UNCHARTED CORNER OF THE UNIVERSE? ANY MORE BRILLIANT THEORIES, FRED?
M-MAYBE IT'S TIME TRAVEL OF SOME KIND? OR PERHAPS WE'RE UNDERGROUND IN SOME FACILITY? THE GOVERNMENT TRYING TO TEST US?
YOU THINK THE GOVERNMENT'S CAPABLE OF CREATING THE KIND OF MONSTERS WE SAW YESTERDAY, MIRIAM?
MAYBE WE'RE DREAMING.
I HOPE WE'RE DREAMING.
SO, REALLY. WE HAVE NOTHING?
I'M A HIGH SCHOOL ENGLISH TEACHER, JOHN. SHE'S A LIBRARIAN. THIS IS A LITTLE BIT OUTSIDE OF OUR WHEELHOUSE.

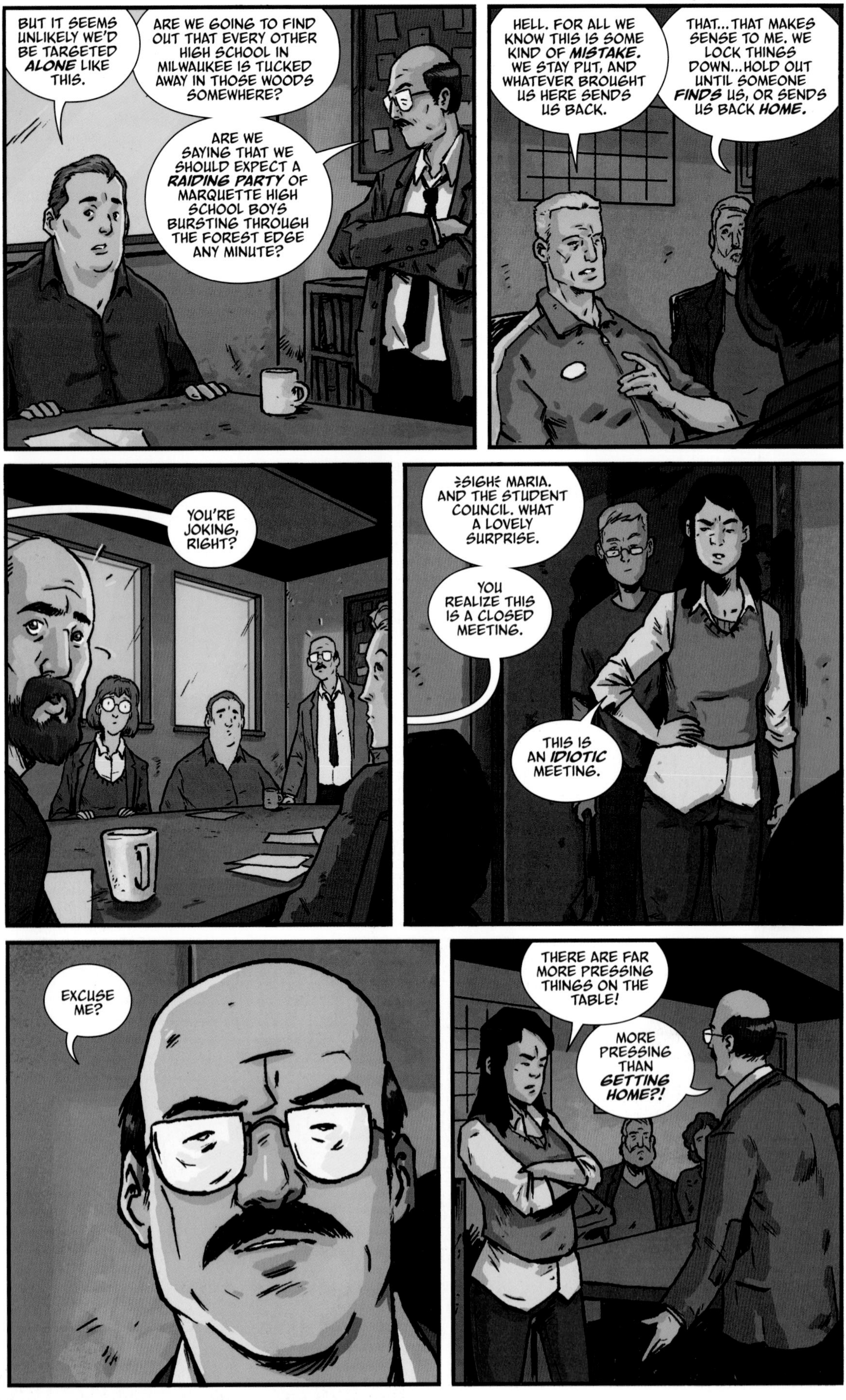
BUT IT SEEMS UNLIKELY WE'D BE TARGETED ALONE LIKE THIS.
ARE WE GOING TO FIND OUT THAT EVERY OTHER HIGH SCHOOL IN MILWAUKEE IS TUCKED AWAY IN THOSE WOODS SOMEWHERE?
ARE WE SAYING THAT WE SHOULD EXPECT A RAIDING PARTY OF MARQUETTE HIGH SCHOOL BOYS BURSTING THROUGH THE FOREST EDGE ANY MINUTE?
HELL. FOR ALL WE KNOW THIS IS SOME KIND OF MISTAKE. WE STAY PUT, AND WHATEVER BROUGHT US HERE SENDS US BACK.
THAT...THAT MAKES SENSE TO ME. WE LOCK THINGS DOWN...HOLD OUT UNTIL SOMEONE FINDS US, OR SENDS US BACK HOME.
YOU'RE JOKING, RIGHT?
SIGH MARIA. AND THE STUDENT COUNCIL. WHAT A LOVELY SURPRISE.
YOU REALIZE THIS IS A CLOSED MEETING.
THIS IS AN IDIOTIC MEETING.
EXCUSE ME?
THERE ARE FAR MORE PRESSING THINGS ON THE TABLE!
MORE PRESSING THAN GETTING HOME?!

YES. THERE'S THE FACT THAT STUDENTS ARE *STRESS-EATING* THROUGH EVERYTHING IN THE CAFETERIA. WE BARELY HAVE ENOUGH TO LAST US A *WEEK.*

AND HAVE YOU NOTICED THE *STENCH* IN HERE? PEOPLE ARE STILL USING THE BATHROOMS DESPITE NO *RUNNING WATER* IN THE BUILDING.

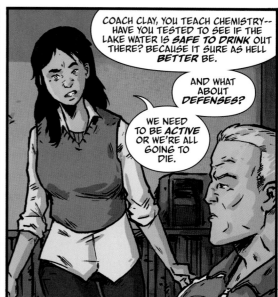

COACH CLAY, YOU TEACH CHEMISTRY-- HAVE YOU TESTED TO SEE IF THE LAKE WATER IS *SAFE TO DRINK* OUT THERE? BECAUSE IT SURE AS HELL *BETTER* BE.

AND WHAT ABOUT *DEFENSES?*

WE NEED TO BE *ACTIVE* OR WE'RE ALL GOING TO DIE.

IT'S OKAY, MS. WINTERS...WE'RE GOING TO BE OKAY. WE JUST HAVE TO *WORK TOGETHER* ON THIS.

OH GOD...OH GOD...

SHE'S RIGHT, JOHN.

WE *APPRECIATE* THAT YOU AND THE REST OF THE STUDENT COUNCIL ARE SO DEDICATED TO GETTING OUR SCHOOL BACK ON TRACK.

BUT RIGHT NOW, THE *ADULTS* NEED TO SIT DOWN AND DECIDE WHAT TO DO.

MR. BEAUMONT--

THAT'S *ENOUGH,* MARIA. YOU'RE DONE.

IF THEY'RE NOT GOING TO DO THIS WITH US, WE'RE GOING TO HAVE TO DO IT OURSELVES... DOES ANYONE REMEMBER HOW DEEP SANAMI SAID A *LATRINE* SHOULD BE?

WHERE THE HELL *IS* SHE, ANYWAY?

TEACHERS LOUNGE

SLAM!

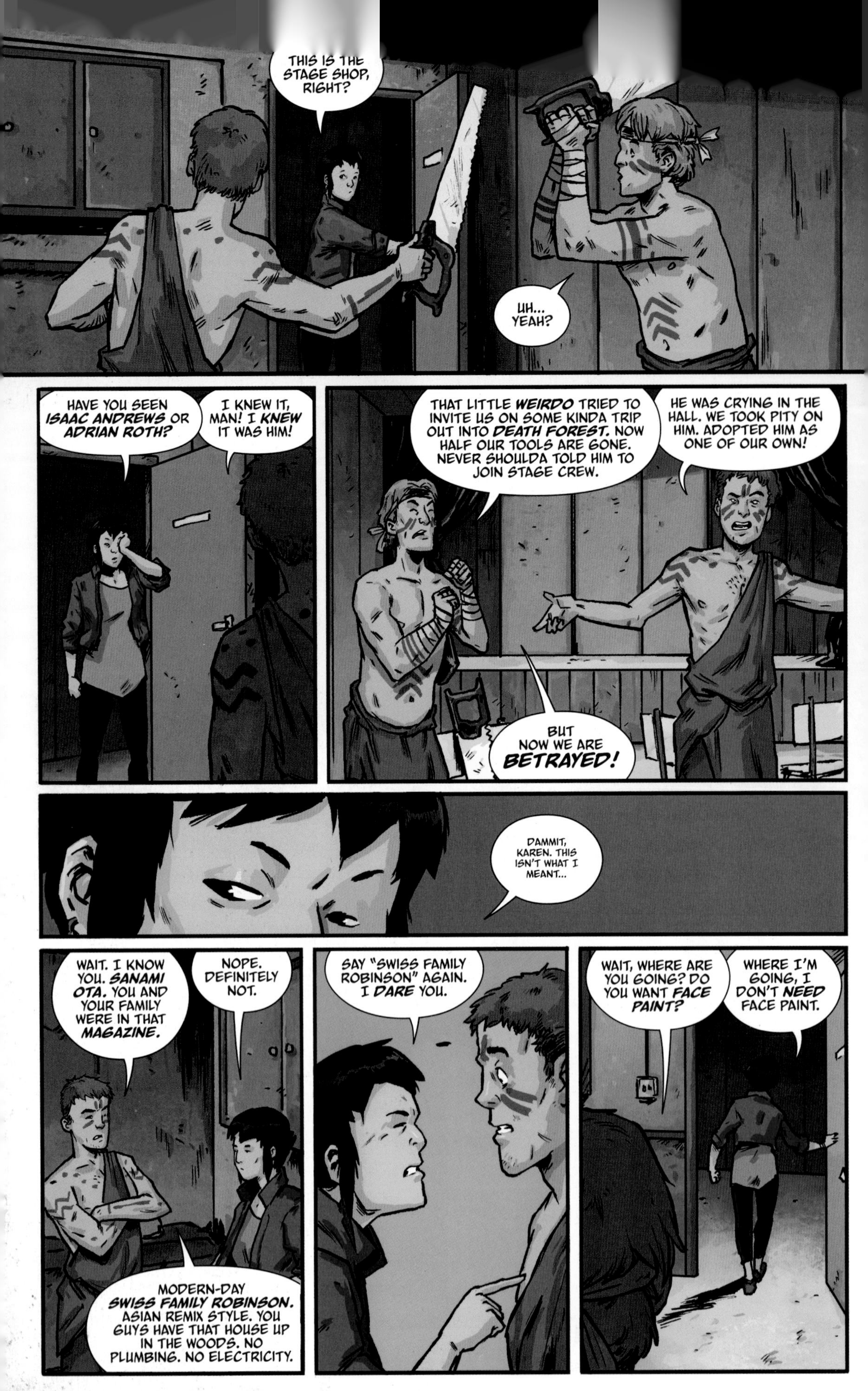
THIS IS THE STAGE SHOP, RIGHT?
UH... YEAH?
HAVE YOU SEEN ISAAC ANDREWS OR ADRIAN ROTH?
I KNEW IT, MAN! I KNEW IT WAS HIM!
THAT LITTLE WEIRDO TRIED TO INVITE US ON SOME KINDA TRIP OUT INTO DEATH FOREST. NOW HALF OUR TOOLS ARE GONE. NEVER SHOULDA TOLD HIM TO JOIN STAGE CREW.
HE WAS CRYING IN THE HALL. WE TOOK PITY ON HIM. ADOPTED HIM AS ONE OF OUR OWN!
BUT NOW WE ARE BETRAYED!
DAMMIT, KAREN. THIS ISN'T WHAT I MEANT...
WAIT. I KNOW YOU. SANAMI OTA. YOU AND YOUR FAMILY WERE IN THAT MAGAZINE.
NOPE. DEFINITELY NOT.
MODERN-DAY SWISS FAMILY ROBINSON. ASIAN REMIX STYLE. YOU GUYS HAVE THAT HOUSE UP IN THE WOODS. NO PLUMBING. NO ELECTRICITY.
SAY "SWISS FAMILY ROBINSON" AGAIN. I DARE YOU.
WAIT, WHERE ARE YOU GOING? DO YOU WANT FACE PAINT?
WHERE I'M GOING, I DON'T NEED FACE PAINT.

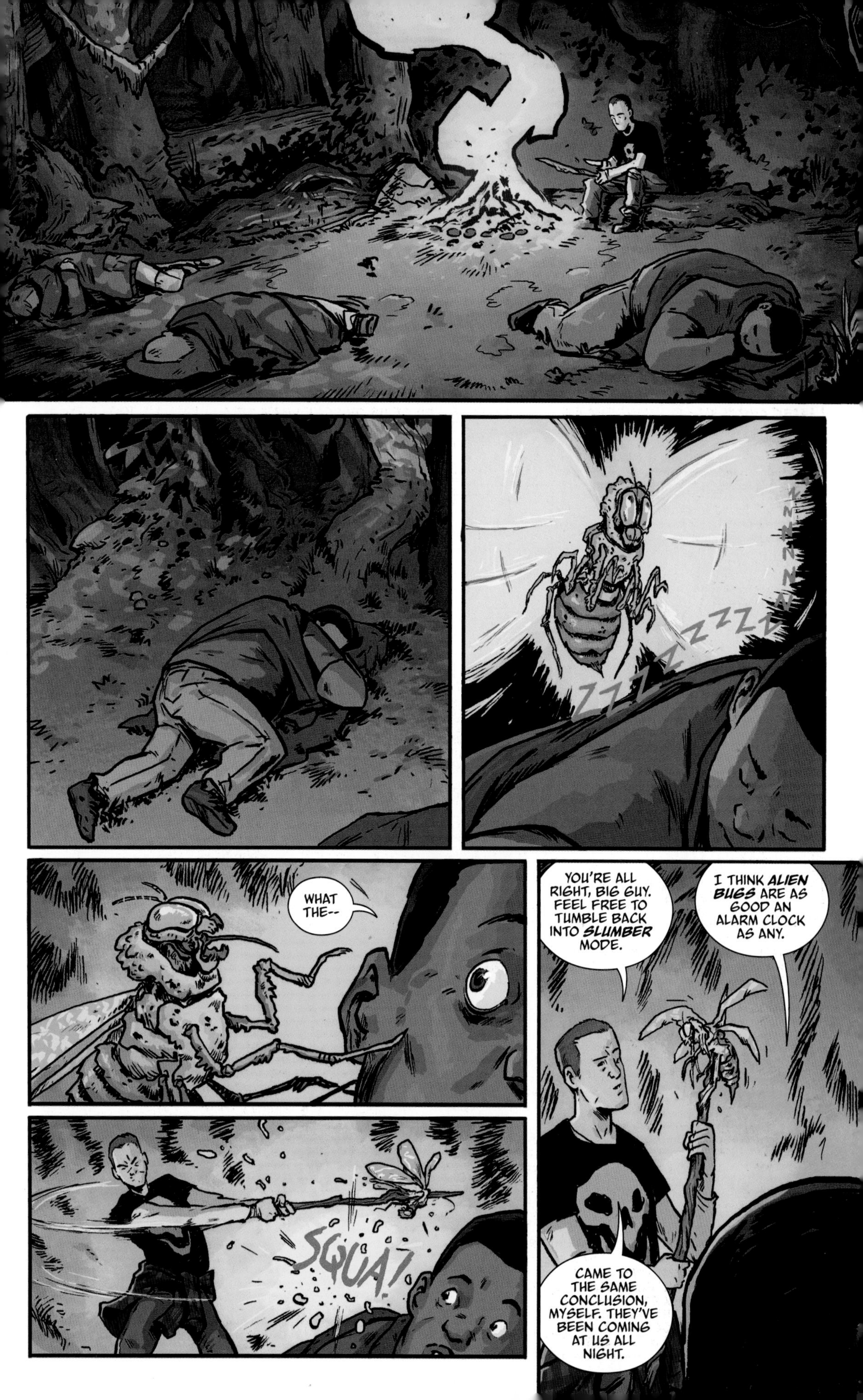
WHAT THE--
SQUA!
YOU'RE ALL RIGHT, BIG GUY. FEEL FREE TO TUMBLE BACK INTO SLUMBER MODE.
I THINK ALIEN BUGS ARE AS GOOD AN ALARM CLOCK AS ANY.
CAME TO THE SAME CONCLUSION, MYSELF. THEY'VE BEEN COMING AT US ALL NIGHT.

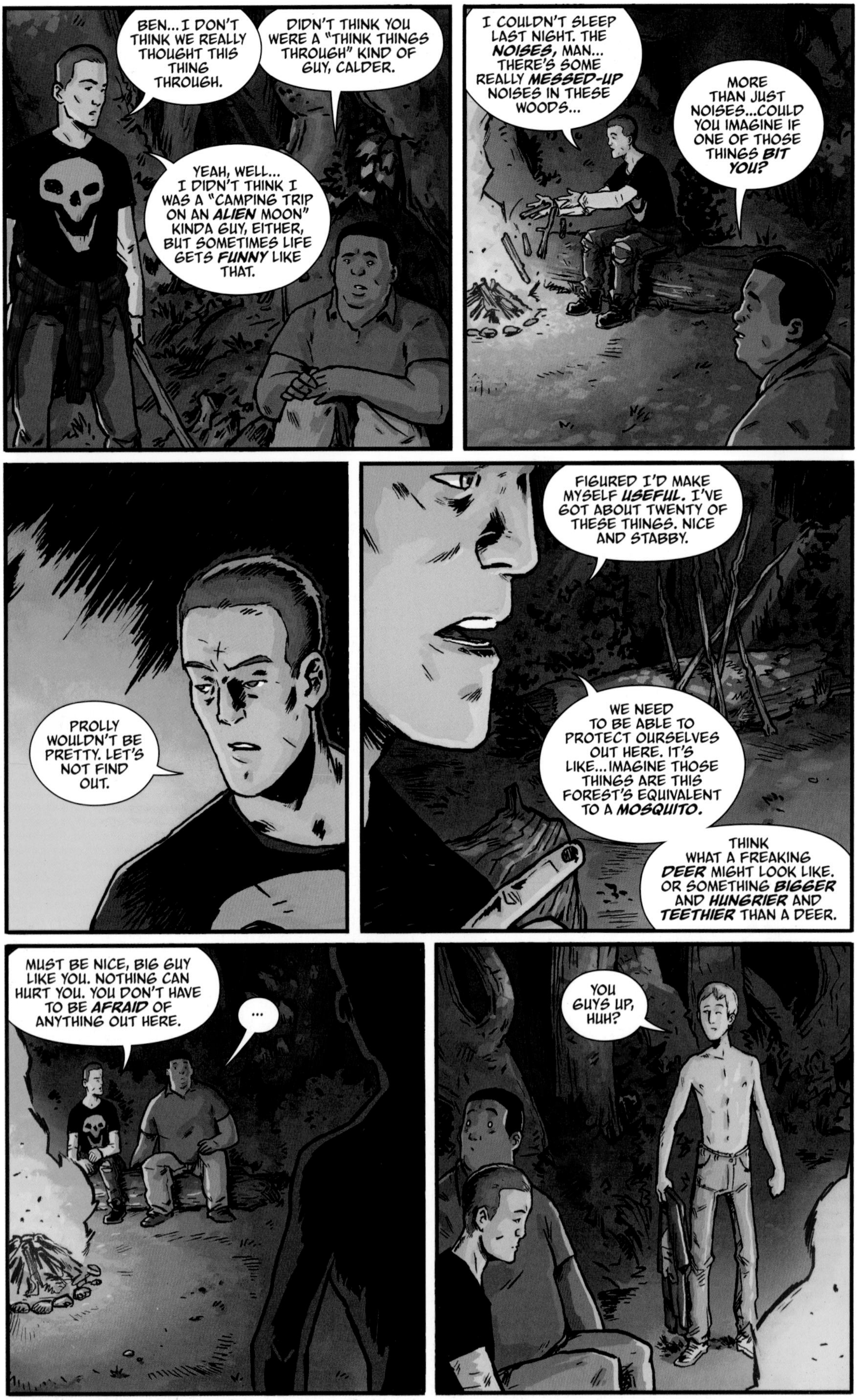
BEN... I DON'T THINK WE REALLY THOUGHT THIS THING THROUGH.
DIDN'T THINK YOU WERE A "THINK THINGS THROUGH" KIND OF GUY, CALDER.
YEAH, WELL... I DIDN'T THINK I WAS A "CAMPING TRIP ON AN ALIEN MOON" KINDA GUY, EITHER, BUT SOMETIMES LIFE GETS FUNNY LIKE THAT.
I COULDN'T SLEEP LAST NIGHT. THE NOISES, MAN... THERE'S SOME REALLY MESSED-UP NOISES IN THESE WOODS...
MORE THAN JUST NOISES...COULD YOU IMAGINE IF ONE OF THOSE THINGS BIT YOU?
PROLLY WOULDN'T BE PRETTY. LET'S NOT FIND OUT.
FIGURED I'D MAKE MYSELF USEFUL. I'VE GOT ABOUT TWENTY OF THESE THINGS. NICE AND STABBY.
WE NEED TO BE ABLE TO PROTECT OURSELVES OUT HERE. IT'S LIKE...IMAGINE THOSE THINGS ARE THIS FOREST'S EQUIVALENT TO A MOSQUITO.
THINK WHAT A FREAKING DEER MIGHT LOOK LIKE. OR SOMETHING BIGGER AND HUNGRIER AND TEETHIER THAN A DEER.
MUST BE NICE, BIG GUY LIKE YOU. NOTHING CAN HURT YOU. YOU DON'T HAVE TO BE AFRAID OF ANYTHING OUT HERE.
...
YOU GUYS UP, HUH?

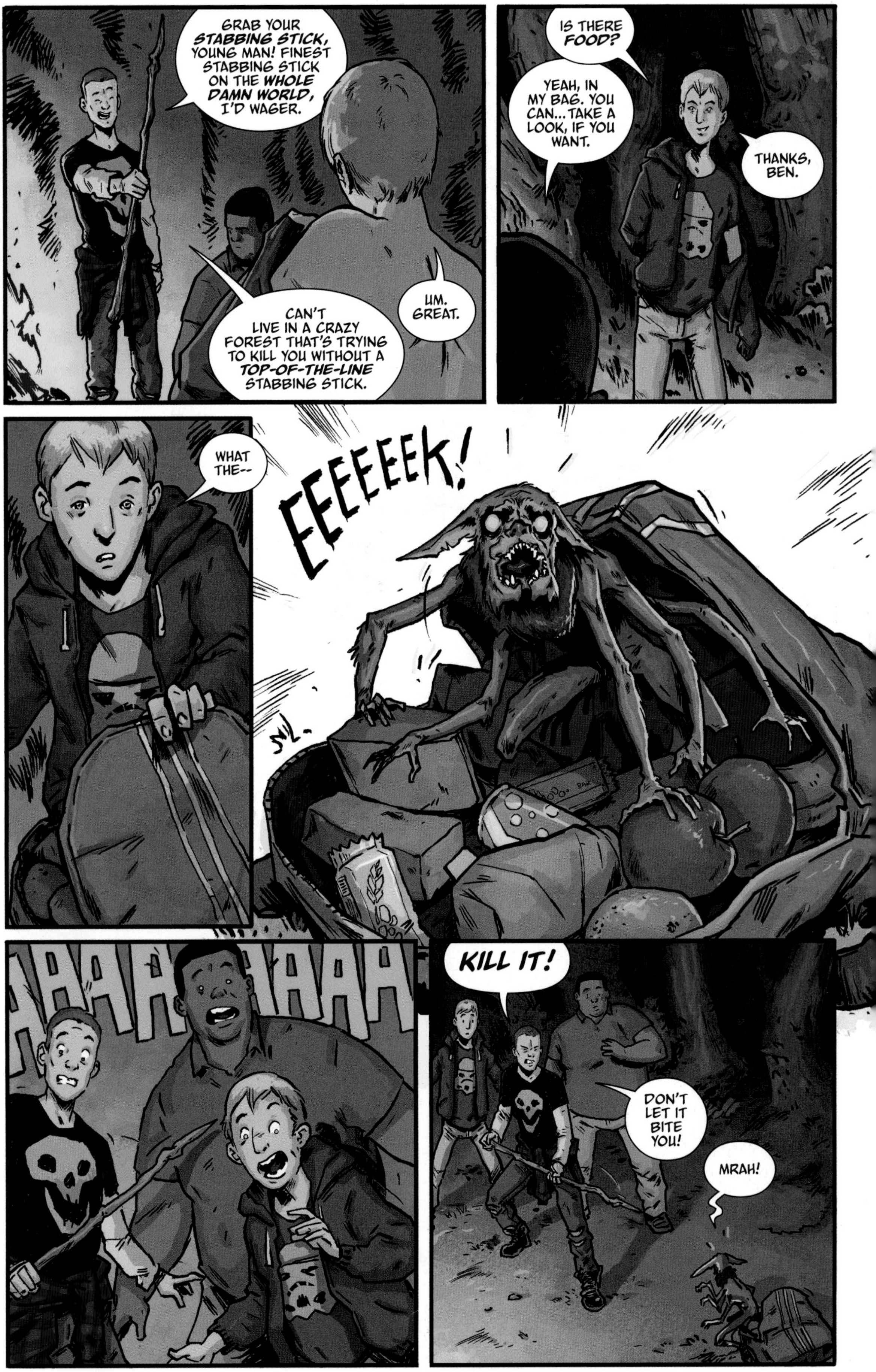
GRAB YOUR STABBING STICK, YOUNG MAN! FINEST STABBING STICK ON THE WHOLE DAMN WORLD, I'D WAGER.
CAN'T LIVE IN A CRAZY FOREST THAT'S TRYING TO KILL YOU WITHOUT A TOP-OF-THE-LINE STABBING STICK.
UM. GREAT.
IS THERE FOOD?
YEAH, IN MY BAG. YOU CAN...TAKE A LOOK, IF YOU WANT.
THANKS, BEN.
WHAT THE--
EEEEEEK!
AAAAAAAAA
KILL IT!
DON'T LET IT BITE YOU!
MRAH!

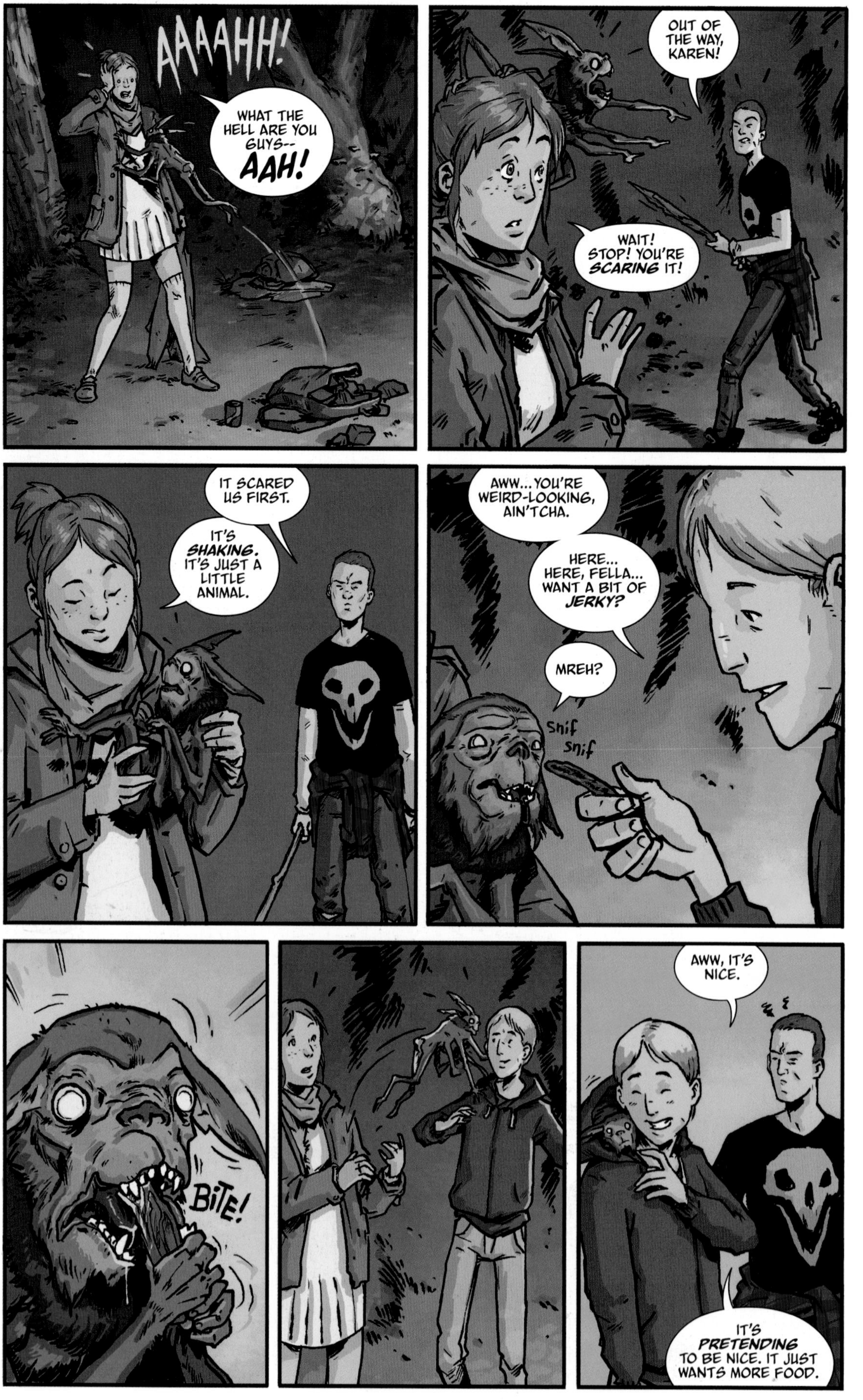
AAAAHH!
WHAT THE HELL ARE YOU GUYS-- AAH!
OUT OF THE WAY, KAREN!
WAIT! STOP! YOU'RE SCARING IT!
IT SCARED US FIRST.
IT'S SHAKING. IT'S JUST A LITTLE ANIMAL.
AWW... YOU'RE WEIRD-LOOKING, AIN'TCHA.
HERE... HERE, FELLA... WANT A BIT OF JERKY?
MREH?
snif snif
BITE!
AWW, IT'S NICE.
IT'S PRETENDING TO BE NICE. IT JUST WANTS MORE FOOD.

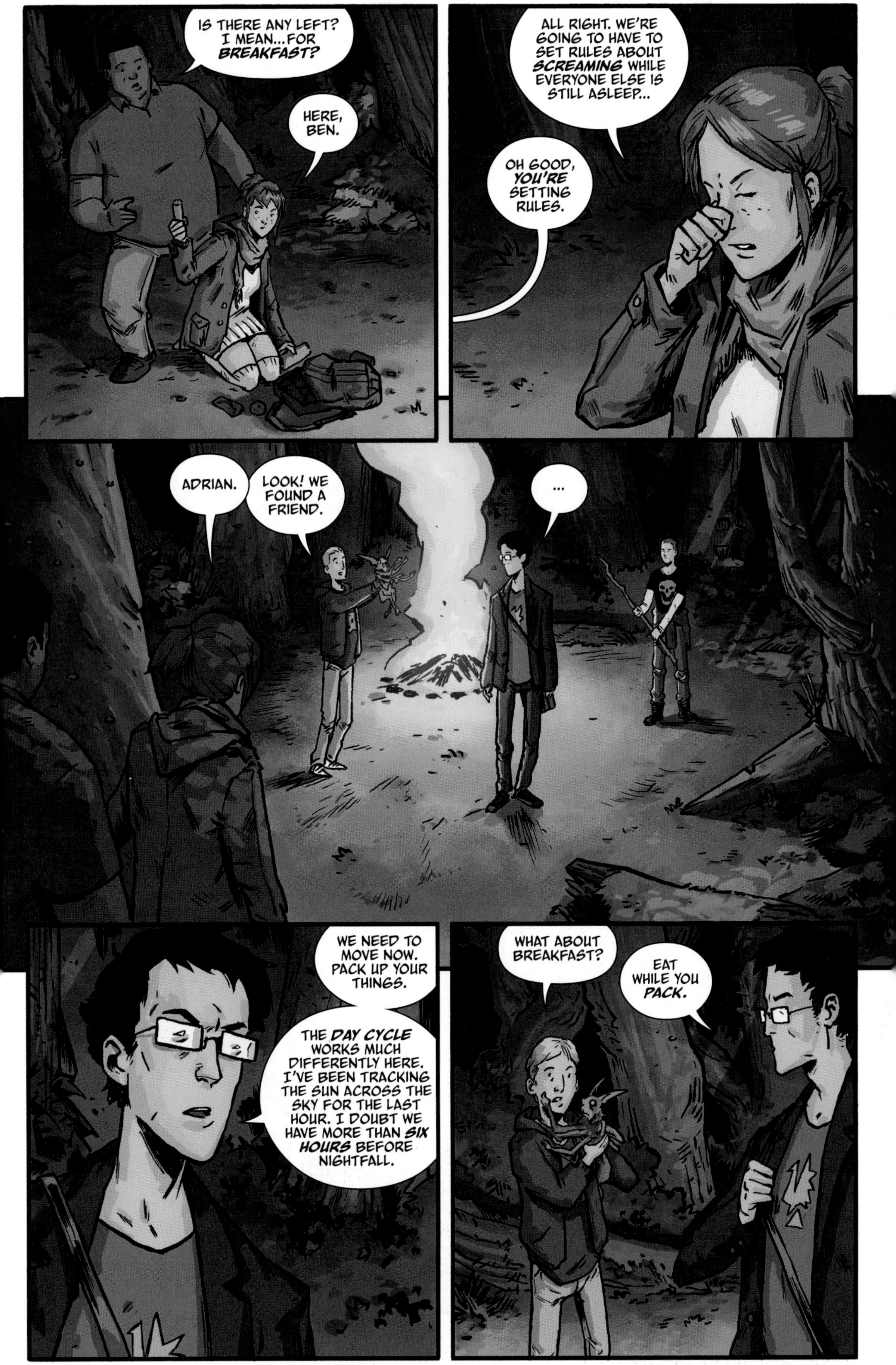
IS THERE ANY LEFT? I MEAN...FOR BREAKFAST?
HERE, BEN.
ALL RIGHT. WE'RE GOING TO HAVE TO SET RULES ABOUT SCREAMING WHILE EVERYONE ELSE IS STILL ASLEEP...
OH GOOD, YOU'RE SETTING RULES.
ADRIAN.
LOOK! WE FOUND A FRIEND.
...
WE NEED TO MOVE NOW. PACK UP YOUR THINGS.
THE DAY CYCLE WORKS MUCH DIFFERENTLY HERE. I'VE BEEN TRACKING THE SUN ACROSS THE SKY FOR THE LAST HOUR. I DOUBT WE HAVE MORE THAN SIX HOURS BEFORE NIGHTFALL.
WHAT ABOUT BREAKFAST?
EAT WHILE YOU PACK.

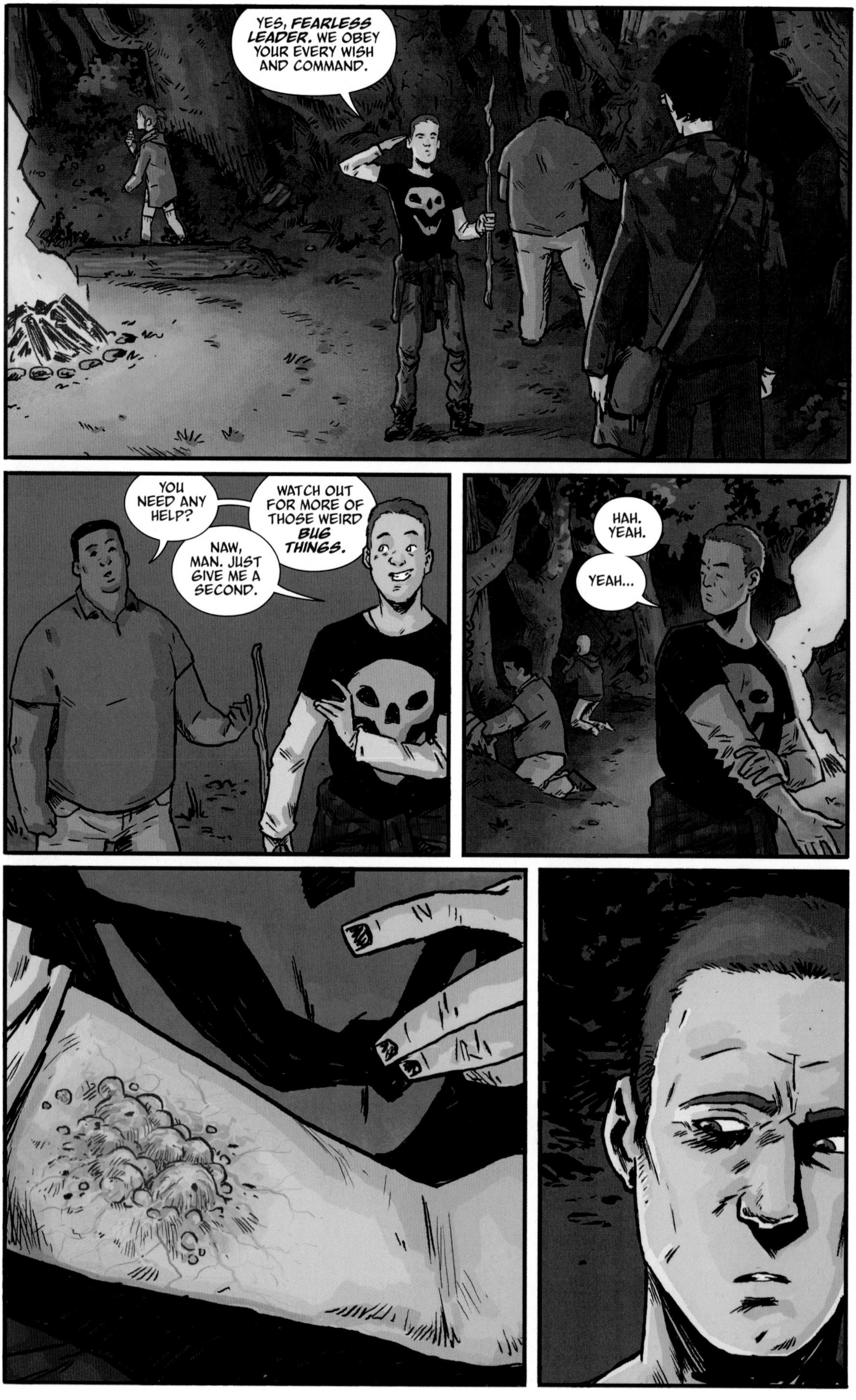

YES, FEARLESS LEADER. WE OBEY YOUR EVERY WISH AND COMMAND.
YOU NEED ANY HELP?
WATCH OUT FOR MORE OF THOSE WEIRD BUG THINGS.
NAW, MAN. JUST GIVE ME A SECOND.
HAH. YEAH.
YEAH...

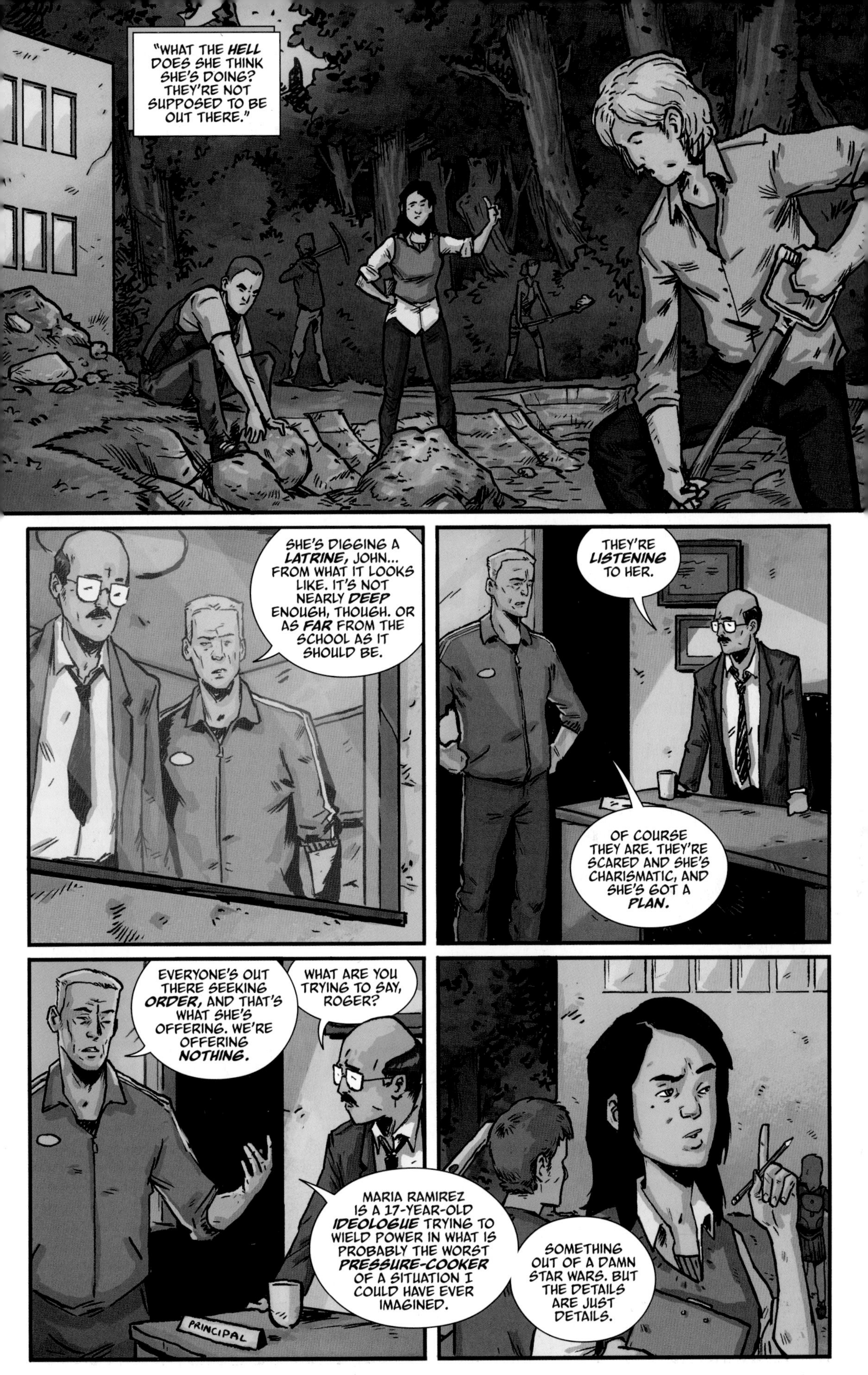
"WHAT THE HELL DOES SHE THINK SHE'S DOING? THEY'RE NOT SUPPOSED TO BE OUT THERE."
SHE'S DIGGING A LATRINE, JOHN... FROM WHAT IT LOOKS LIKE. IT'S NOT NEARLY DEEP ENOUGH, THOUGH. OR AS FAR FROM THE SCHOOL AS IT SHOULD BE.
THEY'RE LISTENING TO HER.
OF COURSE THEY ARE. THEY'RE SCARED AND SHE'S CHARISMATIC, AND SHE'S GOT A PLAN.
EVERYONE'S OUT THERE SEEKING ORDER, AND THAT'S WHAT SHE'S OFFERING. WE'RE OFFERING NOTHING.
WHAT ARE YOU TRYING TO SAY, ROGER?
MARIA RAMIREZ IS A 17-YEAR-OLD IDEOLOGUE TRYING TO WIELD POWER IN WHAT IS PROBABLY THE WORST PRESSURE-COOKER OF A SITUATION I COULD HAVE EVER IMAGINED.
PRINCIPAL
SOMETHING OUT OF A DAMN STAR WARS. BUT THE DETAILS ARE JUST DETAILS.

I'VE SEEN *PLENTY* LIKE HER BEFORE, BACK IN MY TIME WITH THE SPECIAL *FORCES.*

A YOUNG IDEALIST TAKING ADVANTAGE OF A *DESTABILIZED SITUATION* WITH NO REAL KNOWLEDGE OF HOW TO MAKE IT BETTER.

PEOPLE LIKE HER ARE *DANGEROUS,* JOHN. THEY SPREAD DISCORD LIKE AN *INFECTION.* UNTIL EVERYONE'S CAUGHT UP IN IT.

BUT IT DOESN'T HAVE TO BE THAT WAY, DOES IT?

IT DOESN'T?

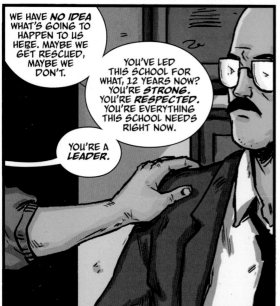

WE HAVE *NO IDEA* WHAT'S GOING TO HAPPEN TO US HERE. MAYBE WE GET RESCUED, MAYBE WE DON'T.

YOU'VE LED THIS SCHOOL FOR WHAT, 12 YEARS NOW? YOU'RE *STRONG.* YOU'RE *RESPECTED.* YOU'RE EVERYTHING THIS SCHOOL NEEDS RIGHT NOW.

YOU'RE A *LEADER.*

THESE ARE *TEENAGERS,* FOR GOD'S SAKE. HALF OF THEM HAVEN'T FIGURED OUT HOW TO USE A STICK OF *DEODORANT.*

WE'VE GOT *MONSTERS.* WE'VE GOT *INFRASTRUCTURE* PROBLEMS. WE'VE GOT A *FOOD SHORTAGE.*

"AND WE HAVE NEARLY *FIVE-HUNDRED* TERRIFIED, HORMONAL KIDS WHO THINK THEY KNOW EVERYTHING ABOUT EVERYTHING.

"I THINK, SIR, THAT IT'S TIME YOU SHOWED THEM THEY'RE *WRONG.*"

"YOU'RE RIGHT, ROGER. YOU'RE RIGHT...GET MY TEAM TOGETHER RIGHT NOW. WE NEED TO ACT *FAST.* THIS HAS GONE ON *LONG ENOUGH.*

"NO MORE OF THIS *CHILD'S PLAY*...AND RAMIREZ...SHE'LL NEED TO BE *DEALT WITH.*"

YES, SIR.

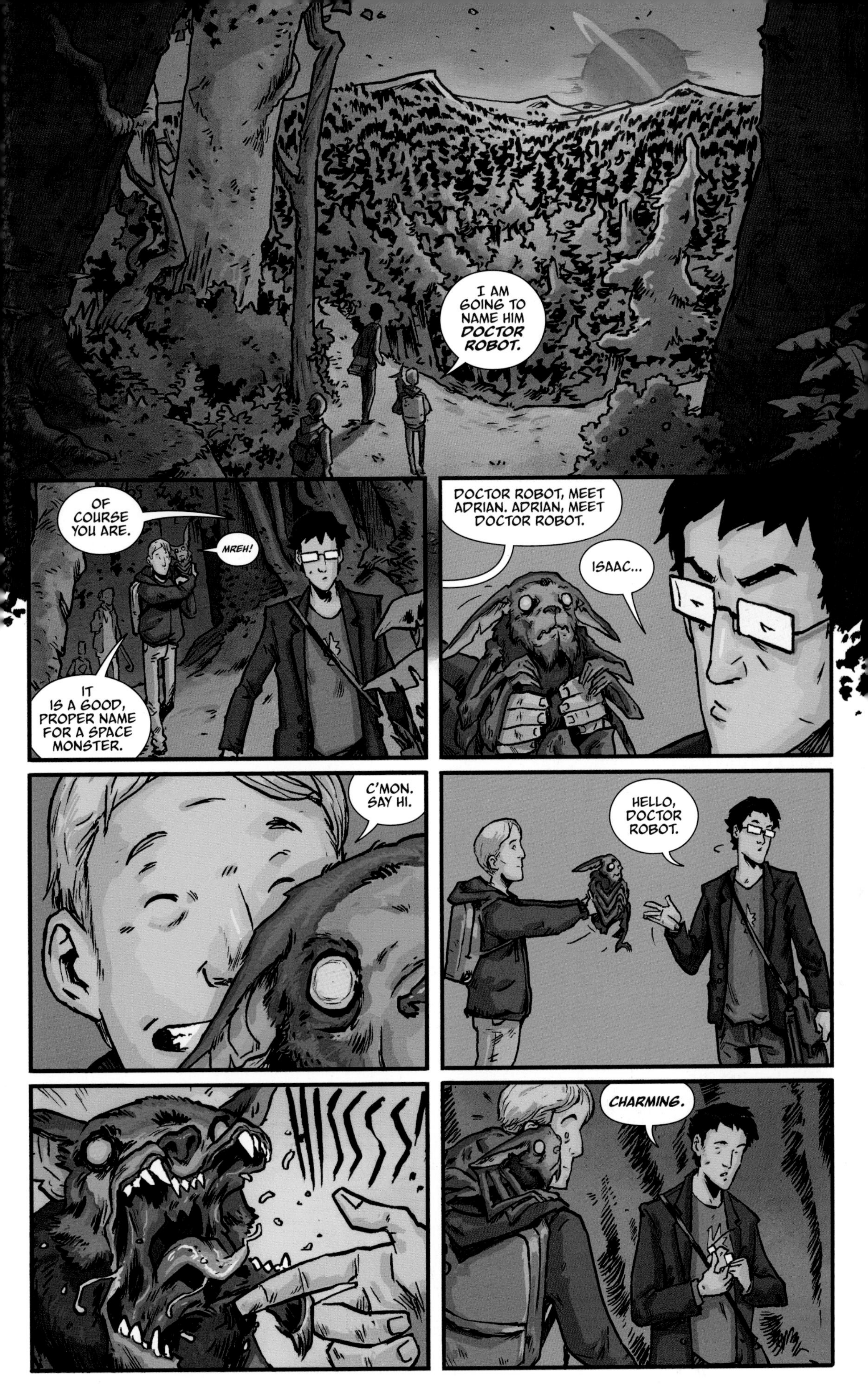
I AM GOING TO NAME HIM *DOCTOR ROBOT.*
OF COURSE YOU ARE.
MREH!
IT IS A GOOD, PROPER NAME FOR A SPACE MONSTER.
DOCTOR ROBOT, MEET ADRIAN. ADRIAN, MEET DOCTOR ROBOT.
ISAAC...
C'MON. SAY HI.
HELLO, DOCTOR ROBOT.
HISSSS!
CHARMING.

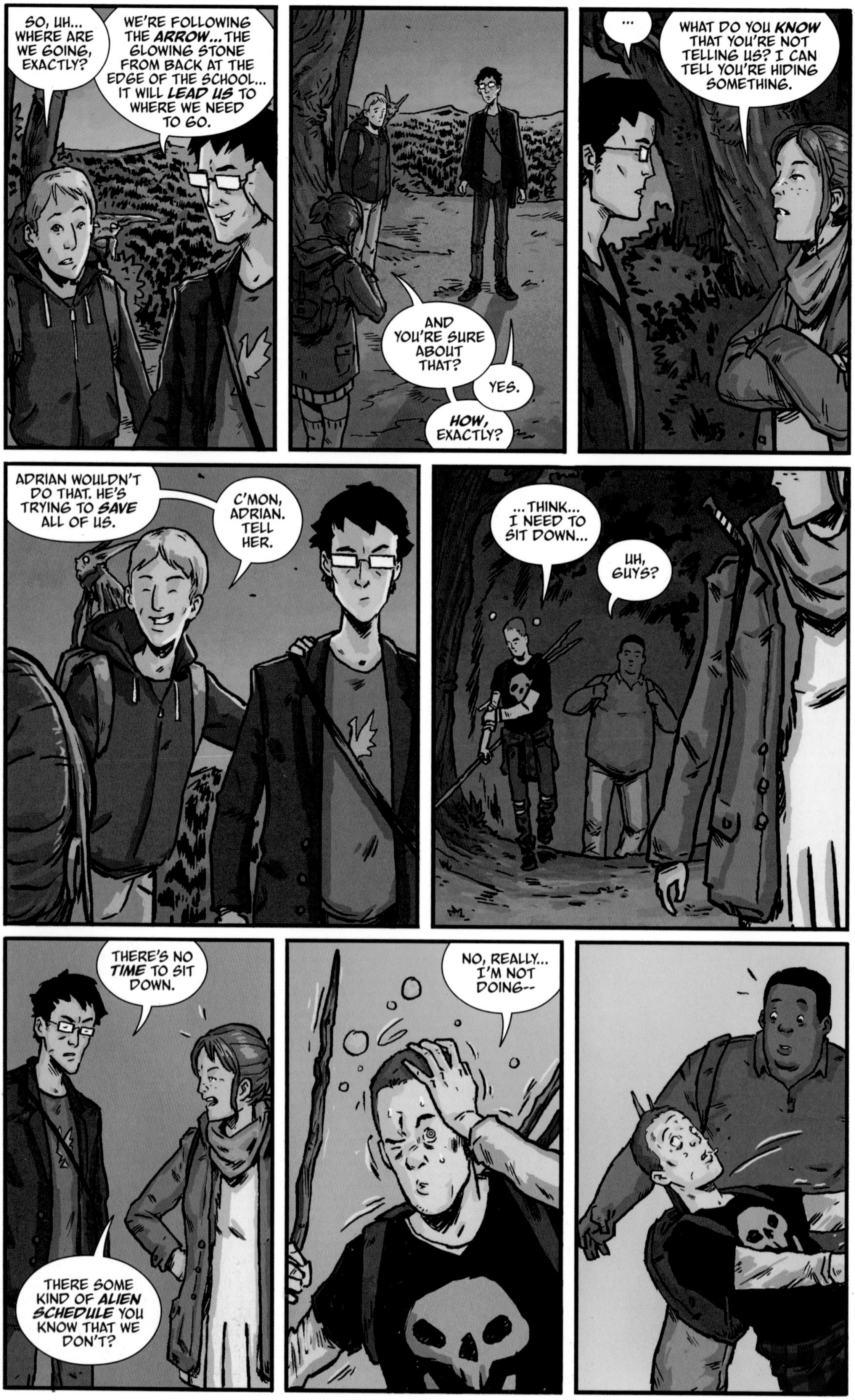
SO, UH... WHERE ARE WE GOING, EXACTLY?
WE'RE FOLLOWING THE ARROW... THE GLOWING STONE FROM BACK AT THE EDGE OF THE SCHOOL... IT WILL LEAD US TO WHERE WE NEED TO GO.
AND YOU'RE SURE ABOUT THAT?
YES.
HOW, EXACTLY?
...
WHAT DO YOU KNOW THAT YOU'RE NOT TELLING US? I CAN TELL YOU'RE HIDING SOMETHING.
ADRIAN WOULDN'T DO THAT. HE'S TRYING TO SAVE ALL OF US.
C'MON, ADRIAN. TELL HER.
...THINK... I NEED TO SIT DOWN...
UH, GUYS?
THERE'S NO TIME TO SIT DOWN.
THERE SOME KIND OF ALIEN SCHEDULE YOU KNOW THAT WE DON'T?
NO, REALLY... I'M NOT DOING--

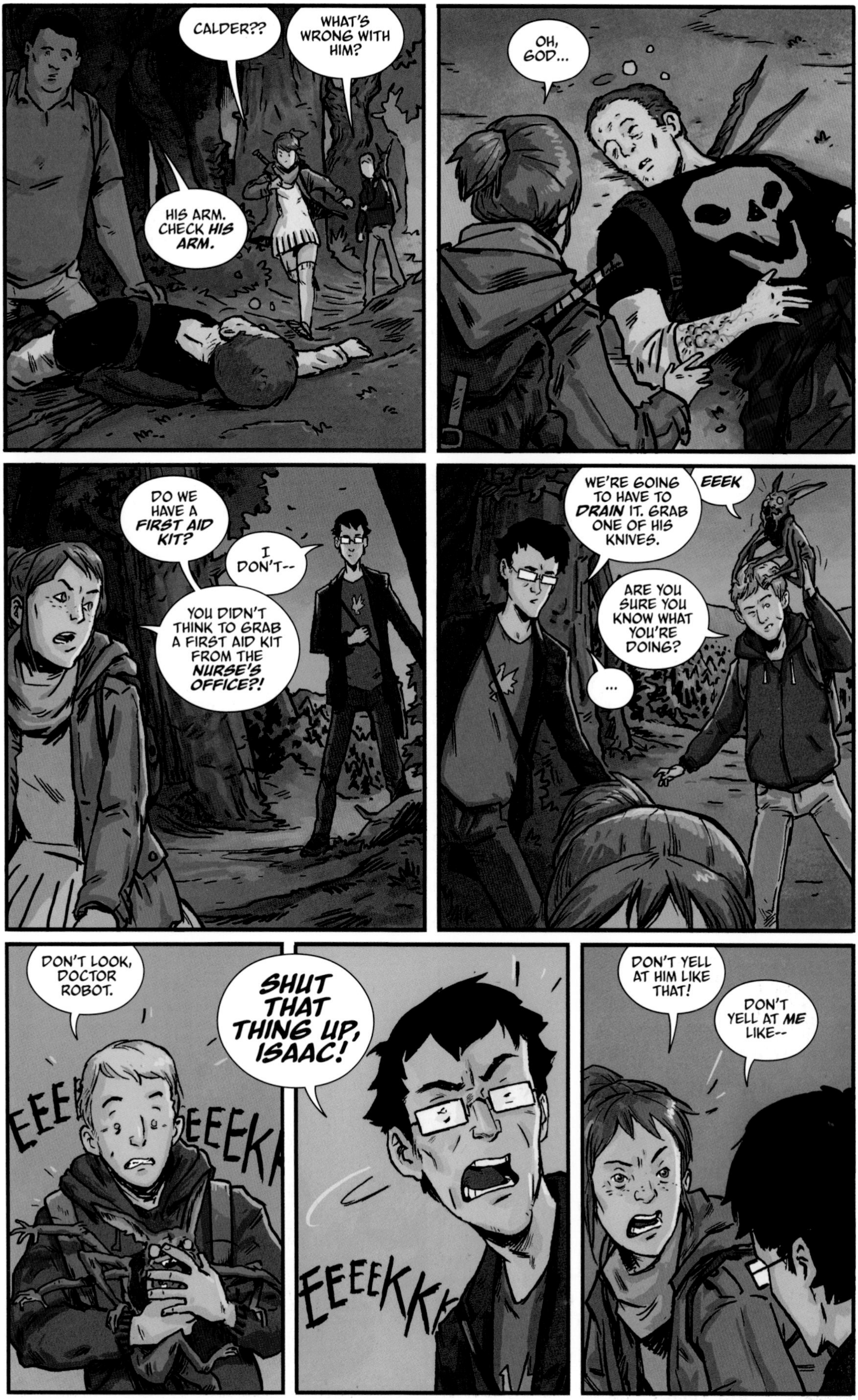
CALDER??
WHAT'S WRONG WITH HIM?
HIS ARM. CHECK HIS ARM.
OH, GOD...
DO WE HAVE A FIRST AID KIT?
I DON'T--
YOU DIDN'T THINK TO GRAB A FIRST AID KIT FROM THE NURSE'S OFFICE?!
WE'RE GOING TO HAVE TO DRAIN IT. GRAB ONE OF HIS KNIVES.
EEEK
ARE YOU SURE YOU KNOW WHAT YOU'RE DOING?
...
DON'T LOOK, DOCTOR ROBOT.
EEEEKK
SHUT THAT THING UP, ISAAC!
EEEKKK
DON'T YELL AT HIM LIKE THAT!
DON'T YELL AT ME LIKE--

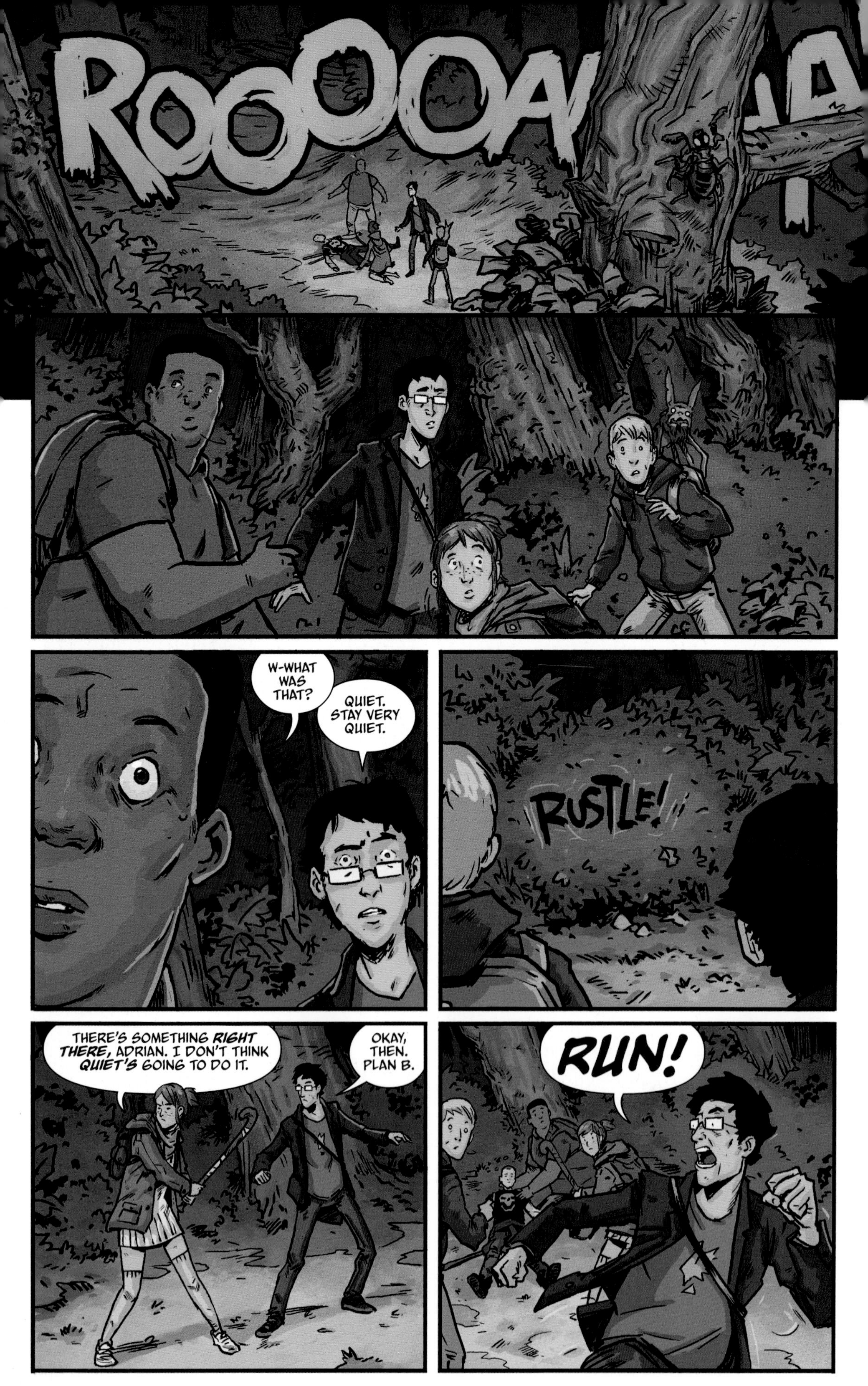
ROOOOA
W-WHAT WAS THAT?
QUIET. STAY VERY QUIET.
RUSTLE!
THERE'S SOMETHING ***RIGHT THERE,*** ADRIAN. I DON'T THINK ***QUIET'S*** GOING TO DO IT.
OKAY, THEN. PLAN B.
RUN!

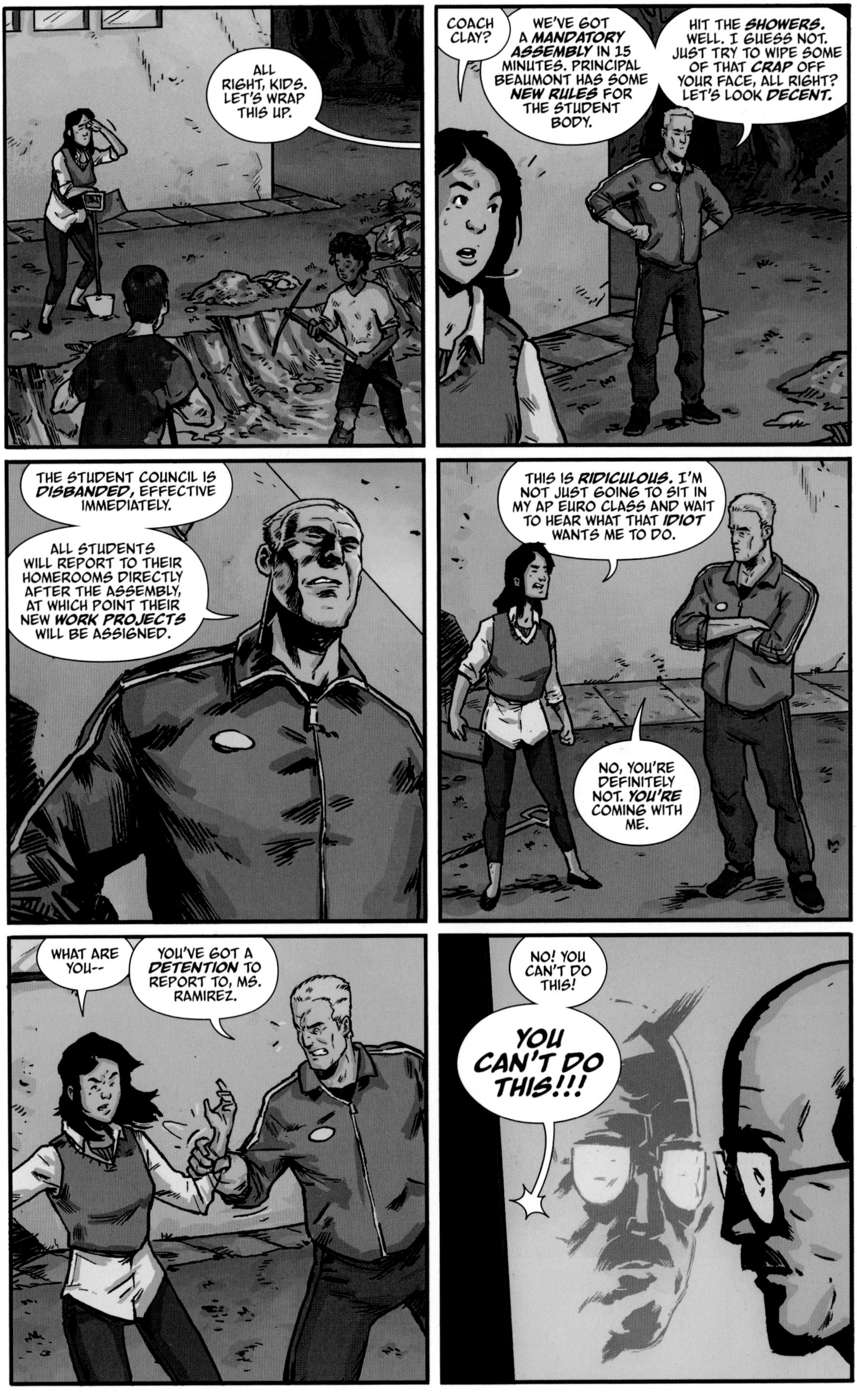
ALL RIGHT, KIDS. LET'S WRAP THIS UP.
COACH CLAY?
WE'VE GOT A MANDATORY ASSEMBLY IN 15 MINUTES. PRINCIPAL BEAUMONT HAS SOME NEW RULES FOR THE STUDENT BODY.
HIT THE SHOWERS. WELL. I GUESS NOT. JUST TRY TO WIPE SOME OF THAT CRAP OFF YOUR FACE, ALL RIGHT? LET'S LOOK DECENT.
THE STUDENT COUNCIL IS DISBANDED, EFFECTIVE IMMEDIATELY.
ALL STUDENTS WILL REPORT TO THEIR HOMEROOMS DIRECTLY AFTER THE ASSEMBLY, AT WHICH POINT THEIR NEW WORK PROJECTS WILL BE ASSIGNED.
THIS IS RIDICULOUS. I'M NOT JUST GOING TO SIT IN MY AP EURO CLASS AND WAIT TO HEAR WHAT THAT IDIOT WANTS ME TO DO.
NO, YOU'RE DEFINITELY NOT. YOU'RE COMING WITH ME.
WHAT ARE YOU--
YOU'VE GOT A DETENTION TO REPORT TO, MS. RAMIREZ.
NO! YOU CAN'T DO THIS!
YOU CAN'T DO THIS!!!

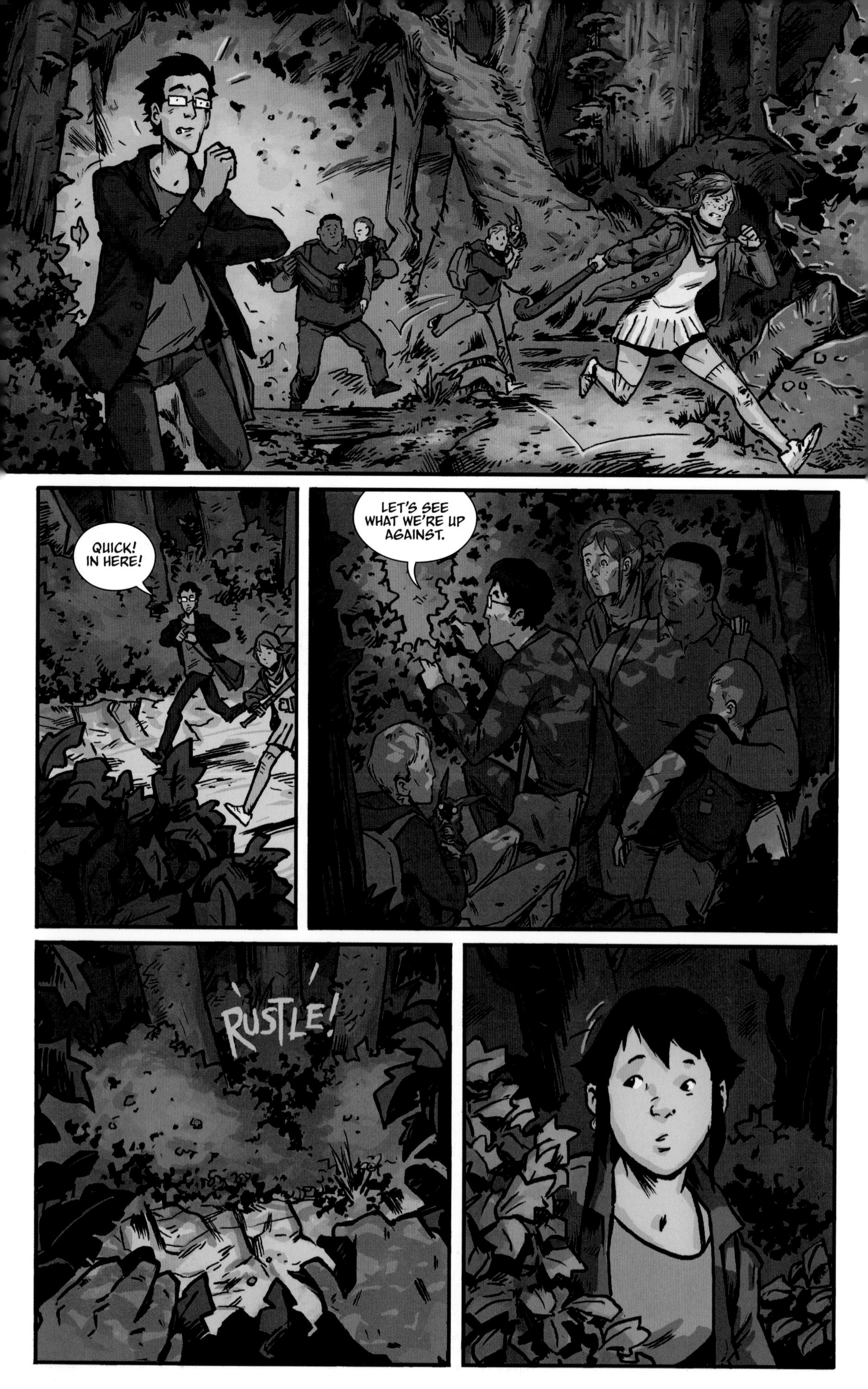
QUICK! IN HERE!
LET'S SEE WHAT WE'RE UP AGAINST.
RUSTLE!

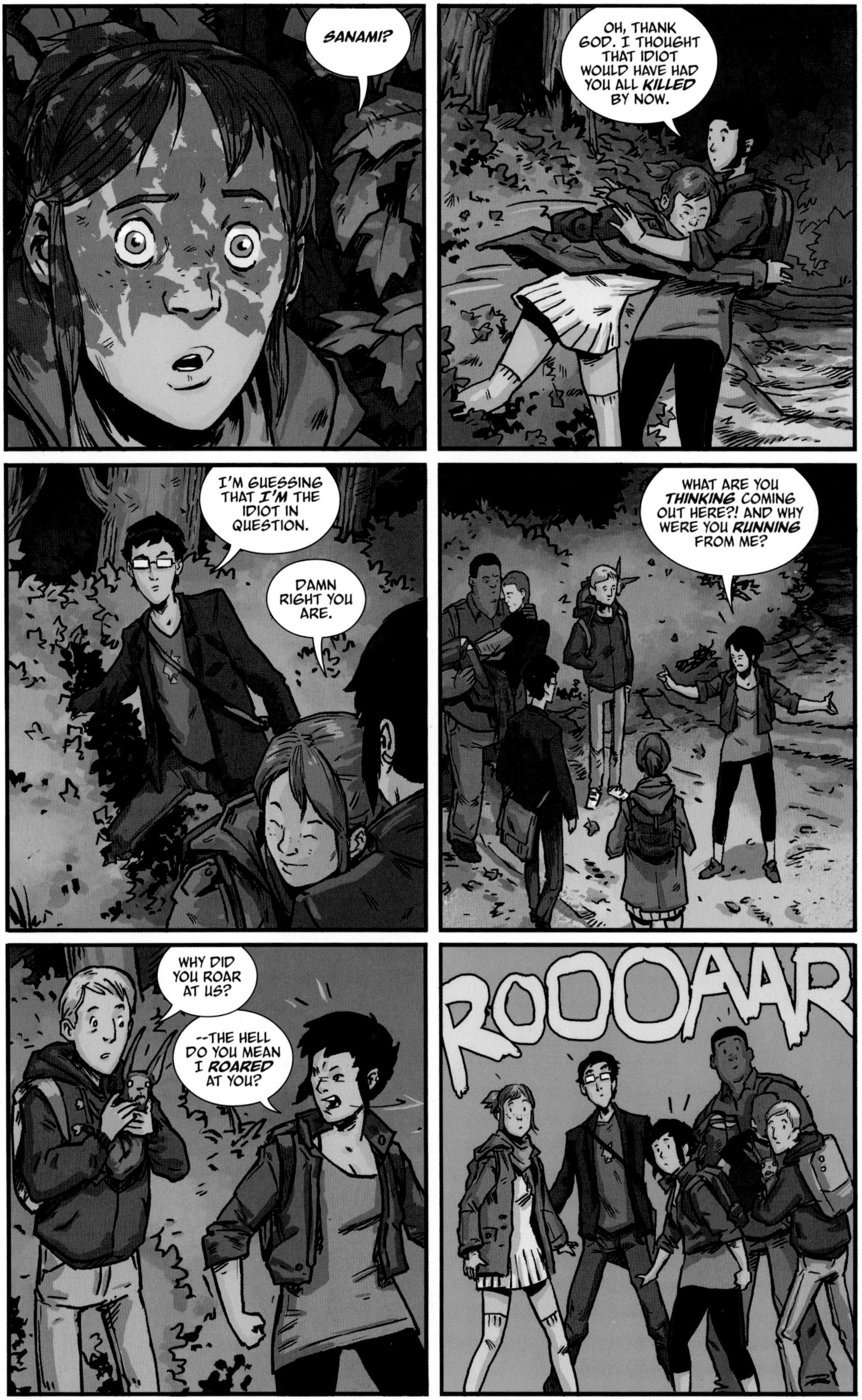
SANAMI?
OH, THANK GOD. I THOUGHT THAT IDIOT WOULD HAVE HAD YOU ALL KILLED BY NOW.
I'M GUESSING THAT I'M THE IDIOT IN QUESTION.
DAMN RIGHT YOU ARE.
WHAT ARE YOU THINKING COMING OUT HERE?! AND WHY WERE YOU RUNNING FROM ME?
WHY DID YOU ROAR AT US?
--THE HELL DO YOU MEAN I ROARED AT YOU?
ROOOAAR

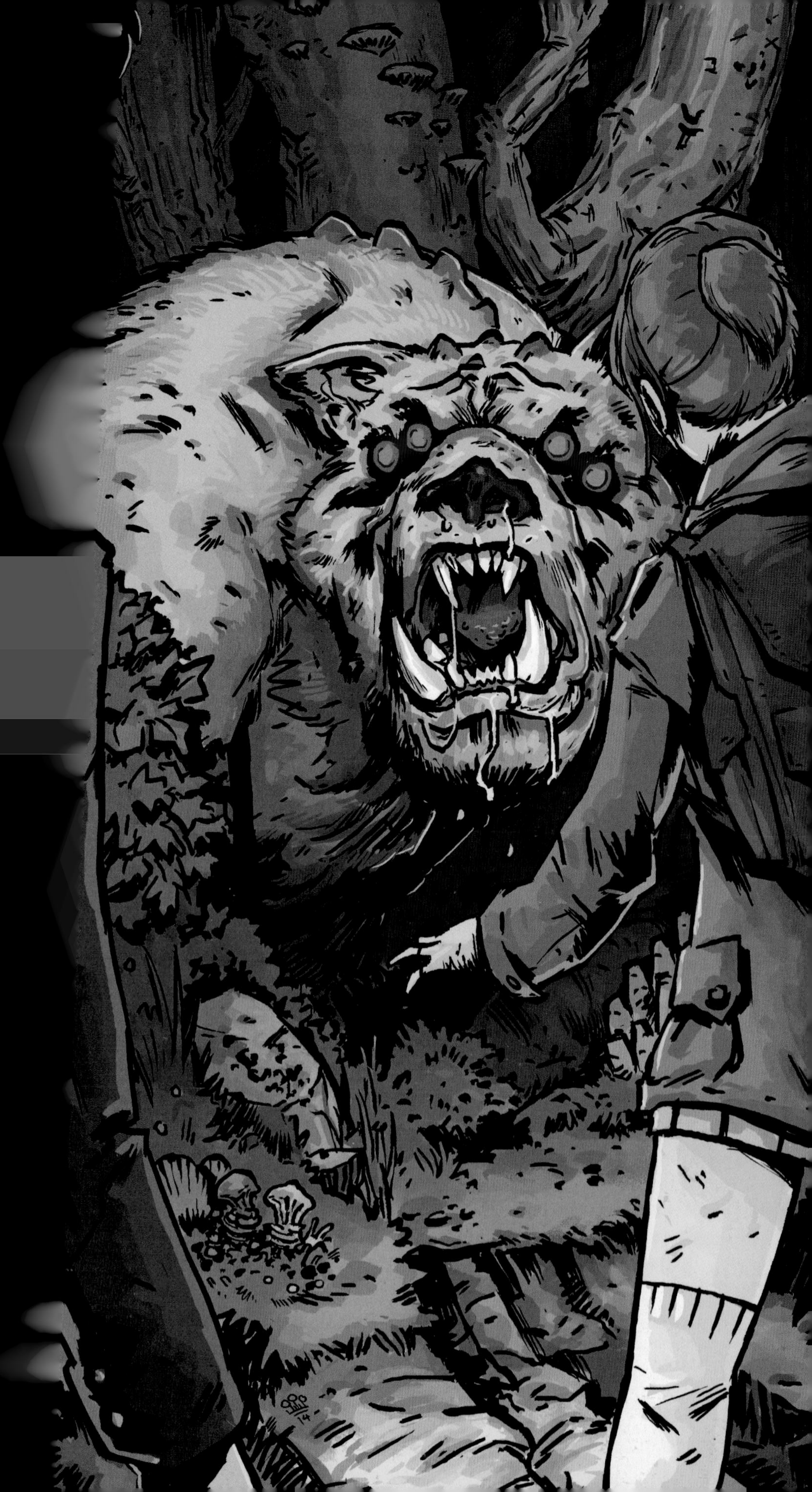

ISSUE TWO COVER **RAMÓN K. PÉREZ**

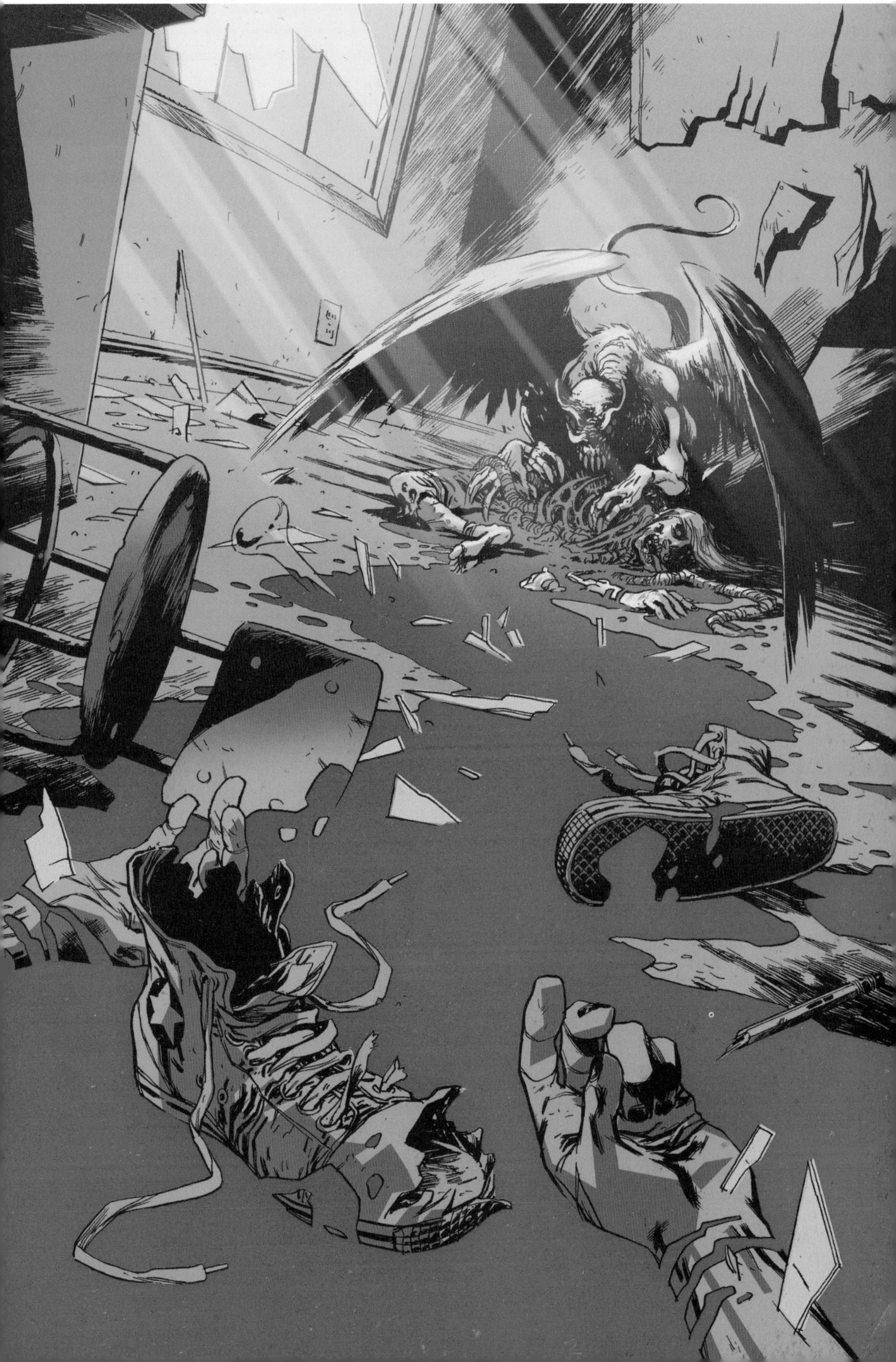

CHAPTER
THREE

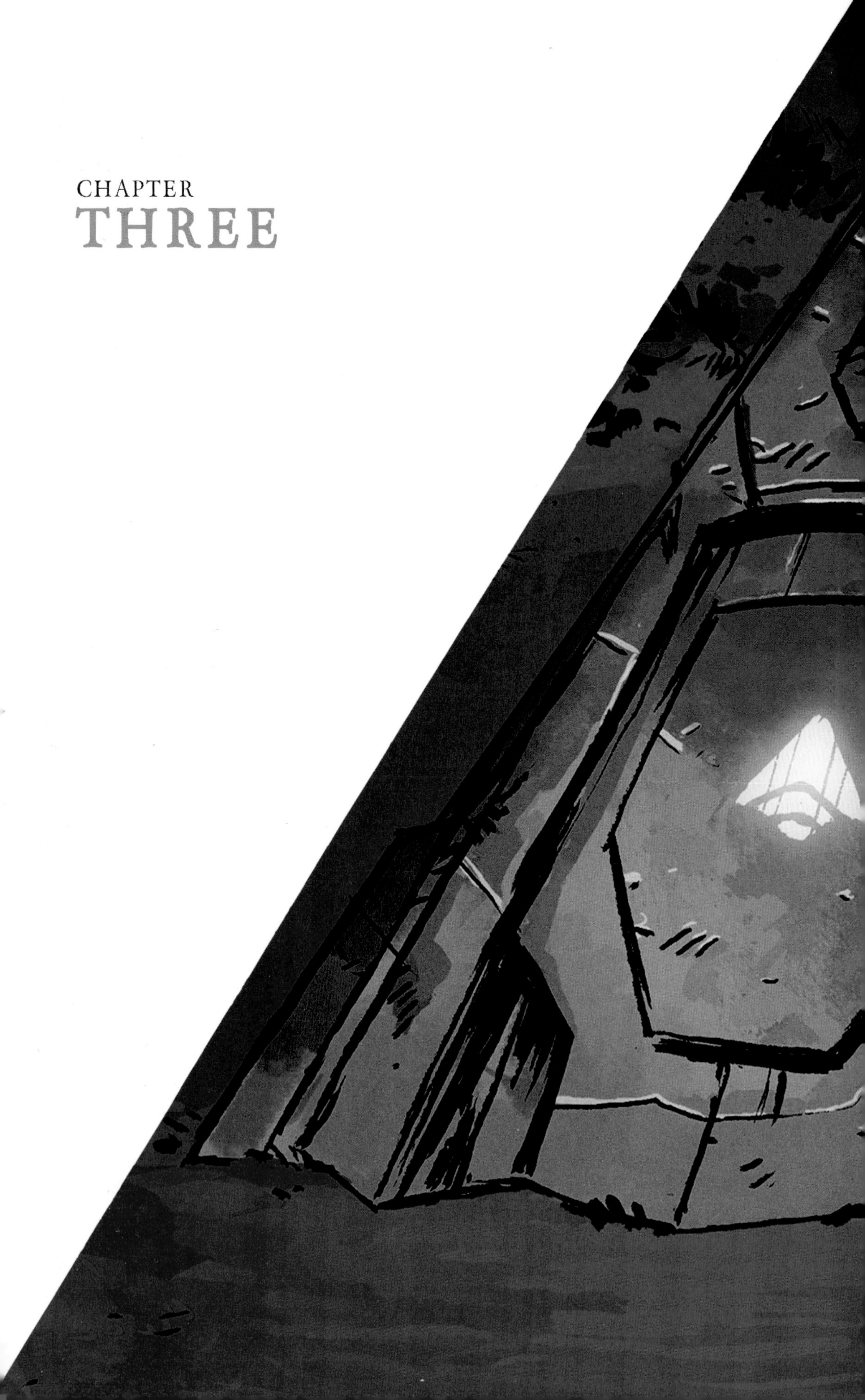

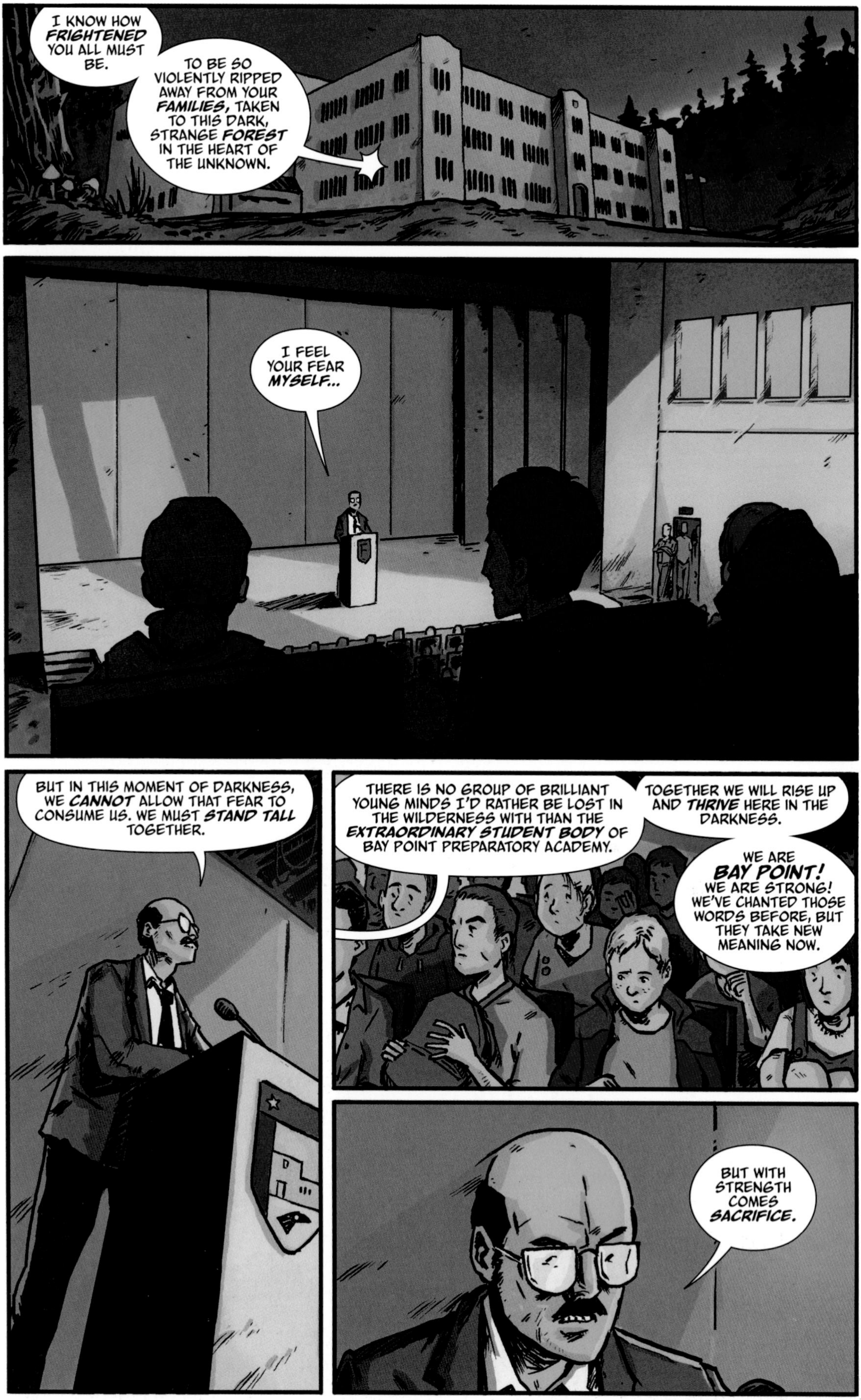
I KNOW HOW FRIGHTENED YOU ALL MUST BE.
TO BE SO VIOLENTLY RIPPED AWAY FROM YOUR FAMILIES, TAKEN TO THIS DARK, STRANGE FOREST IN THE HEART OF THE UNKNOWN.
I FEEL YOUR FEAR MYSELF...
BUT IN THIS MOMENT OF DARKNESS, WE CANNOT ALLOW THAT FEAR TO CONSUME US. WE MUST STAND TALL TOGETHER.
THERE IS NO GROUP OF BRILLIANT YOUNG MINDS I'D RATHER BE LOST IN THE WILDERNESS WITH THAN THE EXTRAORDINARY STUDENT BODY OF BAY POINT PREPARATORY ACADEMY.
TOGETHER WE WILL RISE UP AND THRIVE HERE IN THE DARKNESS.
WE ARE BAY POINT! WE ARE STRONG! WE'VE CHANTED THOSE WORDS BEFORE, BUT THEY TAKE NEW MEANING NOW.
BUT WITH STRENGTH COMES SACRIFICE.

WE MUST BE *DISCIPLINED* TO TAKE ON THIS STORM.

WE, THE *FACULTY* OF BAY POINT, ARE COMING TOGETHER TO DETERMINE OUR FUTURE TOGETHER, AND THE STEPS WE MUST NOW TAKE.

BUT IN THE MEANTIME, YOU WILL *NOT* LEAVE THE CONFINES OF THIS SCHOOL.

YOUR HOMEROOM IS NOW YOUR *HOME*. YOU MUST BE UNDER THE SUPERVISION OF YOUR FACULTY ADVISOR AT *ALL TIMES.*

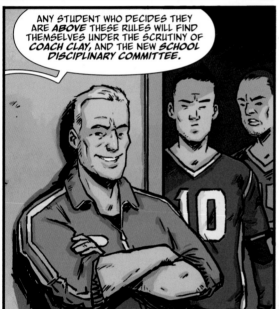

ANY STUDENT WHO DECIDES THEY ARE *ABOVE* THESE RULES WILL FIND THEMSELVES UNDER THE SCRUTINY OF *COACH CLAY*, AND THE NEW *SCHOOL DISCIPLINARY COMMITTEE.*

I DON'T NEED TO REMIND YOU THAT ONE OF OUR STUDENTS, *CARRIE HILL,* DIED IN THE INITIAL ATTACK ON THE SCHOOL.

FIVE MORE OF OUR STUDENTS ARE CURRENTLY *MISSING.*

I WILL *NOT* ALLOW ANY MORE DEATHS. I WILL *NOT* ALLOW THESE WOODS TO CLAIM US.

THUMP!

AND I WILL DO *ANYTHING* IN MY POWER TO KEEP BAY POINT STRONG.

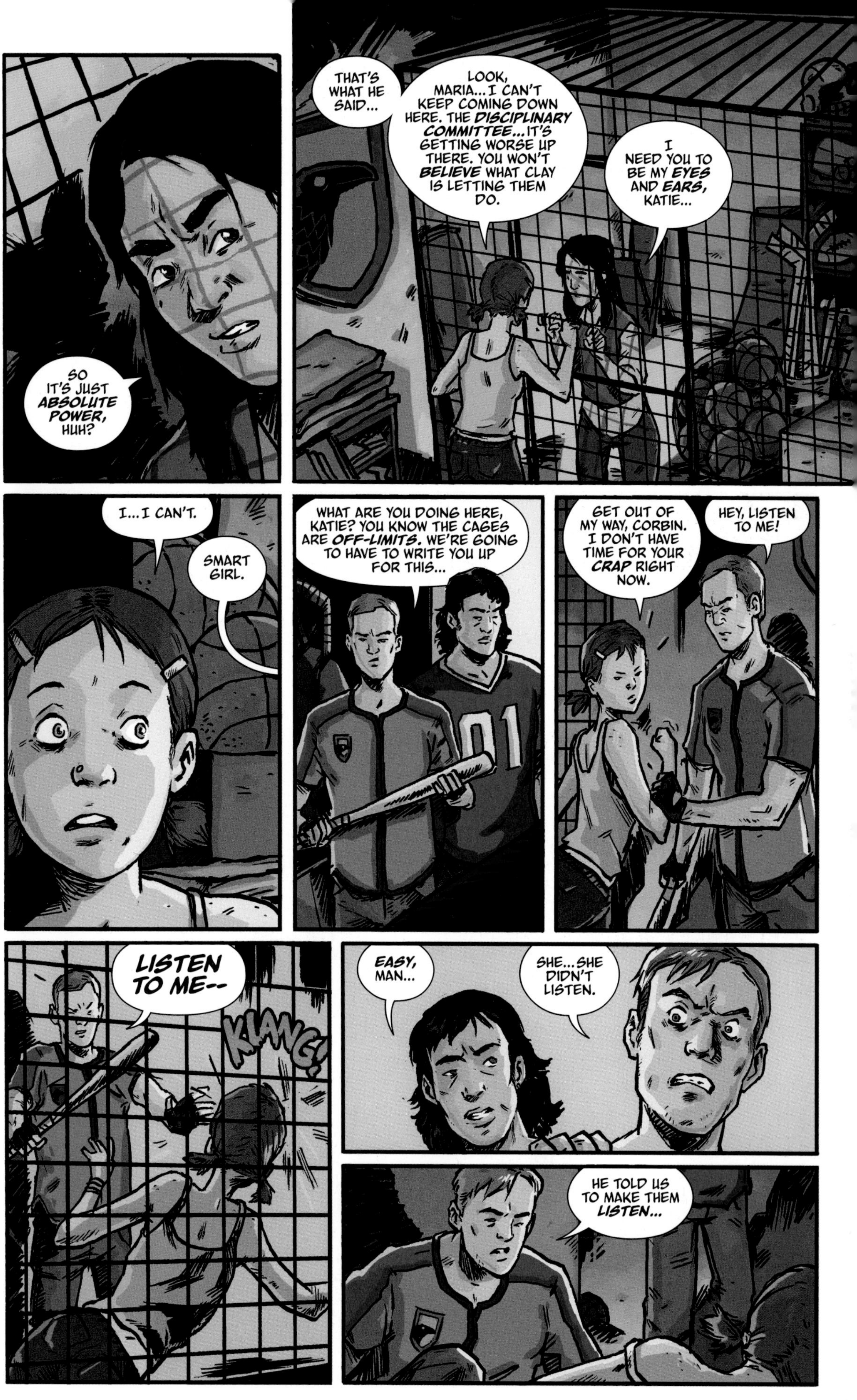
SO IT'S JUST ABSOLUTE POWER, HUH?
THAT'S WHAT HE SAID...
LOOK, MARIA... I CAN'T KEEP COMING DOWN HERE. THE DISCIPLINARY COMMITTEE... IT'S GETTING WORSE UP THERE. YOU WON'T BELIEVE WHAT CLAY IS LETTING THEM DO.
I NEED YOU TO BE MY EYES AND EARS, KATIE...
I... I CAN'T.
SMART GIRL.
WHAT ARE YOU DOING HERE, KATIE? YOU KNOW THE CAGES ARE OFF-LIMITS. WE'RE GOING TO HAVE TO WRITE YOU UP FOR THIS...
GET OUT OF MY WAY, CORBIN. I DON'T HAVE TIME FOR YOUR CRAP RIGHT NOW.
HEY, LISTEN TO ME!
LISTEN TO ME--
KLANG!
EASY, MAN...
SHE... SHE DIDN'T LISTEN.
HE TOLD US TO MAKE THEM LISTEN...

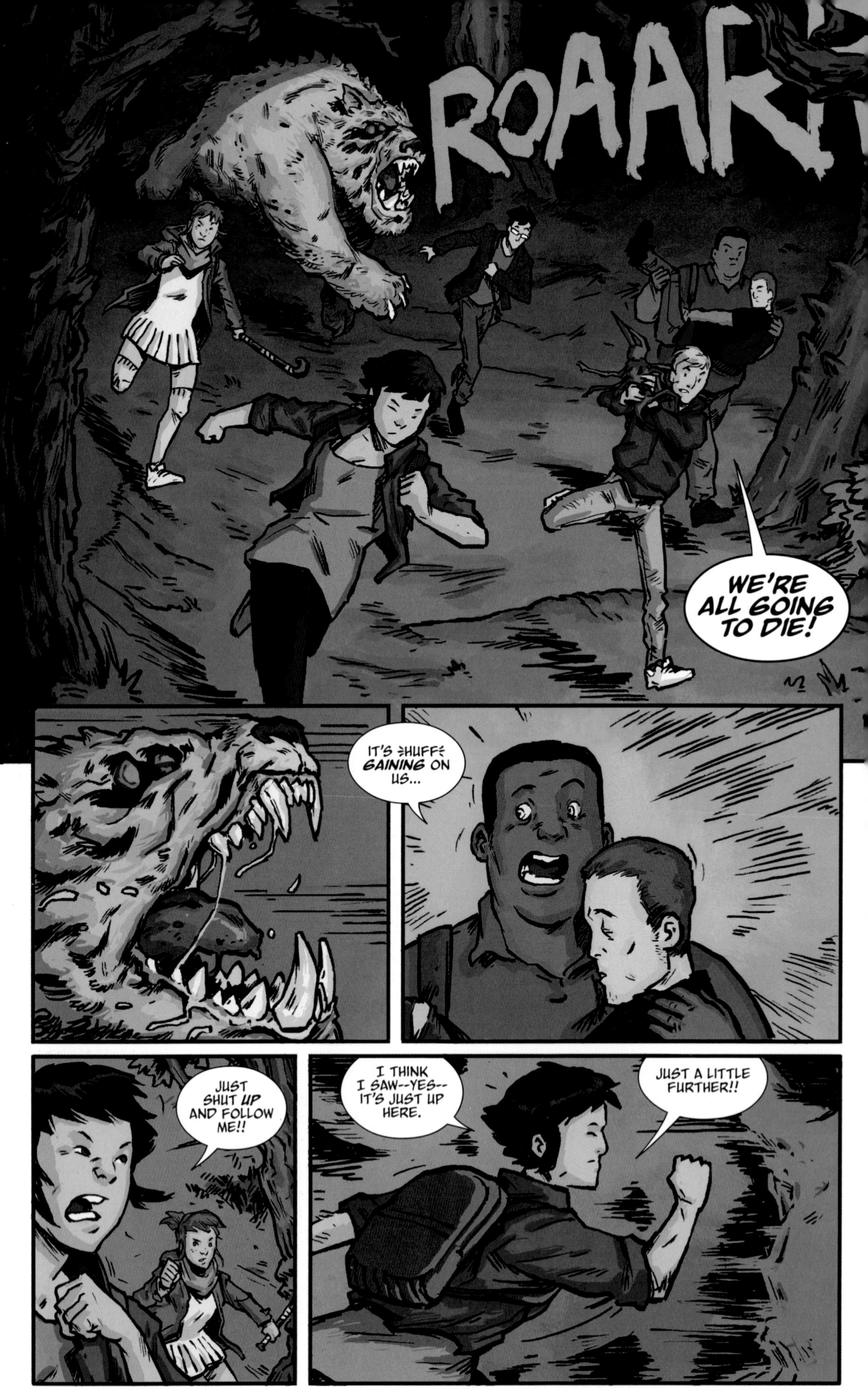
ROAAR!!
WE'RE ALL GOING TO DIE!
IT'S HUFF GAINING ON US...
JUST SHUT UP AND FOLLOW ME!!
I THINK I SAW--YES--IT'S JUST UP HERE.
JUST A LITTLE FURTHER!!

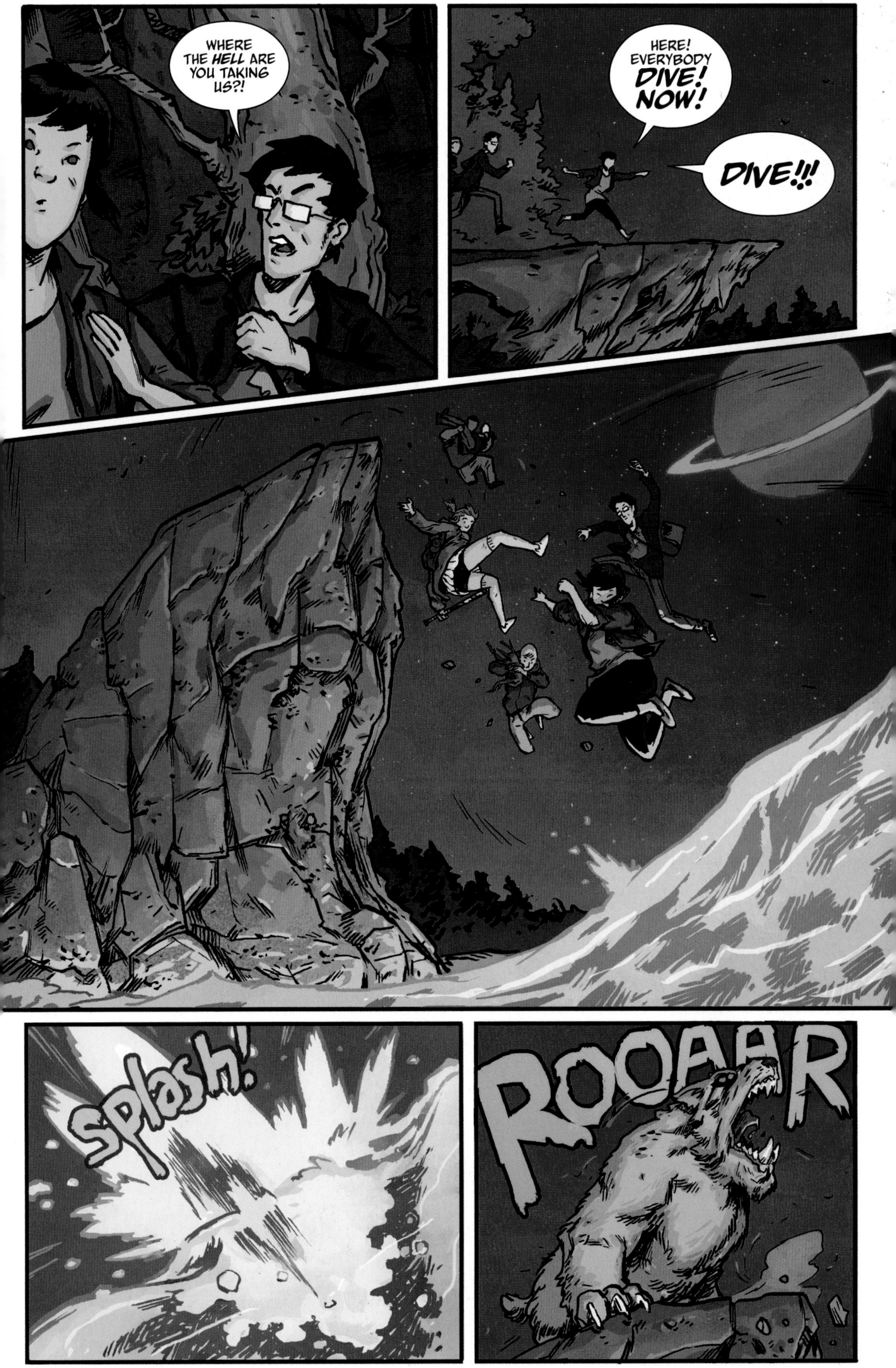
WHERE THE HELL ARE YOU TAKING US?!
HERE! EVERYBODY DIVE! NOW!
DIVE!!!
splash!
ROOAAR

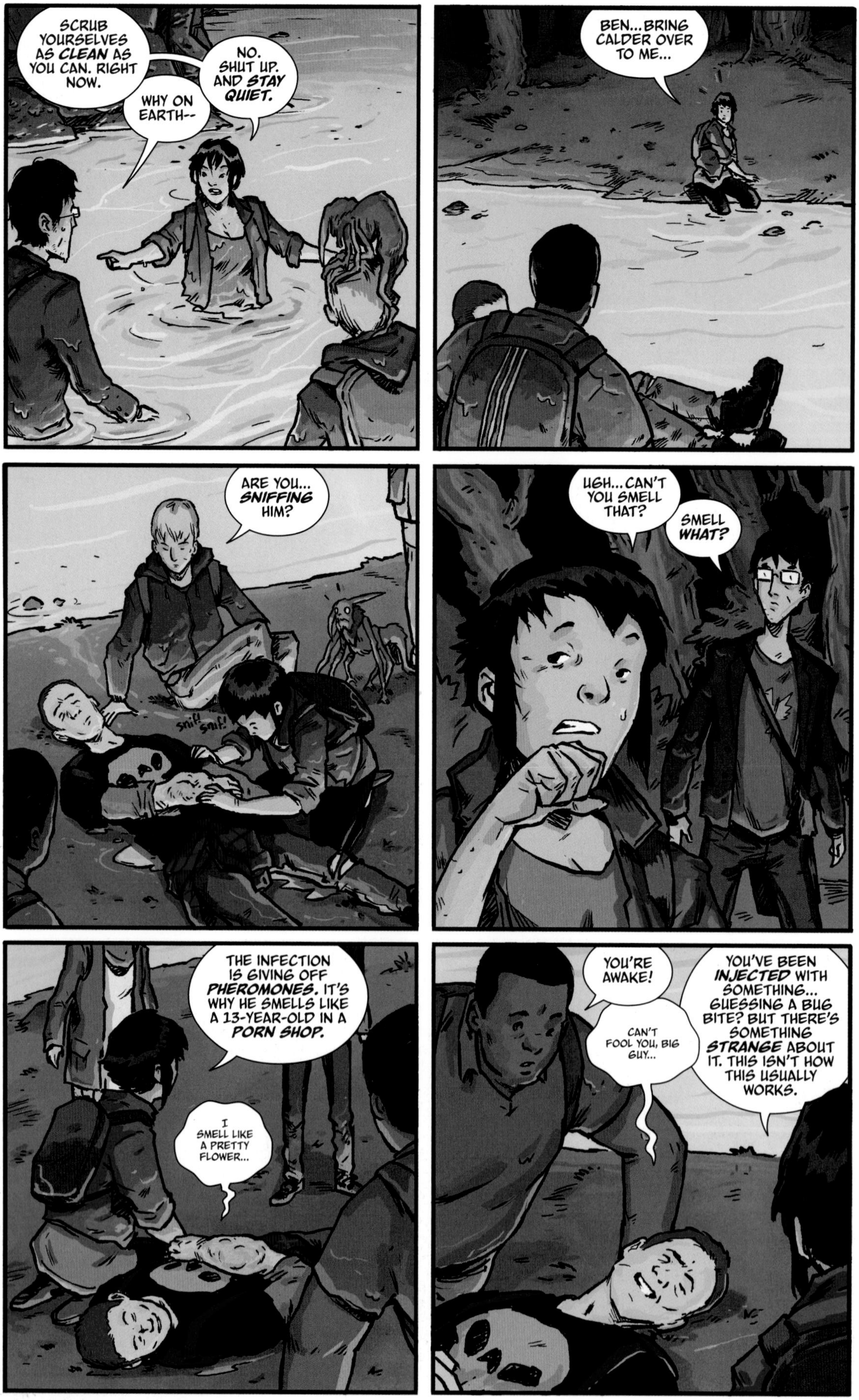
SCRUB YOURSELVES AS CLEAN AS YOU CAN. RIGHT NOW.
WHY ON EARTH--
NO. SHUT UP. AND STAY QUIET.
BEN...BRING CALDER OVER TO ME...
ARE YOU... SNIFFING HIM?
sniff sniff
UGH...CAN'T YOU SMELL THAT?
SMELL WHAT?
THE INFECTION IS GIVING OFF PHEROMONES. IT'S WHY HE SMELLS LIKE A 13-YEAR-OLD IN A PORN SHOP.
I SMELL LIKE A PRETTY FLOWER...
YOU'RE AWAKE!
CAN'T FOOL YOU, BIG GUY...
YOU'VE BEEN INJECTED WITH SOMETHING... GUESSING A BUG BITE? BUT THERE'S SOMETHING STRANGE ABOUT IT. THIS ISN'T HOW THIS USUALLY WORKS.

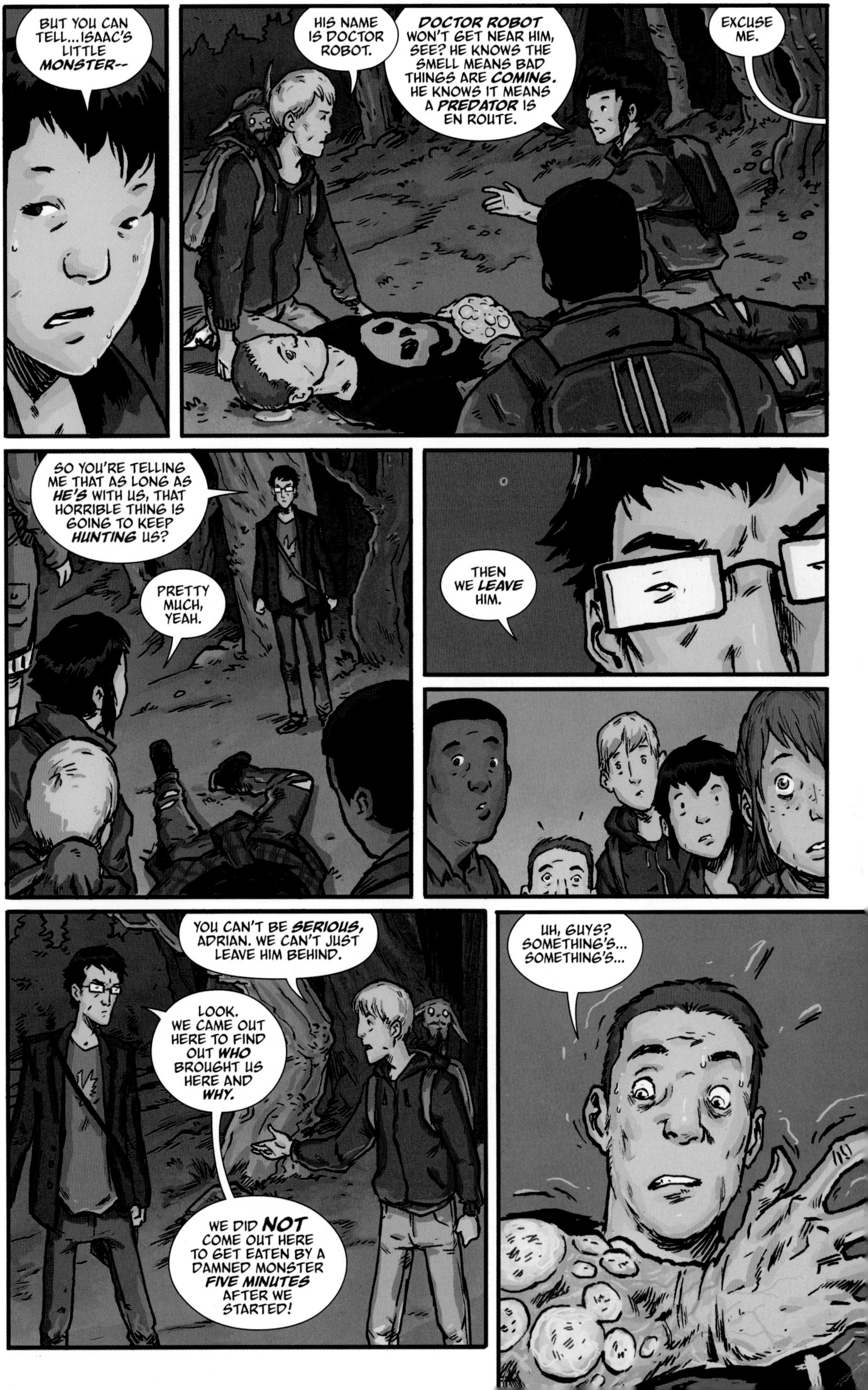
BUT YOU CAN TELL...ISAAC'S LITTLE MONSTER--
HIS NAME IS DOCTOR ROBOT.
DOCTOR ROBOT WON'T GET NEAR HIM, SEE? HE KNOWS THE SMELL MEANS BAD THINGS ARE COMING. HE KNOWS IT MEANS A PREDATOR IS EN ROUTE.
EXCUSE ME.
SO YOU'RE TELLING ME THAT AS LONG AS HE'S WITH US, THAT HORRIBLE THING IS GOING TO KEEP HUNTING US?
PRETTY MUCH, YEAH.
THEN WE LEAVE HIM.
YOU CAN'T BE SERIOUS, ADRIAN. WE CAN'T JUST LEAVE HIM BEHIND.
LOOK. WE CAME OUT HERE TO FIND OUT WHO BROUGHT US HERE AND WHY.
WE DID NOT COME OUT HERE TO GET EATEN BY A DAMNED MONSTER FIVE MINUTES AFTER WE STARTED!
UH, GUYS? SOMETHING'S... SOMETHING'S...

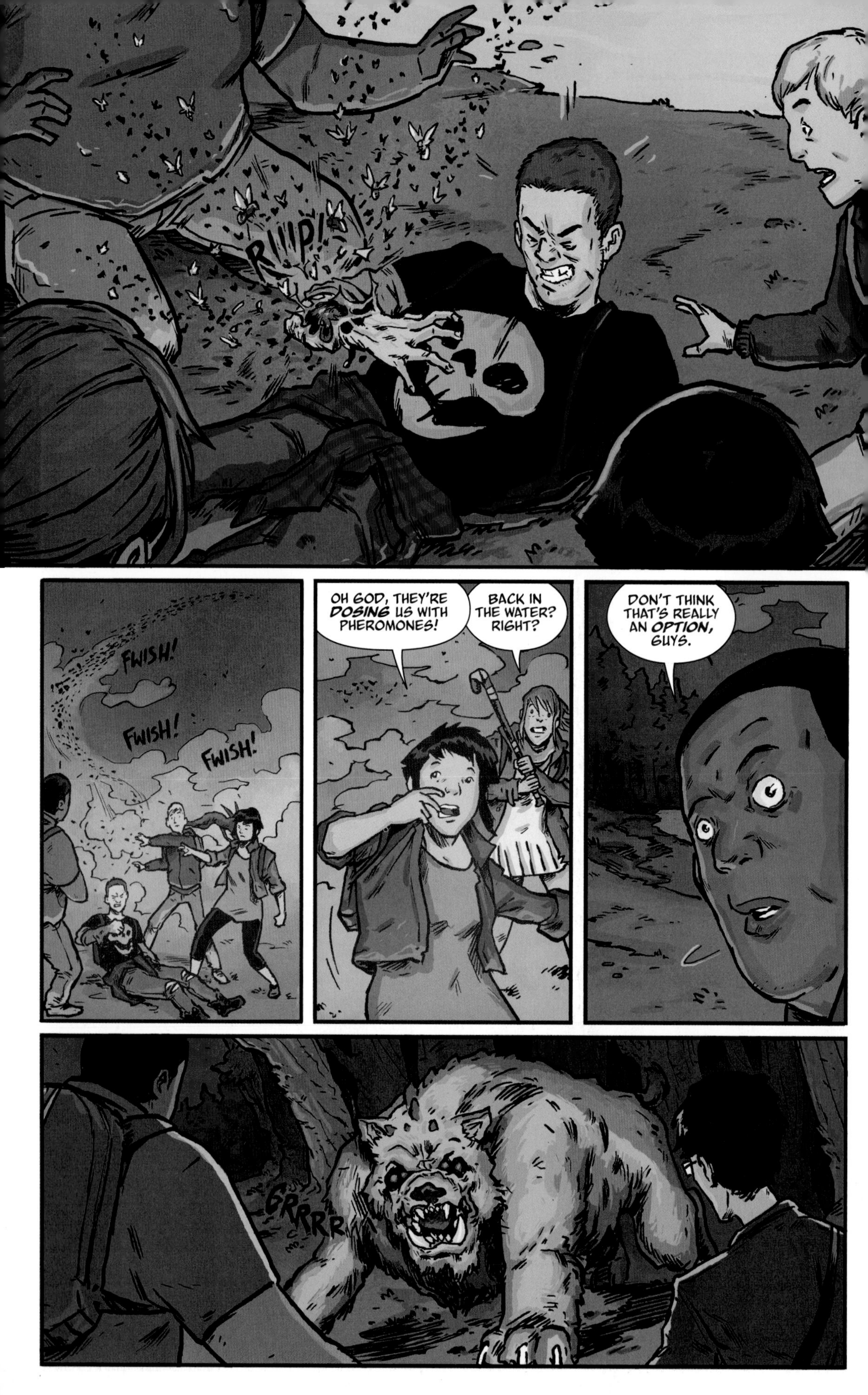
RIIIP!
FWISH!
FWISH!
FWISH!
OH GOD, THEY'RE DOSING US WITH PHEROMONES!
BACK IN THE WATER? RIGHT?
DON'T THINK THAT'S REALLY AN OPTION, GUYS.
GRRRR

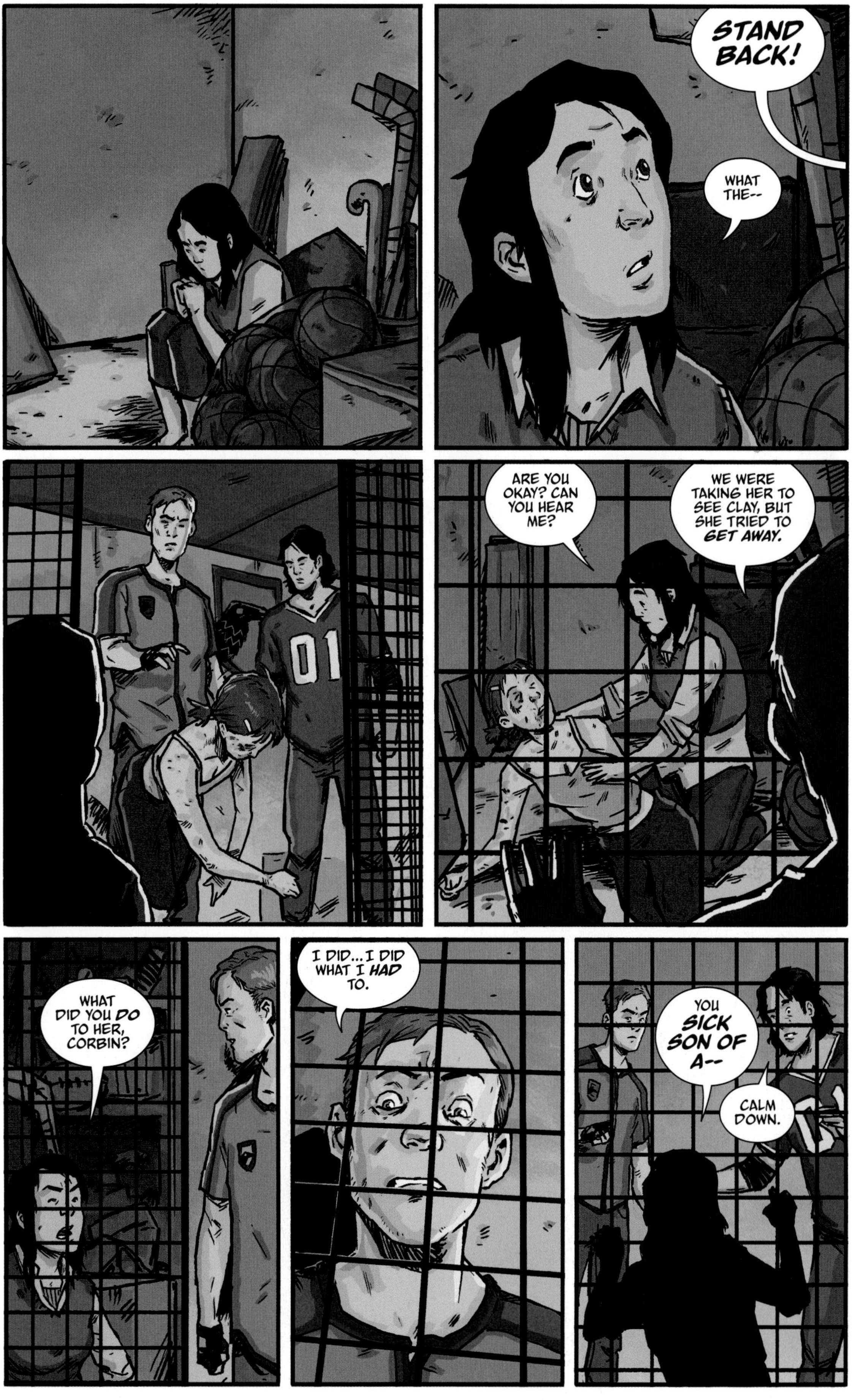
STAND BACK!
WHAT THE--
ARE YOU OKAY? CAN YOU HEAR ME?
WE WERE TAKING HER TO SEE CLAY, BUT SHE TRIED TO GET AWAY.
WHAT DID YOU DO TO HER, CORBIN?
I DID... I DID WHAT I HAD TO.
YOU SICK SON OF A--
CALM DOWN.

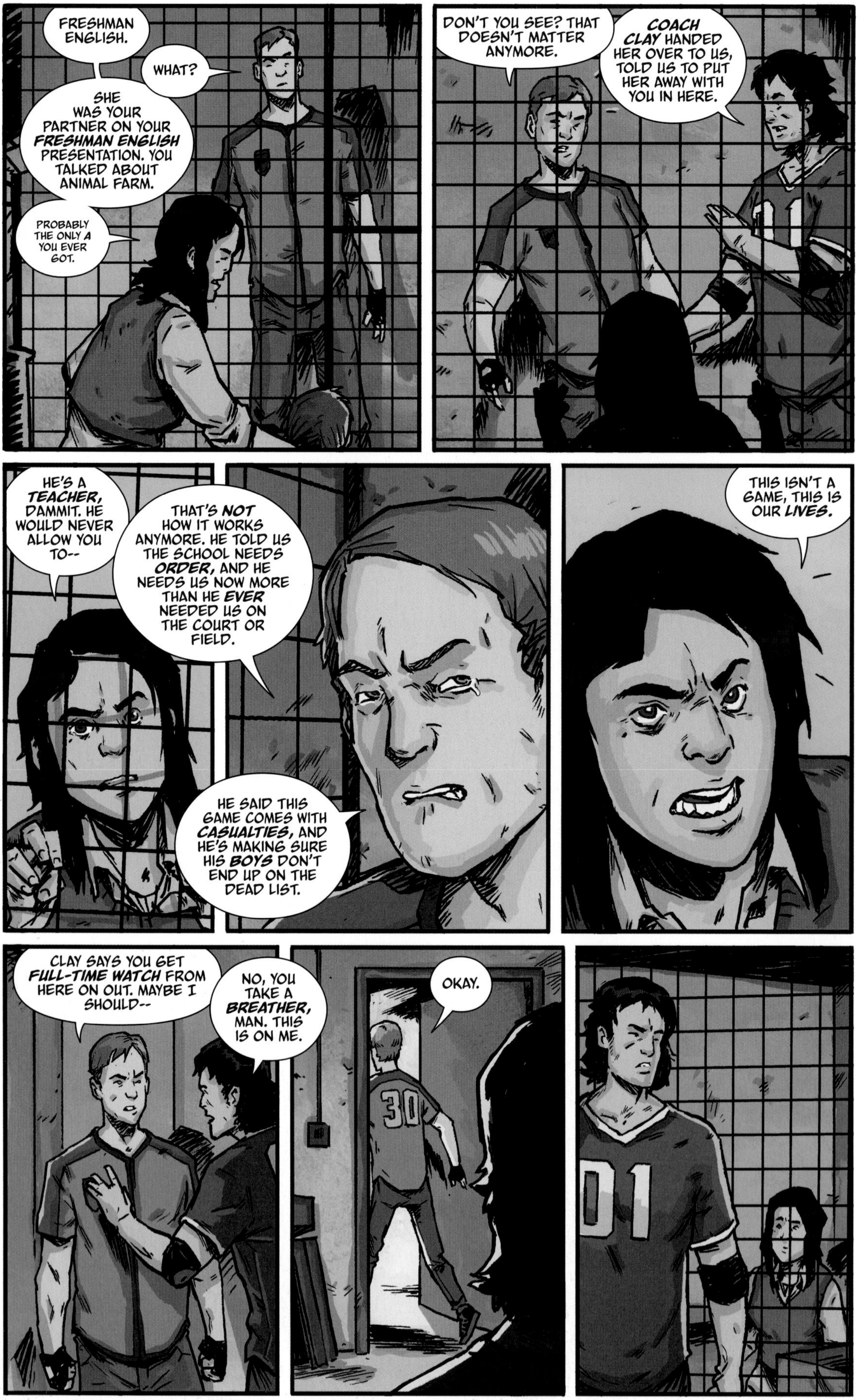
FRESHMAN ENGLISH.
WHAT?
SHE WAS YOUR PARTNER ON YOUR FRESHMAN ENGLISH PRESENTATION. YOU TALKED ABOUT ANIMAL FARM.
PROBABLY THE ONLY A YOU EVER GOT.
DON'T YOU SEE? THAT DOESN'T MATTER ANYMORE.
COACH CLAY HANDED HER OVER TO US, TOLD US TO PUT HER AWAY WITH YOU IN HERE.
HE'S A TEACHER, DAMMIT. HE WOULD NEVER ALLOW YOU TO--
THAT'S NOT HOW IT WORKS ANYMORE. HE TOLD US THE SCHOOL NEEDS ORDER, AND HE NEEDS US NOW MORE THAN HE EVER NEEDED US ON THE COURT OR FIELD.
HE SAID THIS GAME COMES WITH CASUALTIES, AND HE'S MAKING SURE HIS BOYS DON'T END UP ON THE DEAD LIST.
THIS ISN'T A GAME, THIS IS OUR LIVES.
CLAY SAYS YOU GET FULL-TIME WATCH FROM HERE ON OUT. MAYBE I SHOULD--
NO, YOU TAKE A BREATHER, MAN. THIS IS ON ME.
OKAY.

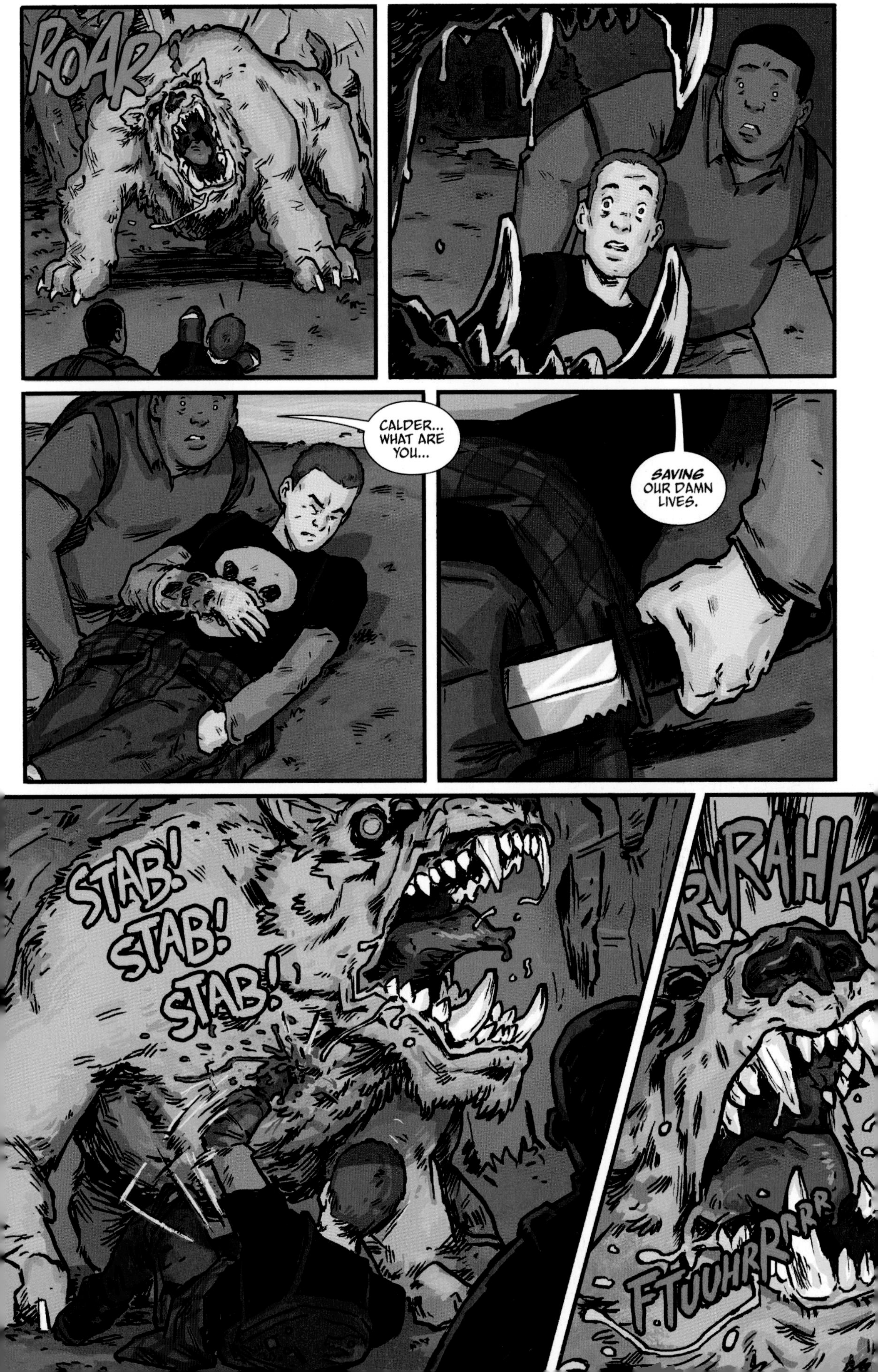
ROAR
CALDER... WHAT ARE YOU...
SAVING OUR DAMN LIVES.
STAB! STAB! STAB!
RVRAHK
FTUUHRRRR

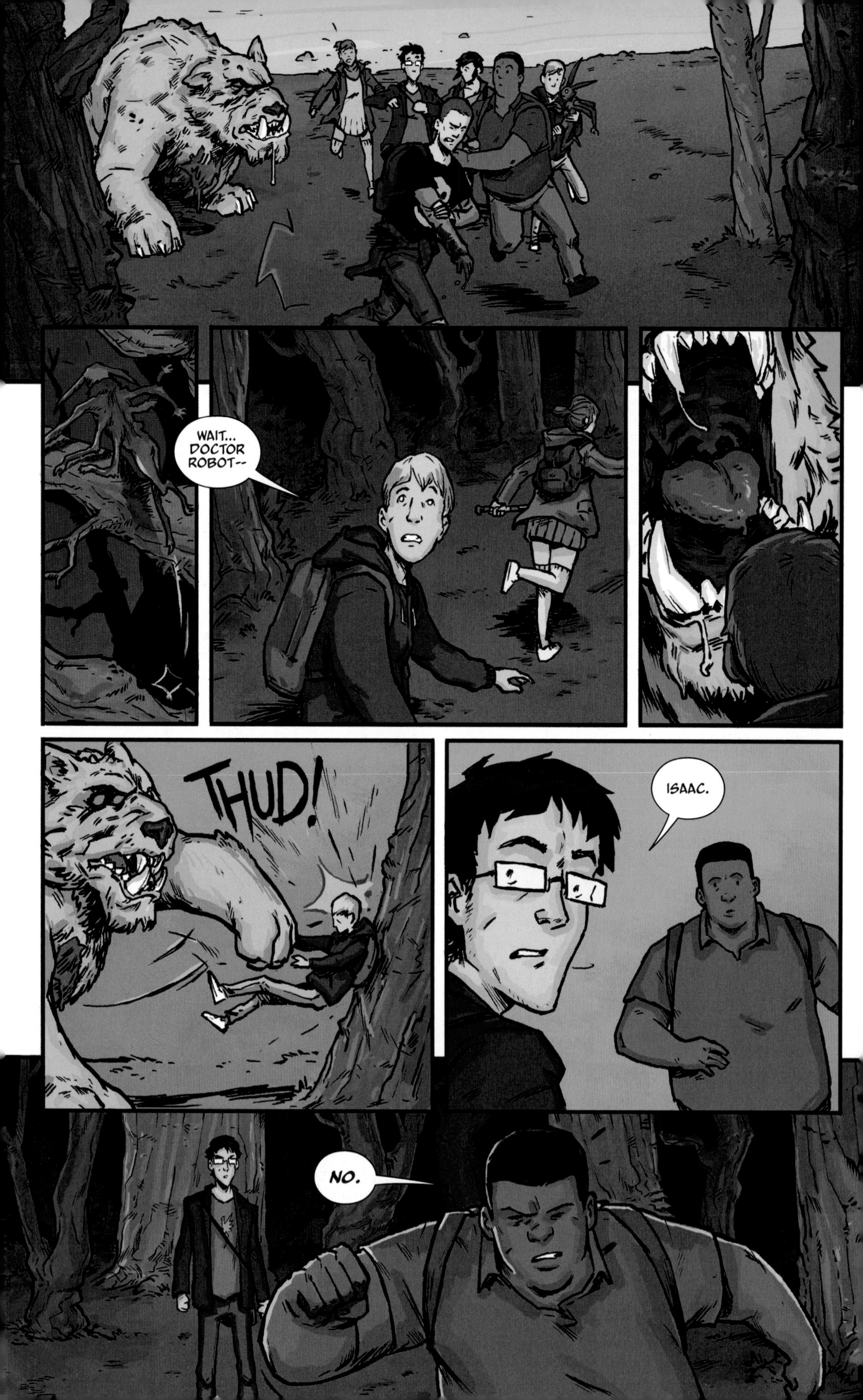
WAIT... DOCTOR ROBOT--
THUD!
ISAAC.
NO.

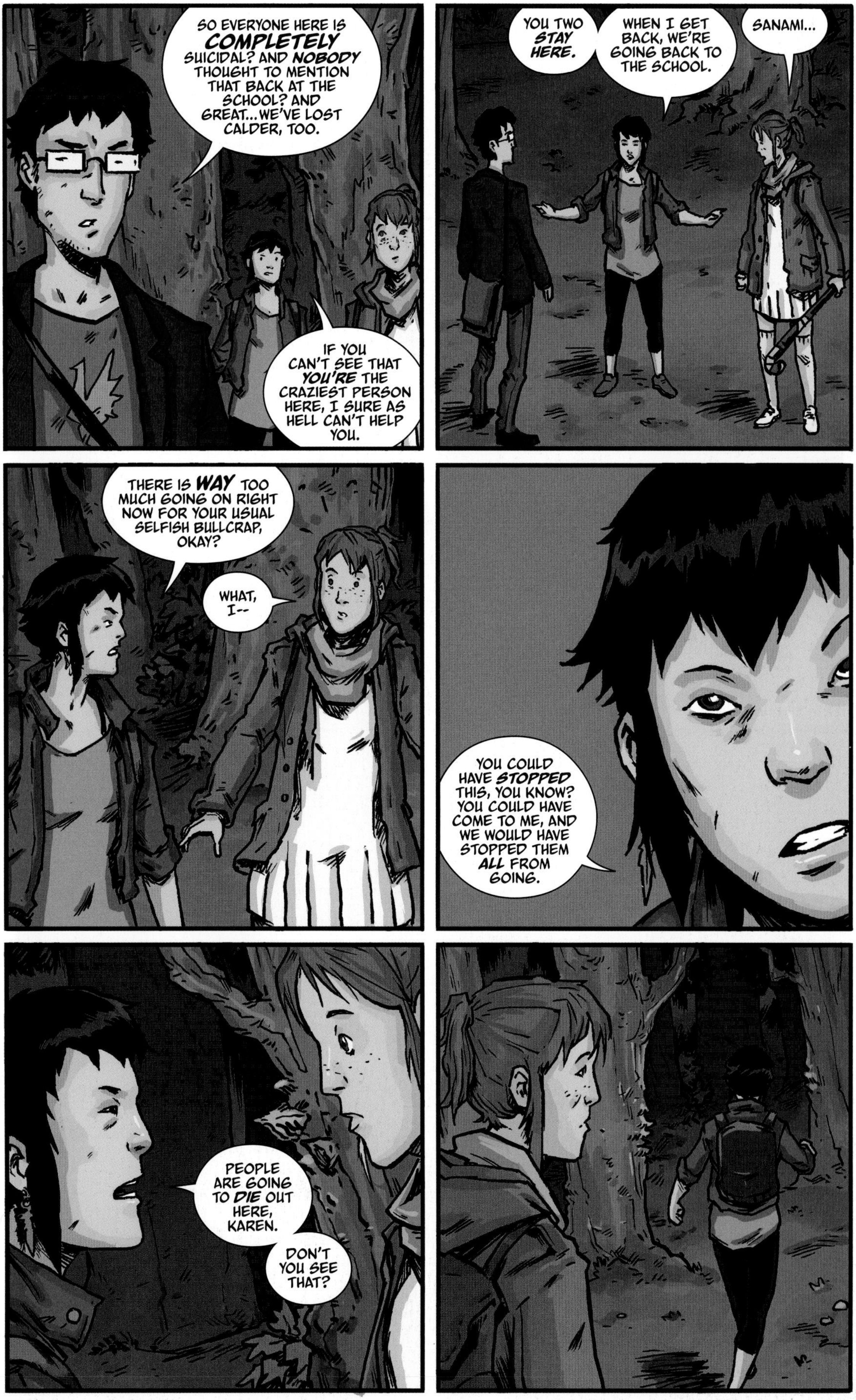

SO EVERYONE HERE IS COMPLETELY SUICIDAL? AND NOBODY THOUGHT TO MENTION THAT BACK AT THE SCHOOL? AND GREAT...WE'VE LOST CALDER, TOO.
IF YOU CAN'T SEE THAT YOU'RE THE CRAZIEST PERSON HERE, I SURE AS HELL CAN'T HELP YOU.
YOU TWO STAY HERE.
WHEN I GET BACK, WE'RE GOING BACK TO THE SCHOOL.
SANAMI...
THERE IS WAY TOO MUCH GOING ON RIGHT NOW FOR YOUR USUAL SELFISH BULLCRAP, OKAY?
WHAT, I--
YOU COULD HAVE STOPPED THIS, YOU KNOW? YOU COULD HAVE COME TO ME, AND WE WOULD HAVE STOPPED THEM ALL FROM GOING.
PEOPLE ARE GOING TO DIE OUT HERE, KAREN.
DON'T YOU SEE THAT?

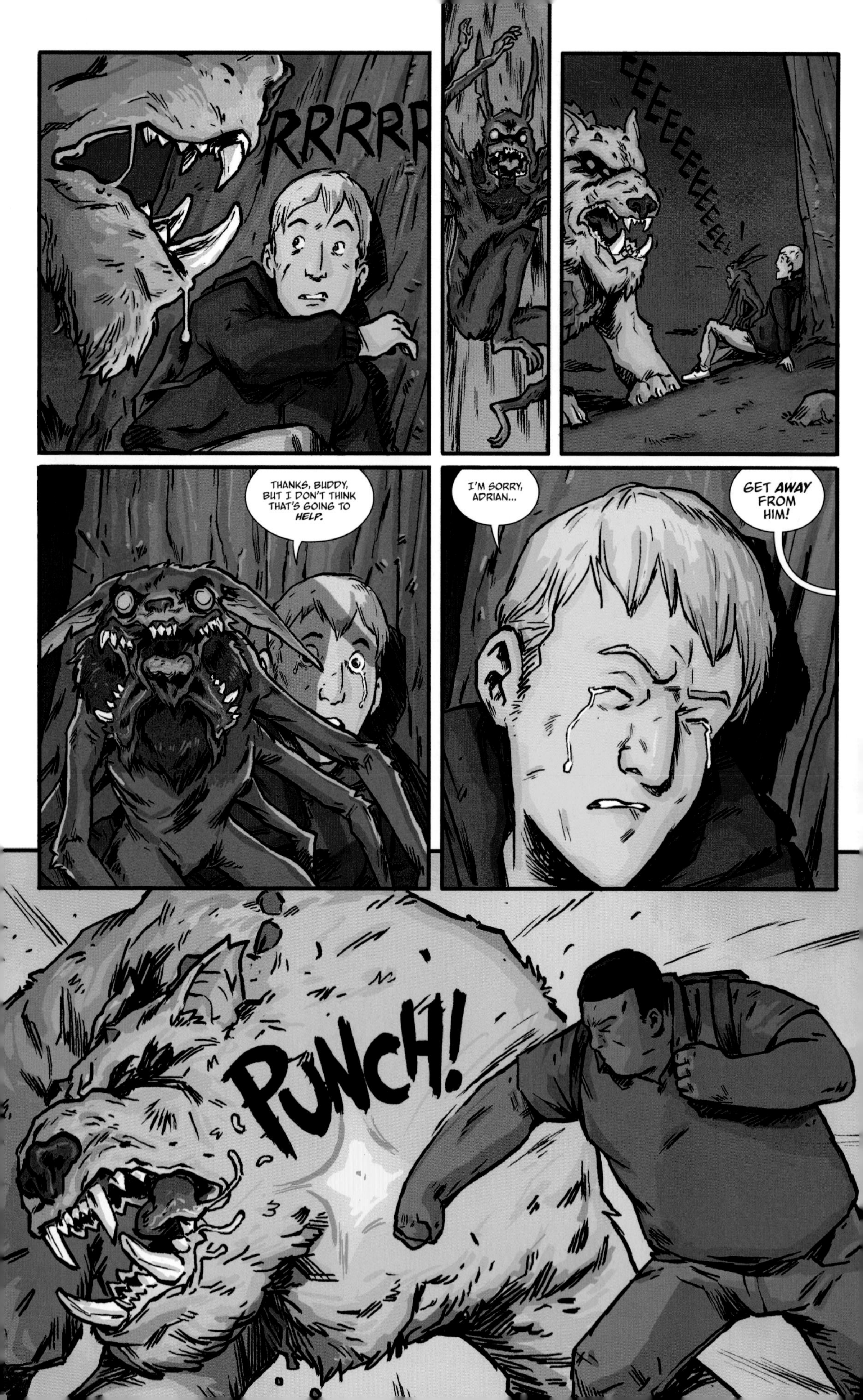
RRRRR
EEEEEEEEEEEEEEEEL
THANKS, BUDDY, BUT I DON'T THINK THAT'S GOING TO HELP.
I'M SORRY, ADRIAN...
GET AWAY FROM HIM!
PUNCH!

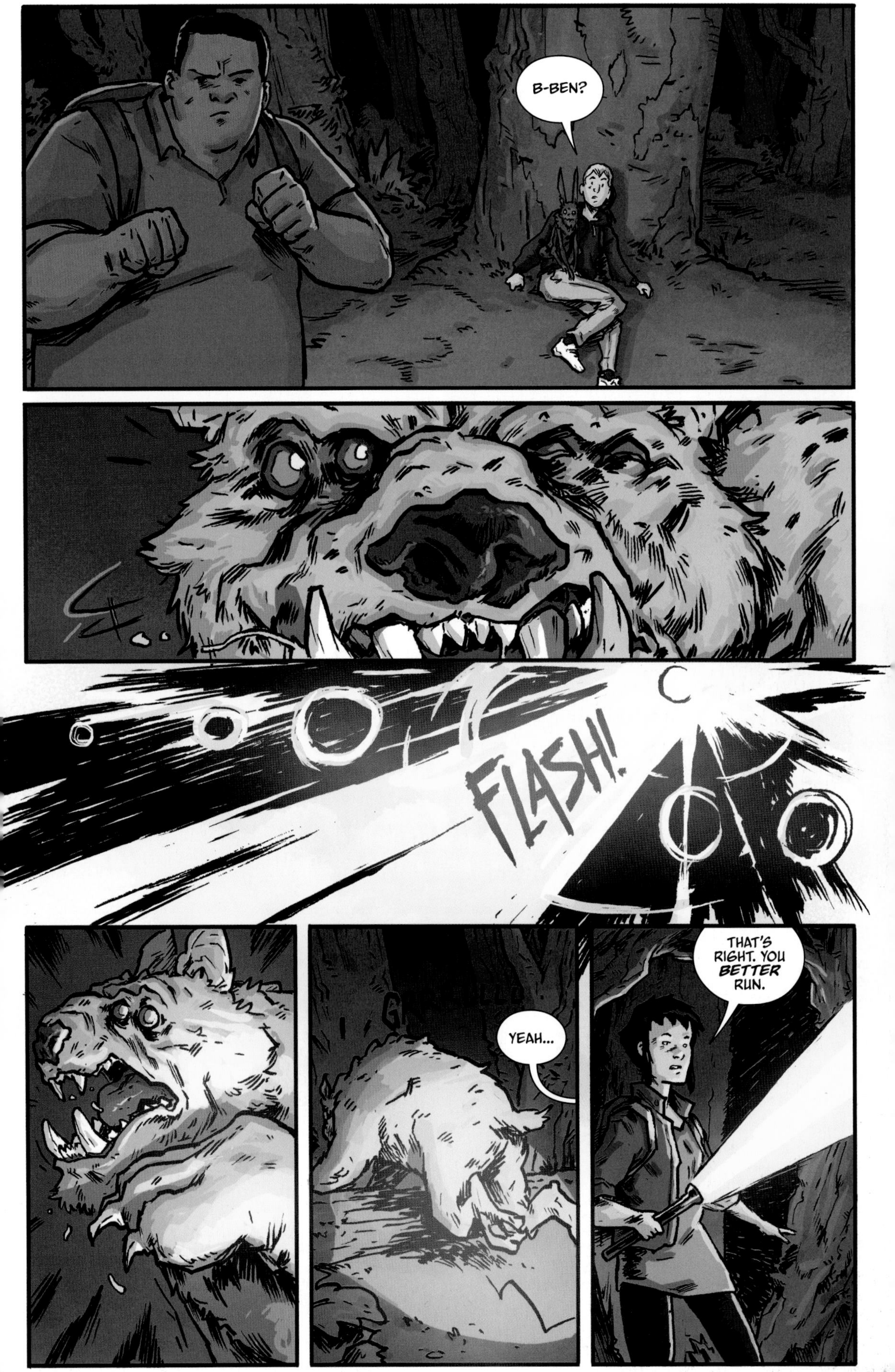
B-BEN?
FLASH!
YEAH...
THAT'S RIGHT. YOU BETTER RUN.

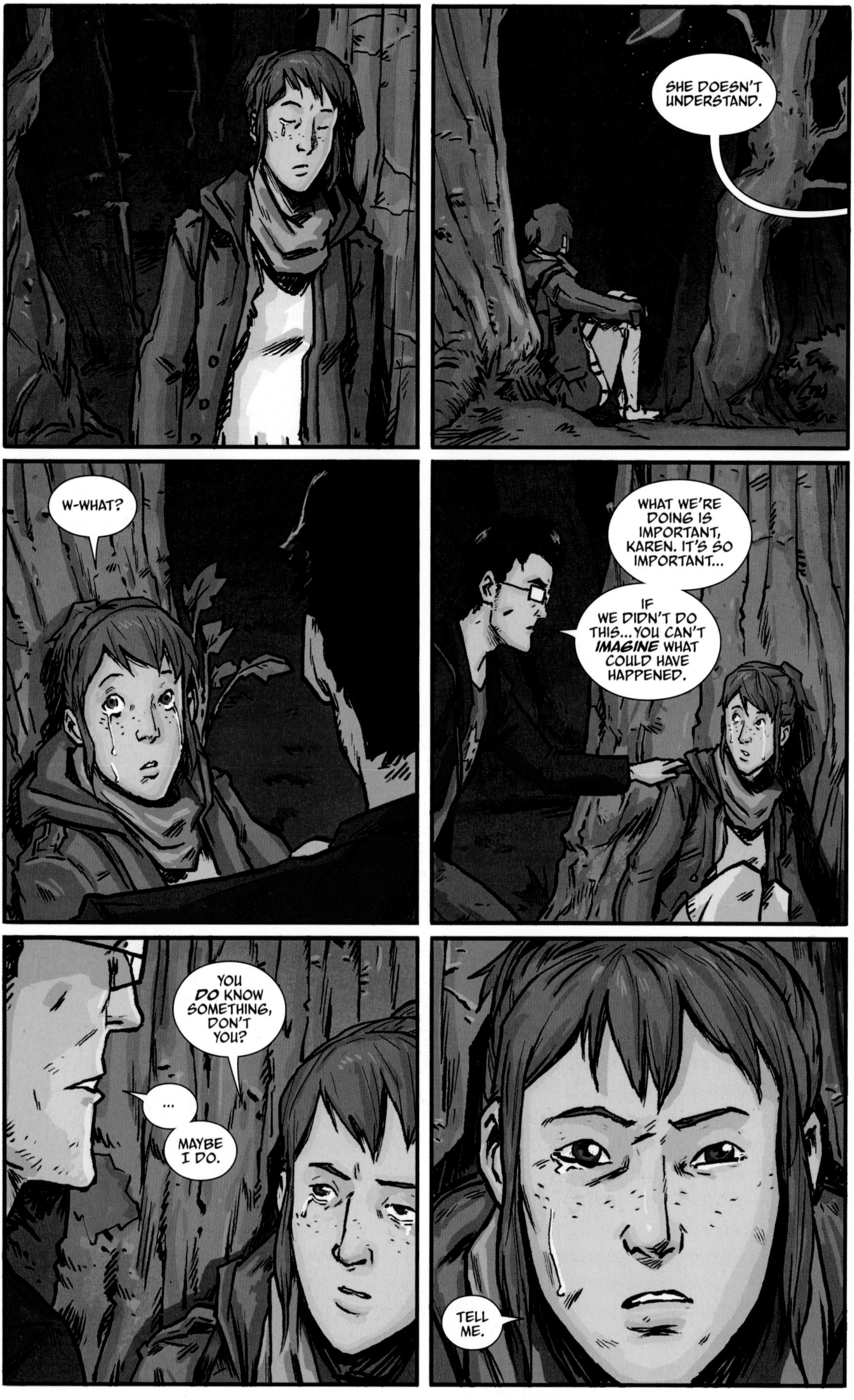
SHE DOESN'T UNDERSTAND.
W-WHAT?
WHAT WE'RE DOING IS IMPORTANT, KAREN. IT'S SO IMPORTANT...
IF WE DIDN'T DO THIS...YOU CAN'T *IMAGINE* WHAT COULD HAVE HAPPENED.
YOU *DO* KNOW SOMETHING, DON'T YOU?
...
MAYBE I DO.
TELL ME.

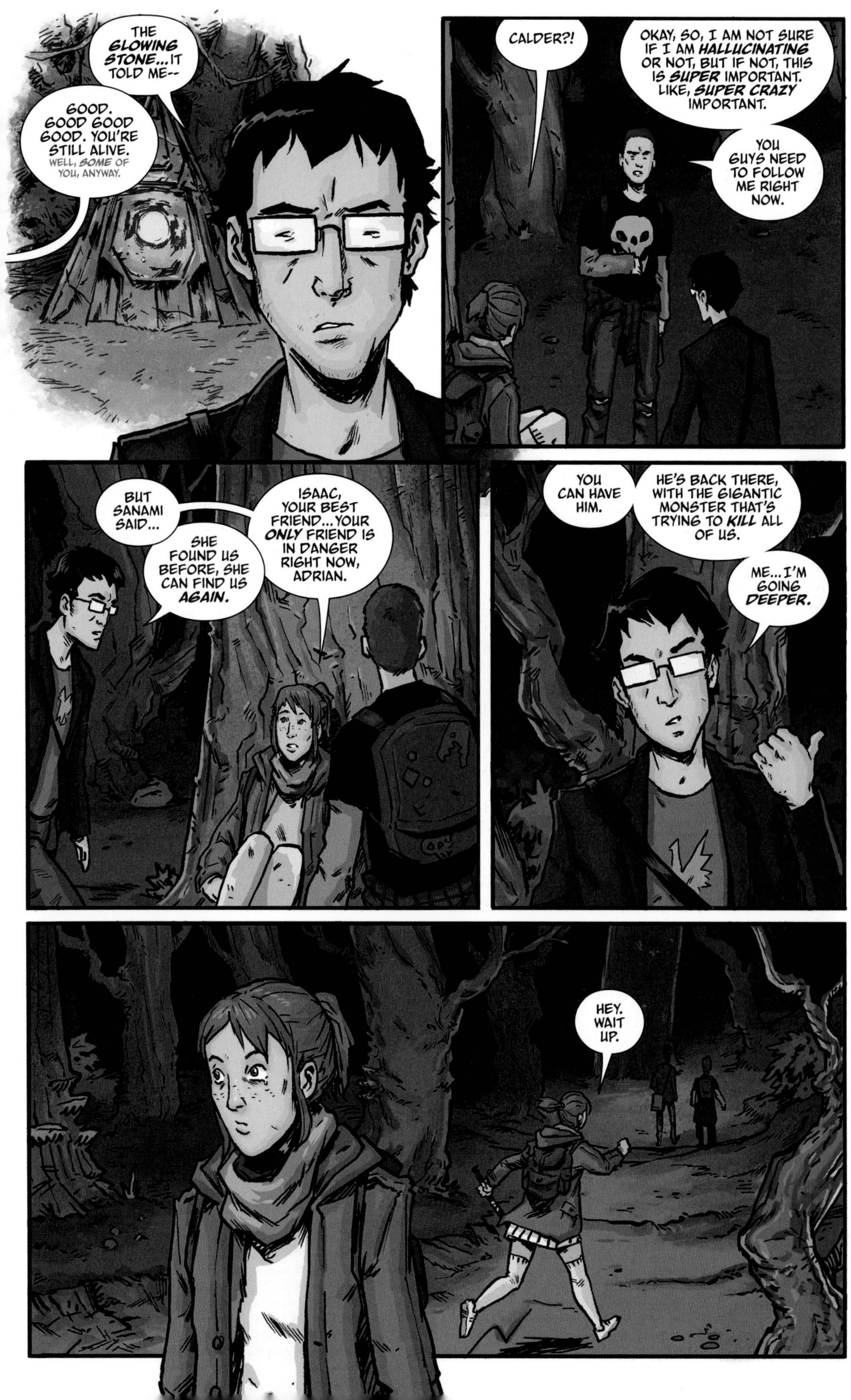
THE GLOWING STONE...IT TOLD ME--
GOOD. GOOD GOOD GOOD. YOU'RE STILL ALIVE. WELL, SOME OF YOU, ANYWAY.
CALDER?!
OKAY, SO, I AM NOT SURE IF I AM HALLUCINATING OR NOT, BUT IF NOT, THIS IS SUPER IMPORTANT. LIKE, SUPER CRAZY IMPORTANT.
YOU GUYS NEED TO FOLLOW ME RIGHT NOW.
BUT SANAMI SAID...
ISAAC, YOUR BEST FRIEND...YOUR ONLY FRIEND IS IN DANGER RIGHT NOW, ADRIAN.
SHE FOUND US BEFORE, SHE CAN FIND US AGAIN.
YOU CAN HAVE HIM.
HE'S BACK THERE, WITH THE GIGANTIC MONSTER THAT'S TRYING TO KILL ALL OF US.
ME...I'M GOING DEEPER.
HEY. WAIT UP.

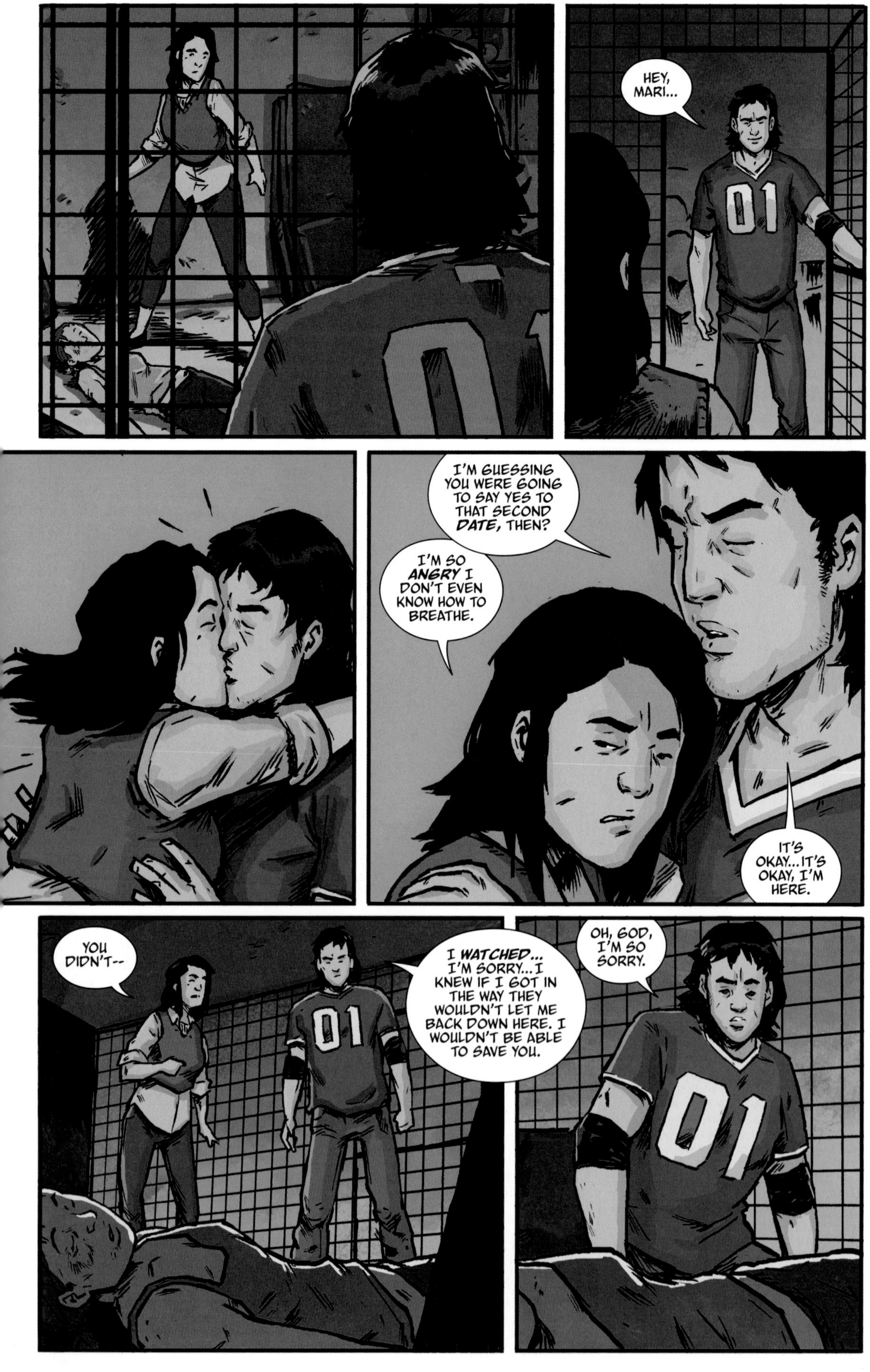
HEY, MARI...
I'M GUESSING YOU WERE GOING TO SAY YES TO THAT SECOND DATE, THEN?
I'M SO ANGRY I DON'T EVEN KNOW HOW TO BREATHE.
IT'S OKAY...IT'S OKAY, I'M HERE.
YOU DIDN'T--
I WATCHED... I'M SORRY...I KNEW IF I GOT IN THE WAY THEY WOULDN'T LET ME BACK DOWN HERE. I WOULDN'T BE ABLE TO SAVE YOU.
OH, GOD, I'M SO SORRY.

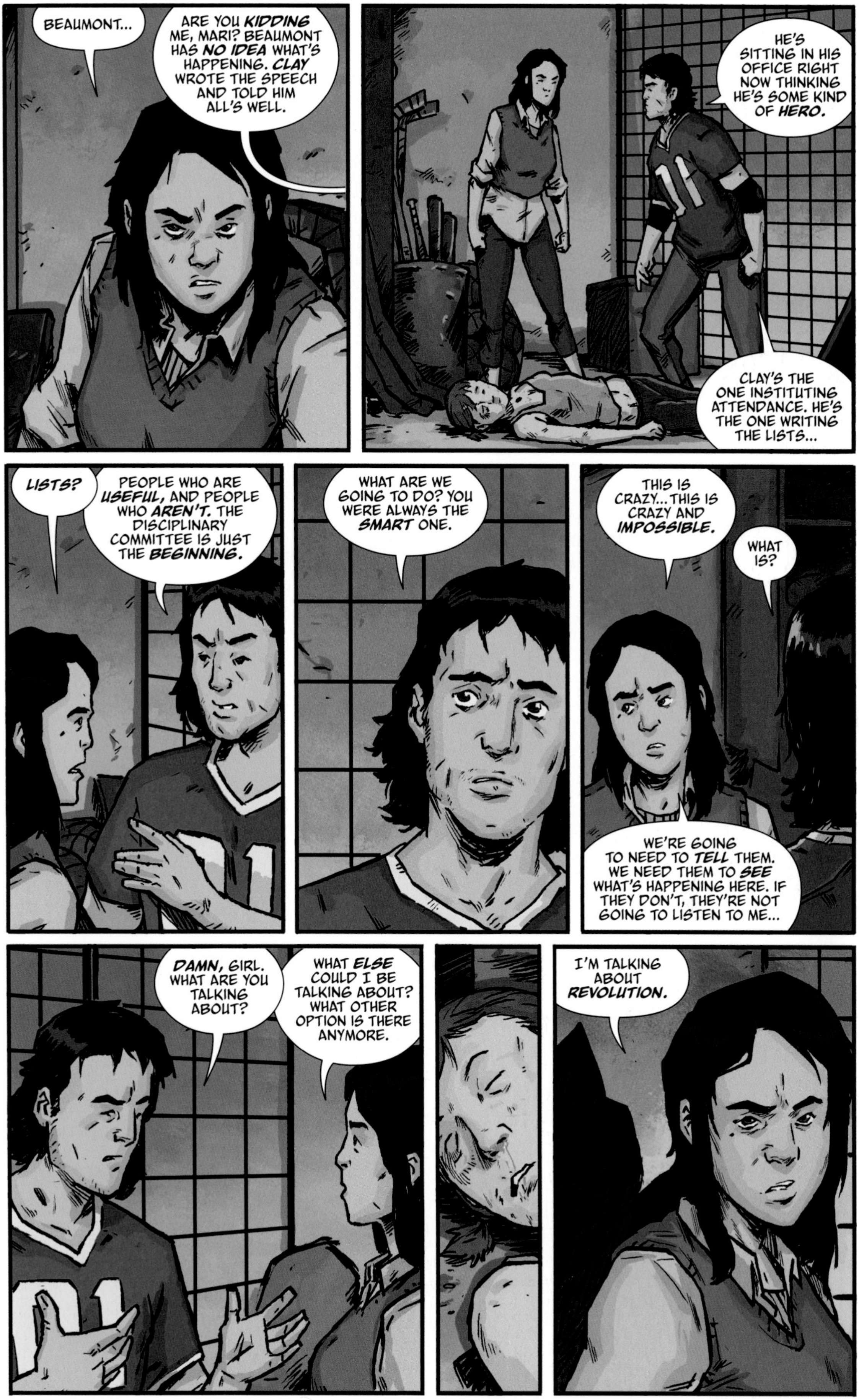
BEAUMONT...
ARE YOU KIDDING ME, MARI? BEAUMONT HAS NO IDEA WHAT'S HAPPENING. CLAY WROTE THE SPEECH AND TOLD HIM ALL'S WELL.
HE'S SITTING IN HIS OFFICE RIGHT NOW THINKING HE'S SOME KIND OF HERO.
CLAY'S THE ONE INSTITUTING ATTENDANCE. HE'S THE ONE WRITING THE LISTS...
LISTS?
PEOPLE WHO ARE USEFUL, AND PEOPLE WHO AREN'T. THE DISCIPLINARY COMMITTEE IS JUST THE BEGINNING.
WHAT ARE WE GOING TO DO? YOU WERE ALWAYS THE SMART ONE.
THIS IS CRAZY...THIS IS CRAZY AND IMPOSSIBLE.
WHAT IS?
WE'RE GOING TO NEED TO TELL THEM. WE NEED THEM TO SEE WHAT'S HAPPENING HERE. IF THEY DON'T, THEY'RE NOT GOING TO LISTEN TO ME...
DAMN, GIRL. WHAT ARE YOU TALKING ABOUT?
WHAT ELSE COULD I BE TALKING ABOUT? WHAT OTHER OPTION IS THERE ANYMORE.
I'M TALKING ABOUT REVOLUTION.

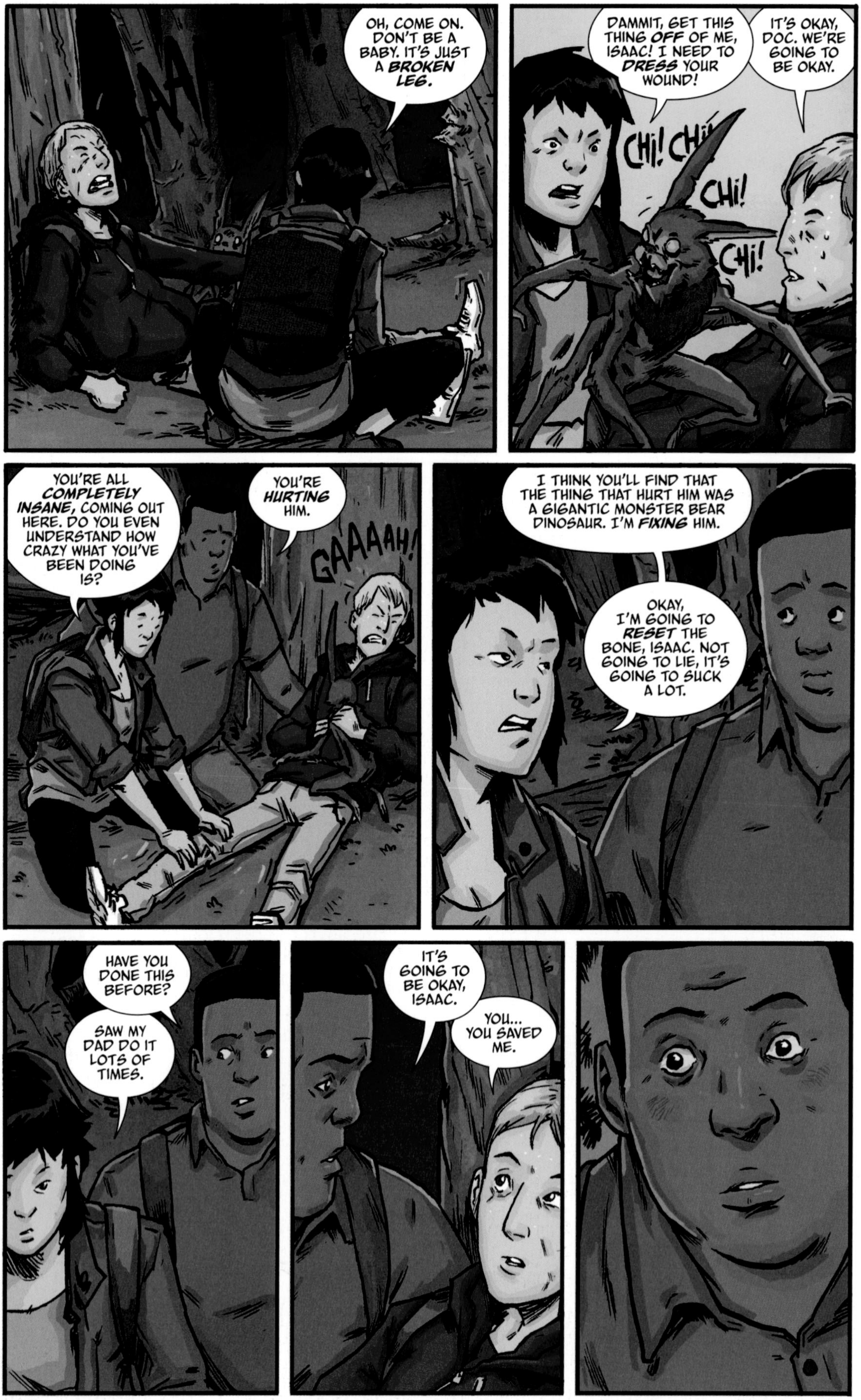
AA
OH, COME ON. DON'T BE A BABY. IT'S JUST A BROKEN LEG.
DAMMIT, GET THIS THING OFF OF ME, ISAAC! I NEED TO DRESS YOUR WOUND!
CHI! CHI!
CHI!
CHI!
IT'S OKAY, DOC. WE'RE GOING TO BE OKAY.
YOU'RE ALL COMPLETELY INSANE, COMING OUT HERE. DO YOU EVEN UNDERSTAND HOW CRAZY WHAT YOU'VE BEEN DOING IS?
YOU'RE HURTING HIM.
GAAAAH!
I THINK YOU'LL FIND THAT THE THING THAT HURT HIM WAS A GIGANTIC MONSTER BEAR DINOSAUR. I'M FIXING HIM.
OKAY, I'M GOING TO RESET THE BONE, ISAAC. NOT GOING TO LIE, IT'S GOING TO SUCK A LOT.
HAVE YOU DONE THIS BEFORE?
SAW MY DAD DO IT LOTS OF TIMES.
IT'S GOING TO BE OKAY, ISAAC.
YOU... YOU SAVED ME.

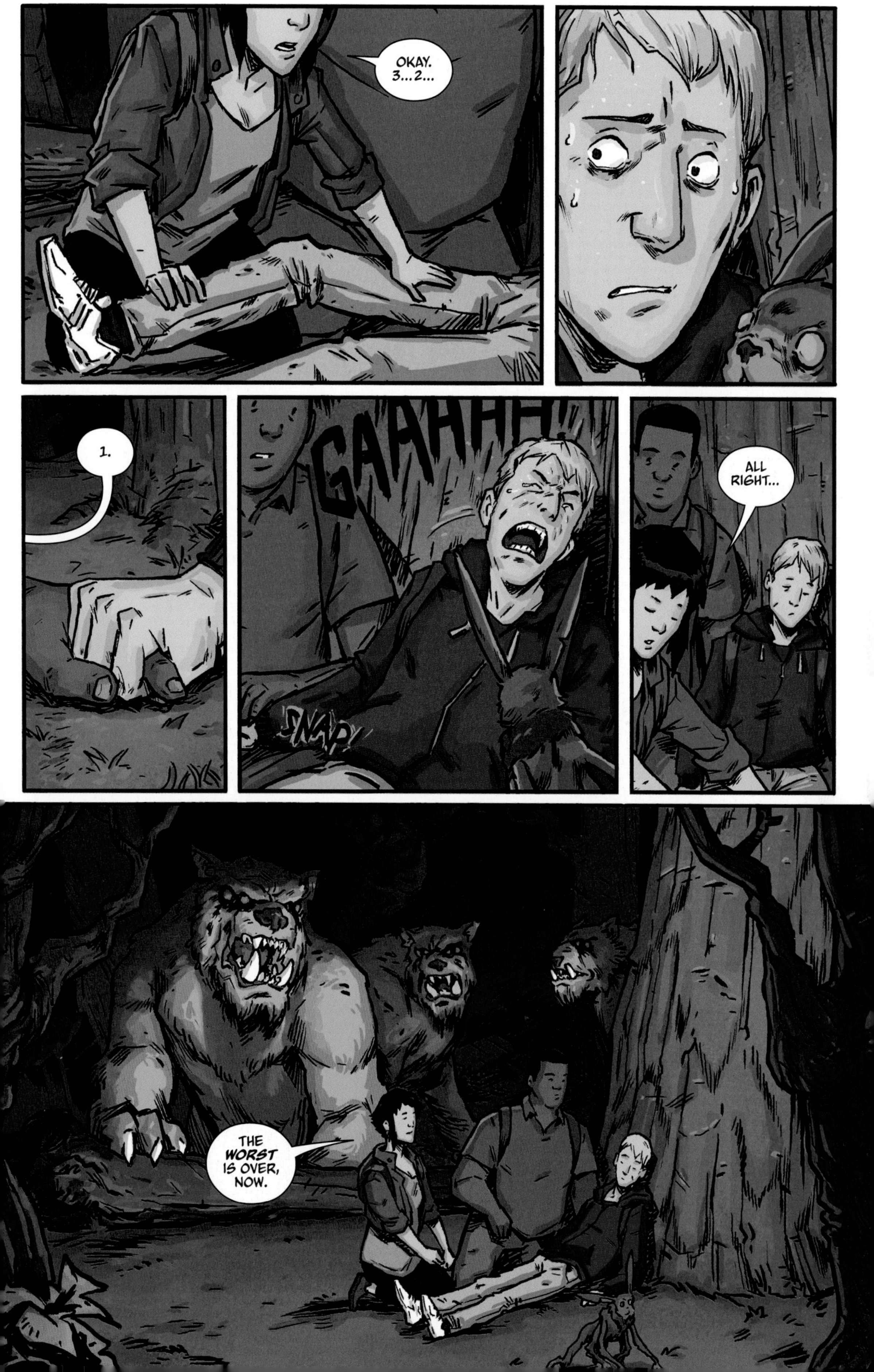
OKAY.
3...2...
1.
GAAHHH!!
SNAP!
ALL
RIGHT...
THE
WORST
IS OVER,
NOW.

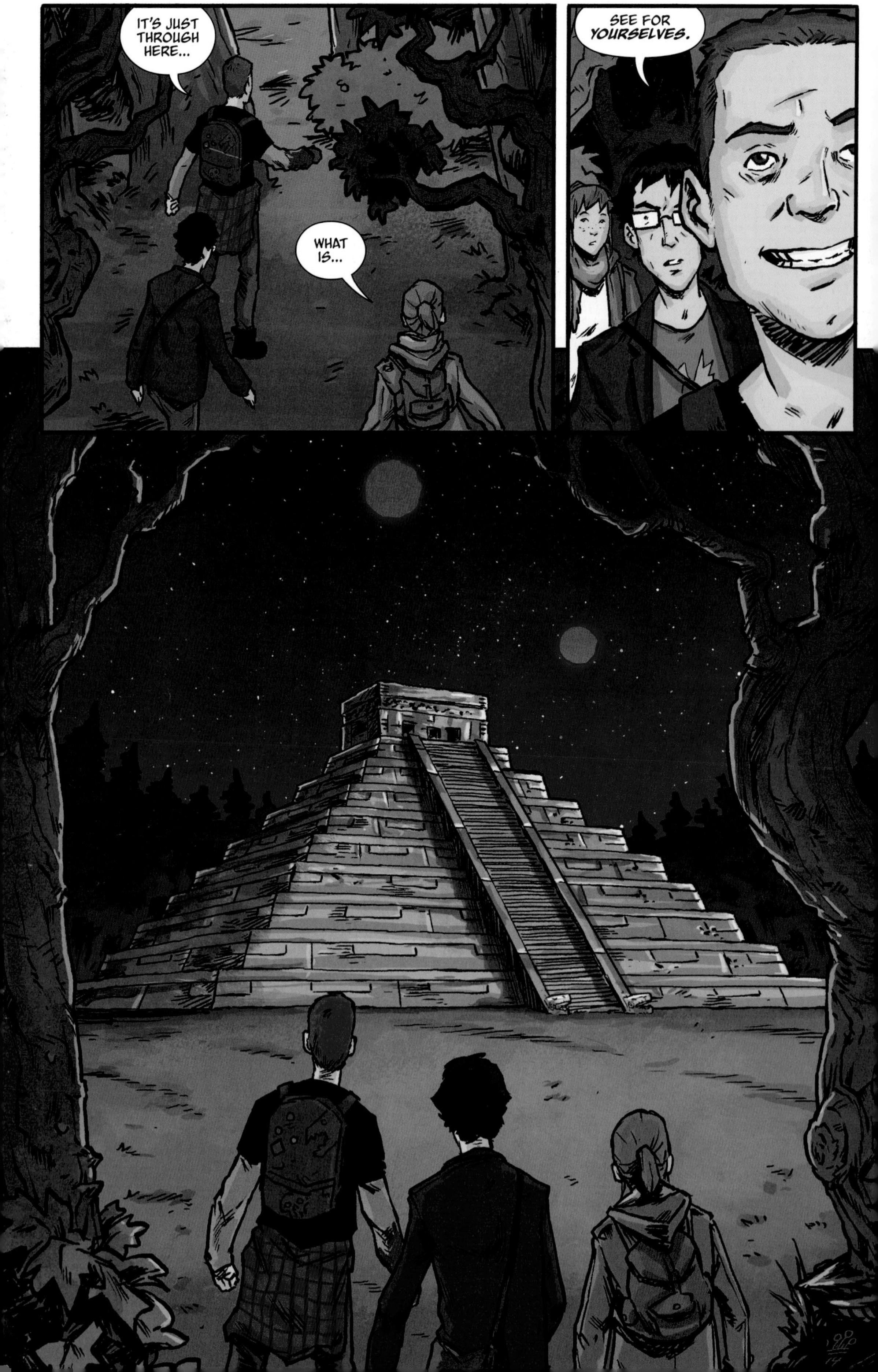
IT'S JUST THROUGH HERE...
WHAT IS...
SEE FOR YOURSELVES.

ISSUE THREE COVER **RAMÓN K. PÉREZ**

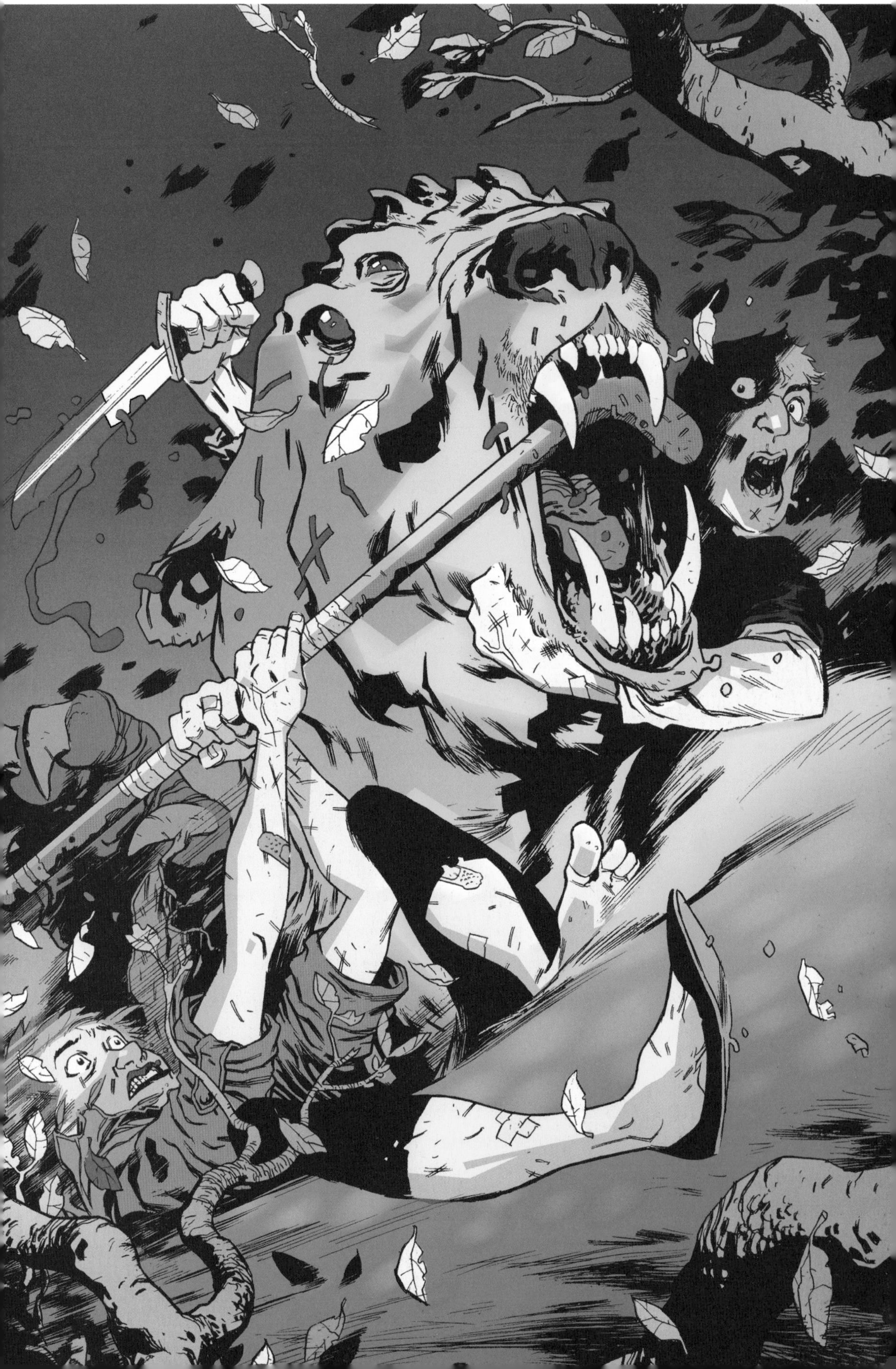

CHAPTER
FOUR

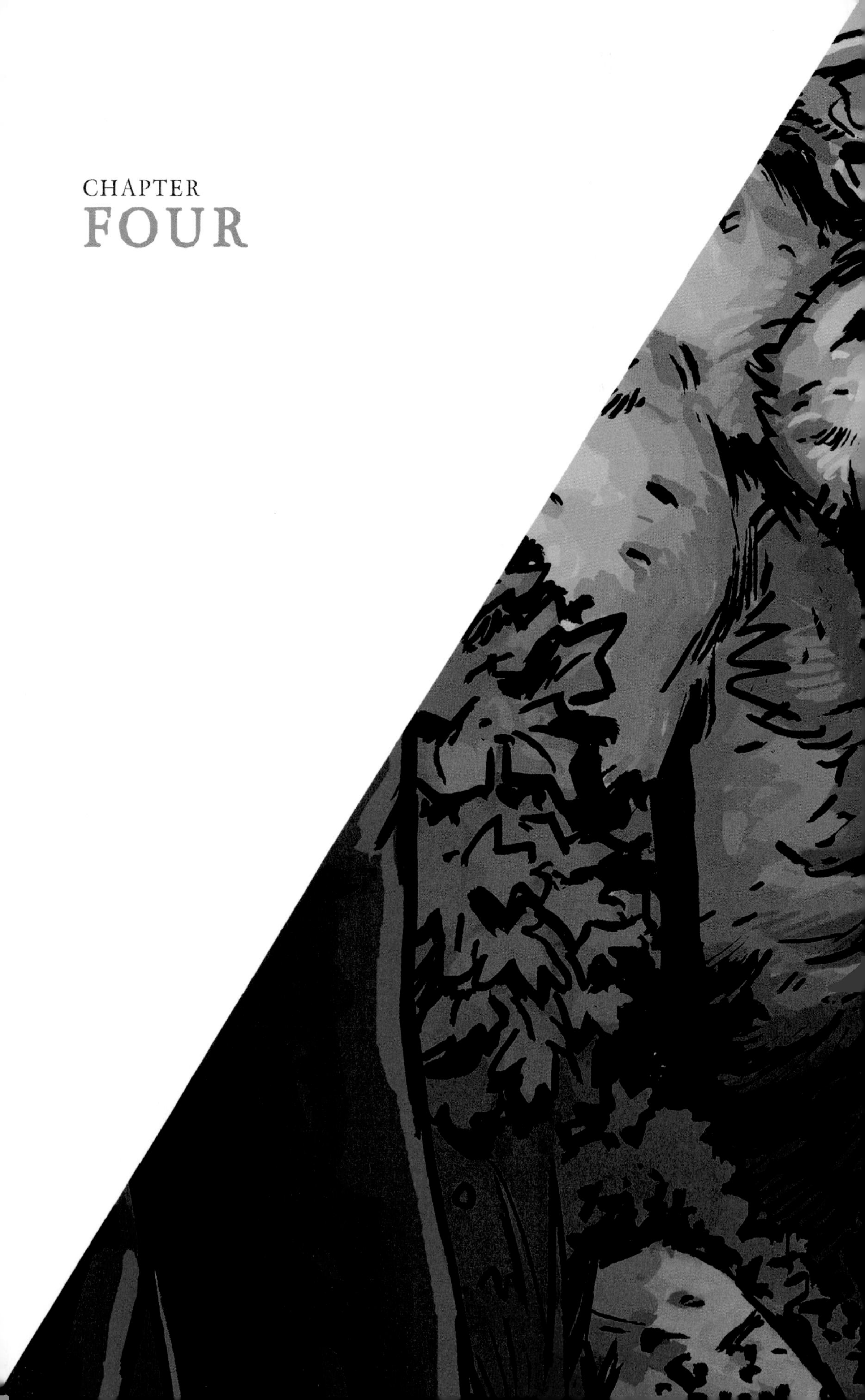

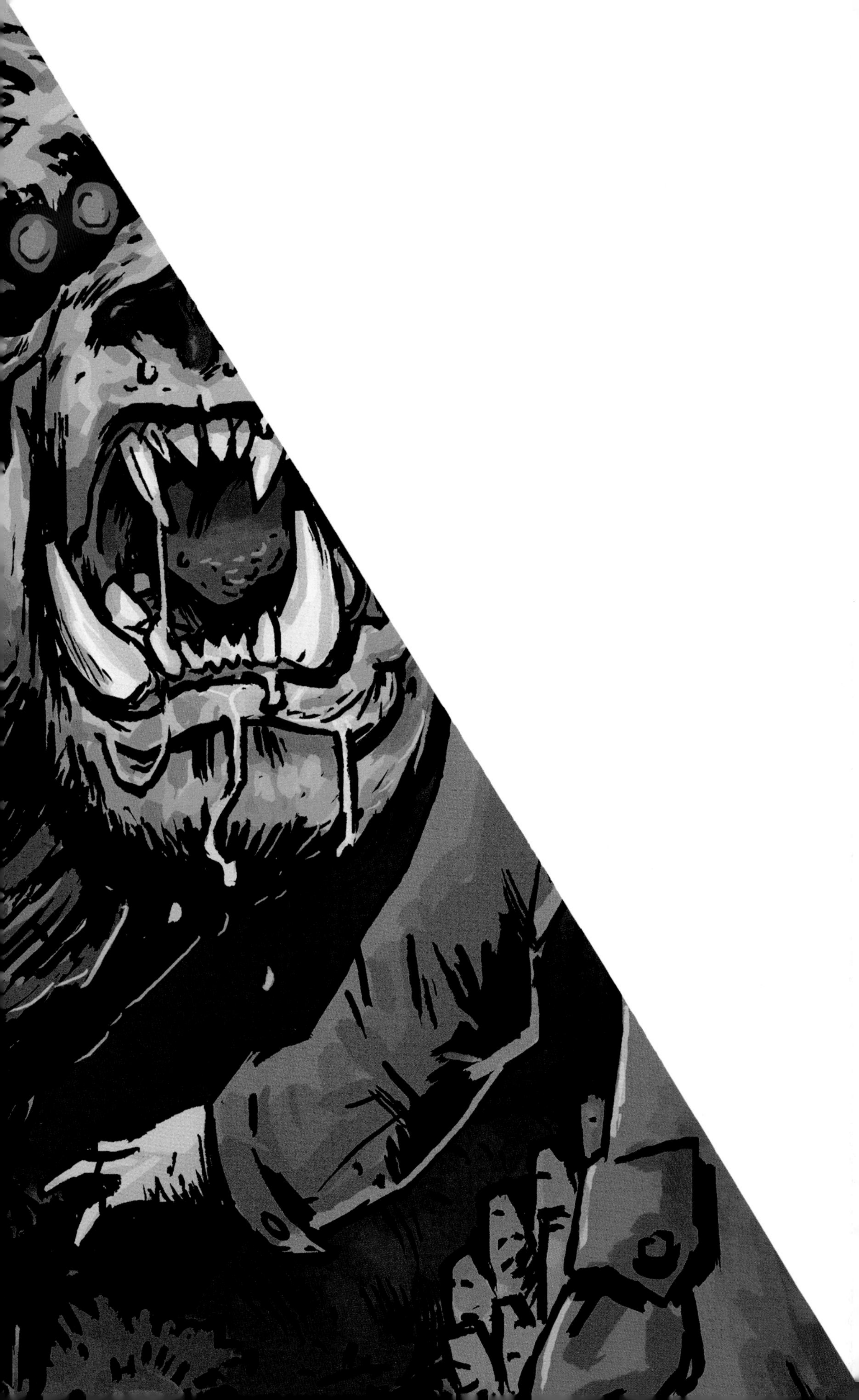

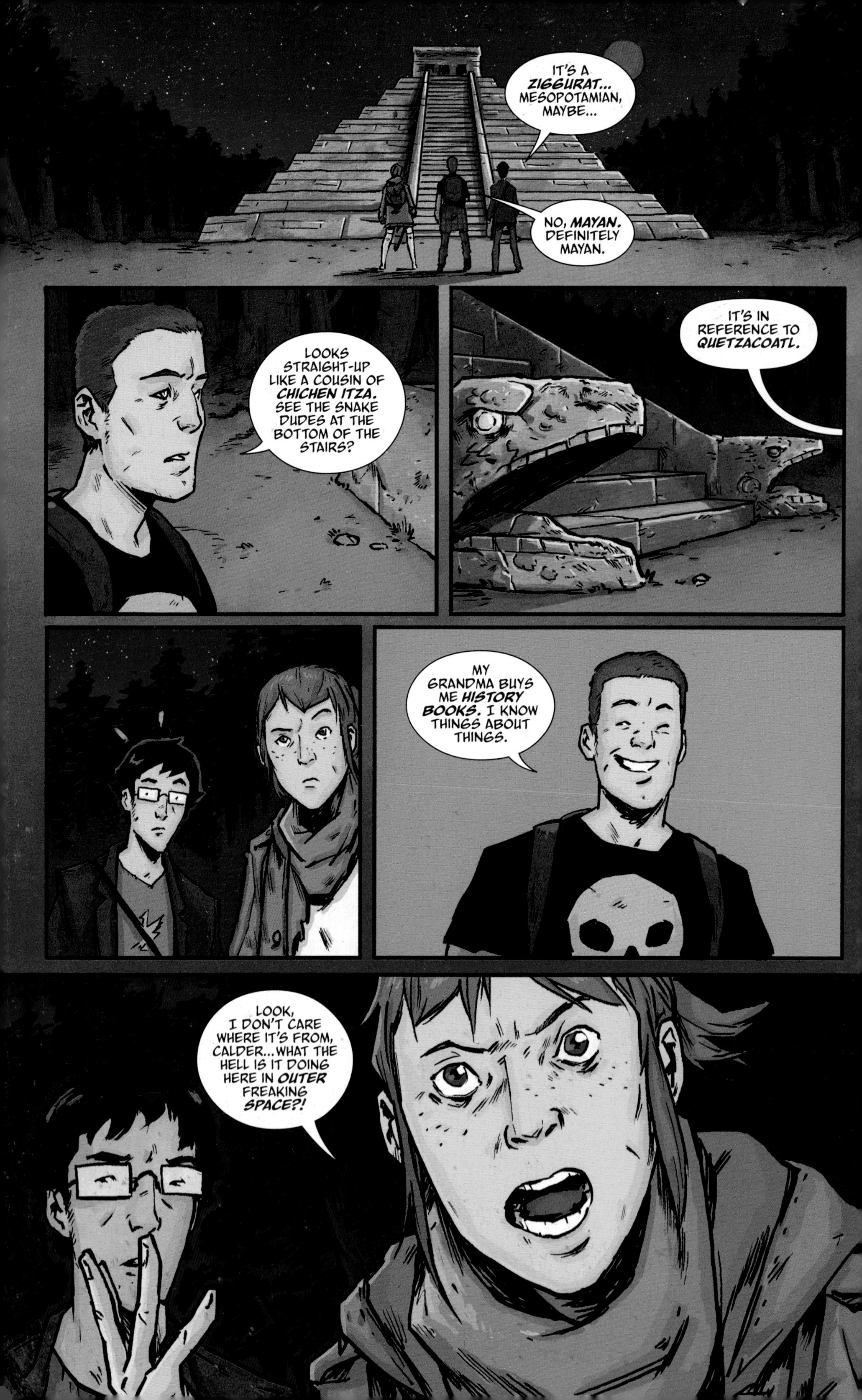
IT'S A ZIGGURAT... MESOPOTAMIAN, MAYBE...
NO, MAYAN. DEFINITELY MAYAN.
LOOKS STRAIGHT-UP LIKE A COUSIN OF CHICHEN ITZA. SEE THE SNAKE DUDES AT THE BOTTOM OF THE STAIRS?
IT'S IN REFERENCE TO QUETZACOATL.
MY GRANDMA BUYS ME HISTORY BOOKS. I KNOW THINGS ABOUT THINGS.
LOOK, I DON'T CARE WHERE IT'S FROM, CALDER... WHAT THE HELL IS IT DOING HERE IN OUTER FREAKING SPACE?!

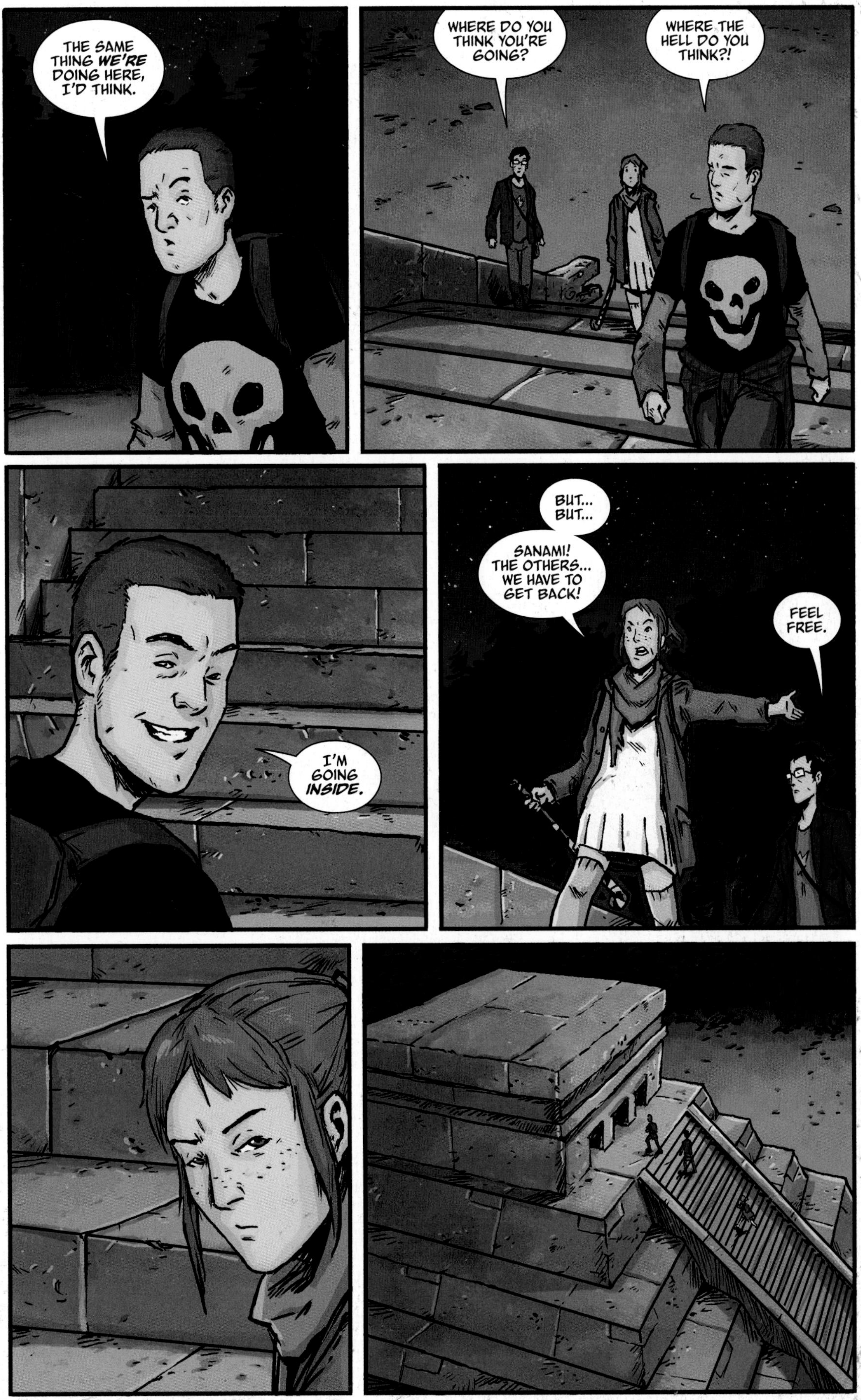
THE SAME THING WE'RE DOING HERE, I'D THINK.
WHERE DO YOU THINK YOU'RE GOING?
WHERE THE HELL DO YOU THINK?!
I'M GOING INSIDE.
BUT... BUT...
SANAMI! THE OTHERS... WE HAVE TO GET BACK!
FEEL FREE.

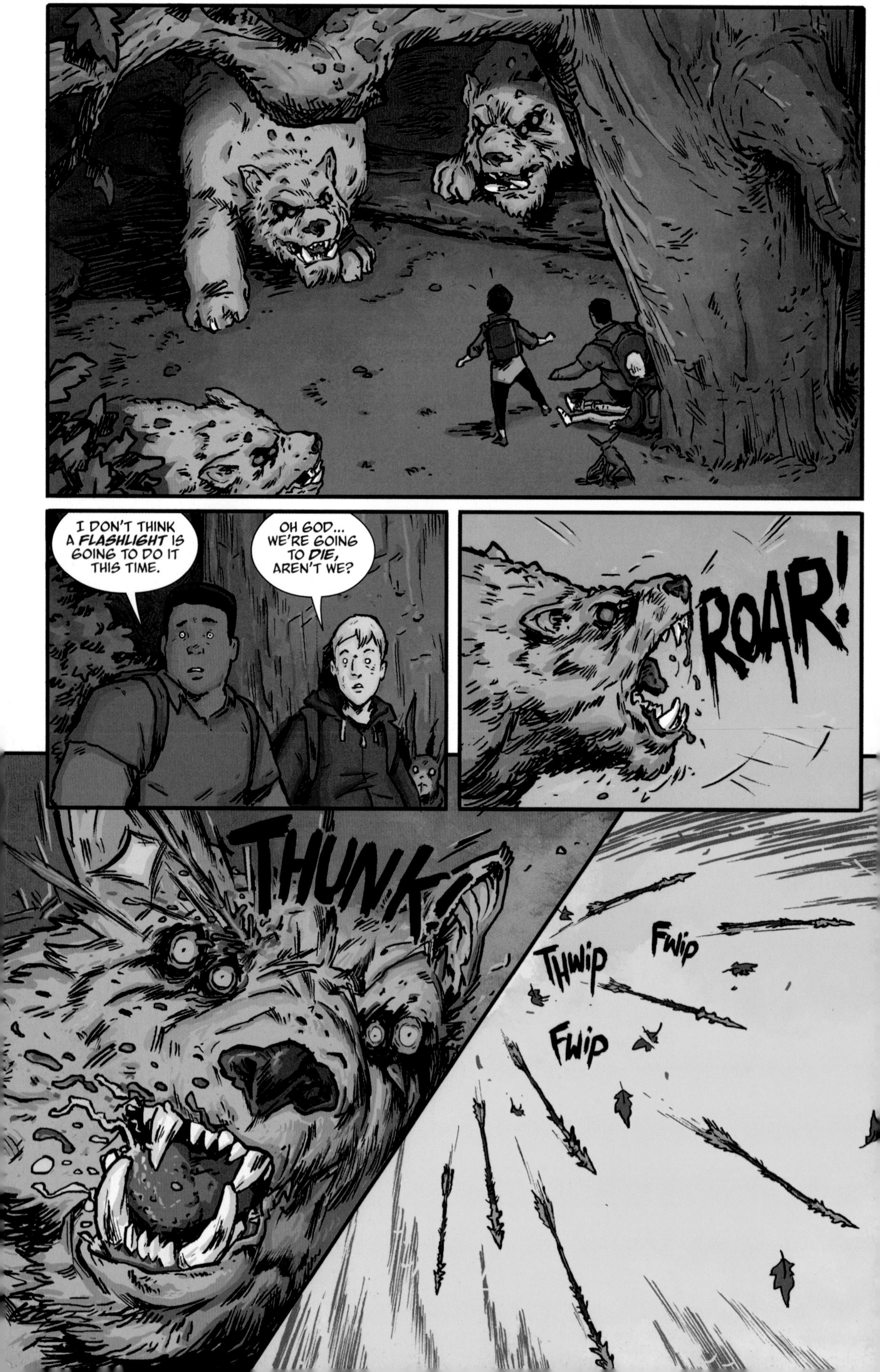

I DON'T THINK A FLASHLIGHT IS GOING TO DO IT THIS TIME.
OH GOD... WE'RE GOING TO DIE, AREN'T WE?
ROAR!
THUNK!
THWIP
FWIP
FWIP

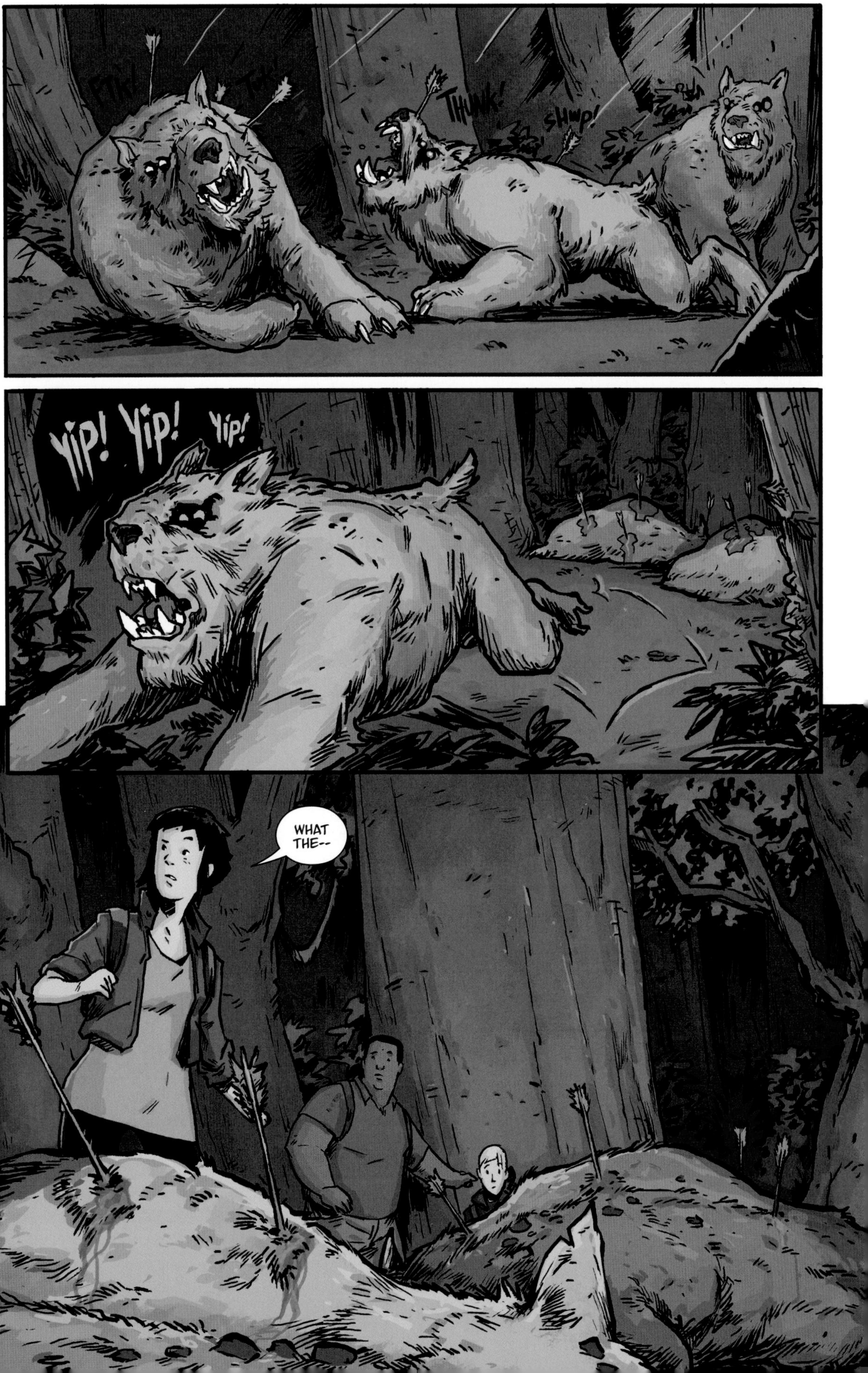
FTIK!
TUK!
THUNK!
SHWP!
YIP! YIP!
YIP!
WHAT THE--

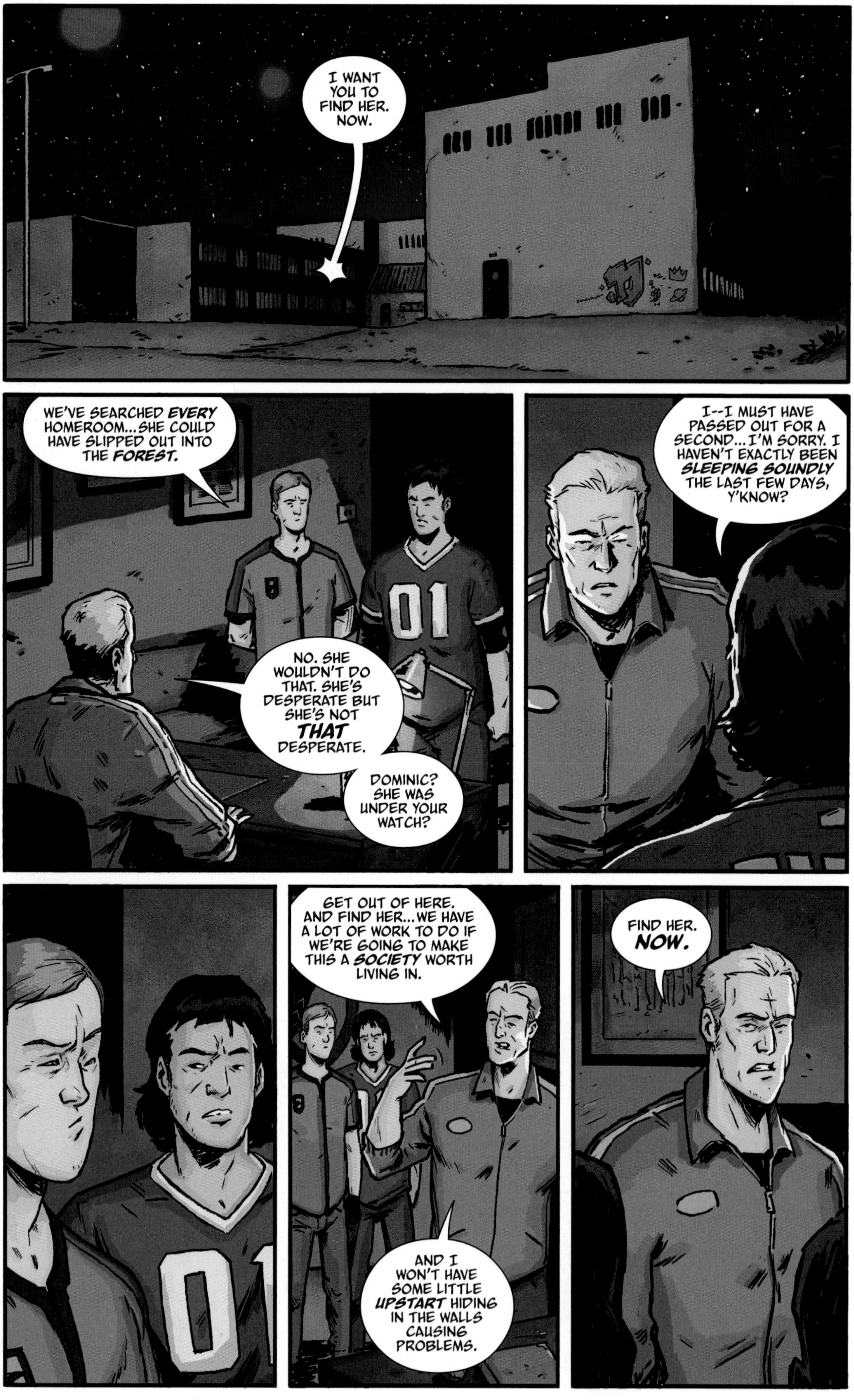
I WANT YOU TO FIND HER. NOW.
WE'VE SEARCHED EVERY HOMEROOM...SHE COULD HAVE SLIPPED OUT INTO THE FOREST.
NO. SHE WOULDN'T DO THAT. SHE'S DESPERATE BUT SHE'S NOT THAT DESPERATE.
DOMINIC? SHE WAS UNDER YOUR WATCH?
I--I MUST HAVE PASSED OUT FOR A SECOND...I'M SORRY. I HAVEN'T EXACTLY BEEN SLEEPING SOUNDLY THE LAST FEW DAYS, Y'KNOW?
GET OUT OF HERE. AND FIND HER...WE HAVE A LOT OF WORK TO DO IF WE'RE GOING TO MAKE THIS A SOCIETY WORTH LIVING IN.
AND I WON'T HAVE SOME LITTLE UPSTART HIDING IN THE WALLS CAUSING PROBLEMS.
FIND HER. NOW.

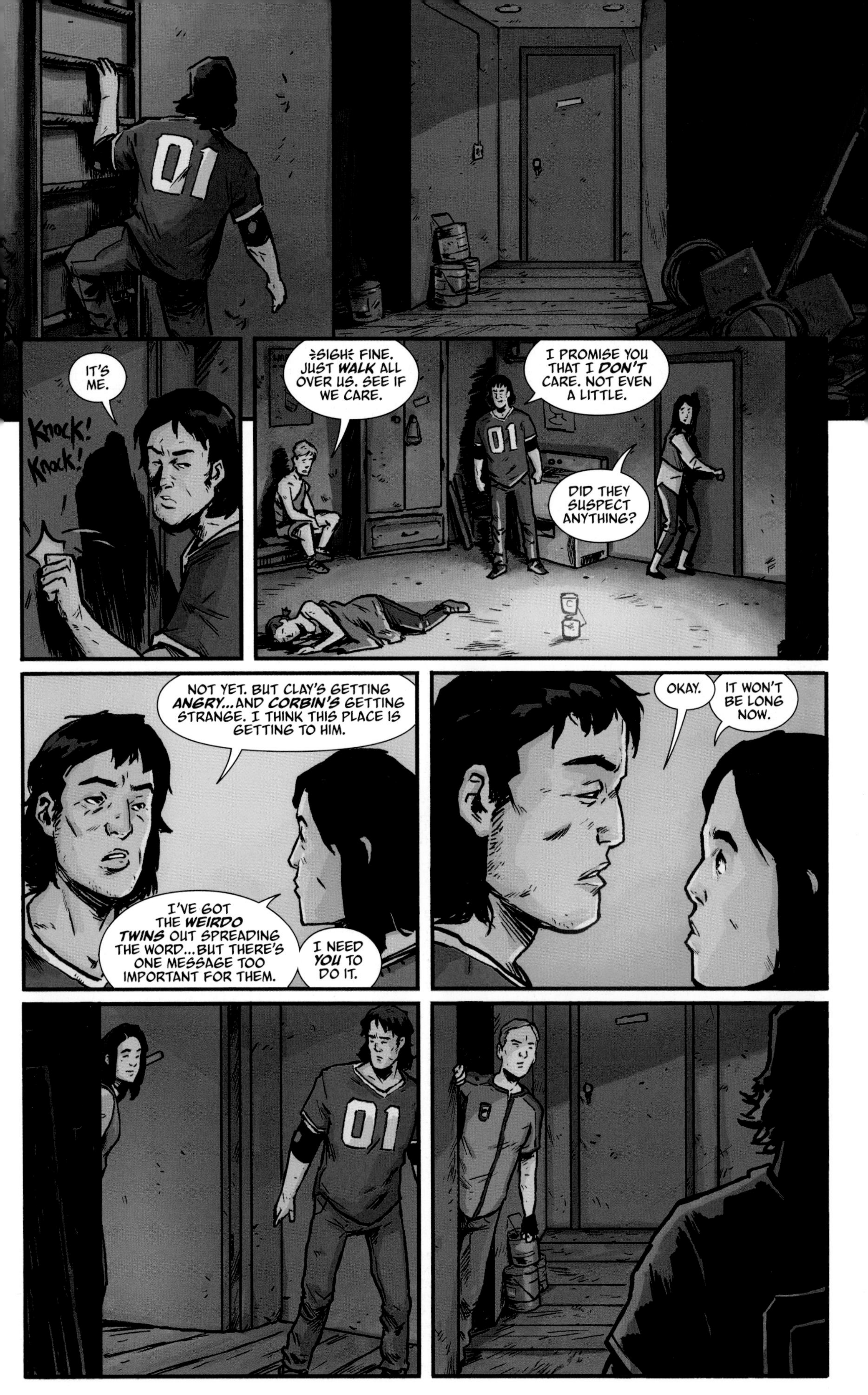
IT'S ME.
KNOCK! KNOCK!
≈SIGH≈ FINE. JUST WALK ALL OVER US. SEE IF WE CARE.
I PROMISE YOU THAT I DON'T CARE. NOT EVEN A LITTLE.
DID THEY SUSPECT ANYTHING?
NOT YET. BUT CLAY'S GETTING ANGRY...AND CORBIN'S GETTING STRANGE. I THINK THIS PLACE IS GETTING TO HIM.
I'VE GOT THE WEIRDO TWINS OUT SPREADING THE WORD...BUT THERE'S ONE MESSAGE TOO IMPORTANT FOR THEM.
I NEED YOU TO DO IT.
OKAY.
IT WON'T BE LONG NOW.

HMM... LOOK AT *THIS*.

THAT'S *CYRILLIC* TEXT, ISN'T IT?

Остерегайтесь лесу.

CYRILLIC?

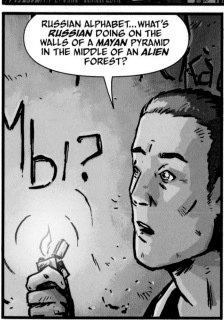

RUSSIAN ALPHABET... WHAT'S *RUSSIAN* DOING ON THE WALLS OF A *MAYAN* PYRAMID IN THE MIDDLE OF AN *ALIEN* FOREST?

МЫ?

WHAT IF WE'RE NOT THE *FIRST* HUMANS TAKEN TO THIS PLACE?

Чер

THIS... THIS DOESN'T MAKE ANY SENSE. THESE LOOK LIKE THEY WERE CARVED IN *CENTURIES* APART.

¿Dónde estamos?

ГДе МЫ?

La Roche noire Sail

Η Μαύρη Πόλη.

IT WAS RIGHT THERE IN THE BULLSEYE...

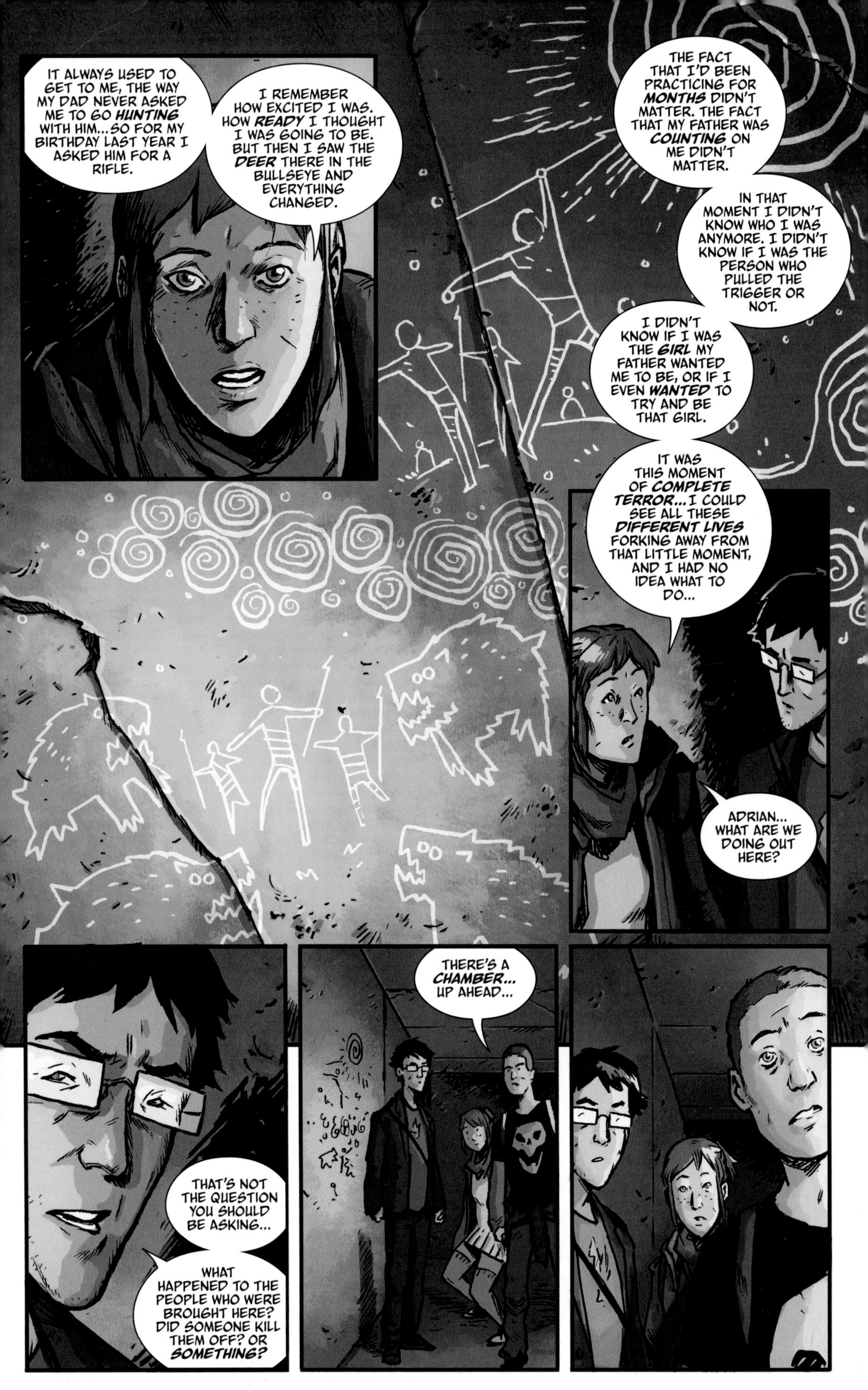
IT ALWAYS USED TO GET TO ME, THE WAY MY DAD NEVER ASKED ME TO GO HUNTING WITH HIM...SO FOR MY BIRTHDAY LAST YEAR I ASKED HIM FOR A RIFLE.
I REMEMBER HOW EXCITED I WAS. HOW READY I THOUGHT I WAS GOING TO BE. BUT THEN I SAW THE DEER THERE IN THE BULLSEYE AND EVERYTHING CHANGED.
THE FACT THAT I'D BEEN PRACTICING FOR MONTHS DIDN'T MATTER. THE FACT THAT MY FATHER WAS COUNTING ON ME DIDN'T MATTER.
IN THAT MOMENT I DIDN'T KNOW WHO I WAS ANYMORE. I DIDN'T KNOW IF I WAS THE PERSON WHO PULLED THE TRIGGER OR NOT.
I DIDN'T KNOW IF I WAS THE GIRL MY FATHER WANTED ME TO BE, OR IF I EVEN WANTED TO TRY AND BE THAT GIRL.
IT WAS THIS MOMENT OF COMPLETE TERROR... I COULD SEE ALL THESE DIFFERENT LIVES FORKING AWAY FROM THAT LITTLE MOMENT, AND I HAD NO IDEA WHAT TO DO...
ADRIAN... WHAT ARE WE DOING OUT HERE?
THAT'S NOT THE QUESTION YOU SHOULD BE ASKING...
WHAT HAPPENED TO THE PEOPLE WHO WERE BROUGHT HERE? DID SOMEONE KILL THEM OFF? OR SOMETHING?
THERE'S A CHAMBER... UP AHEAD...

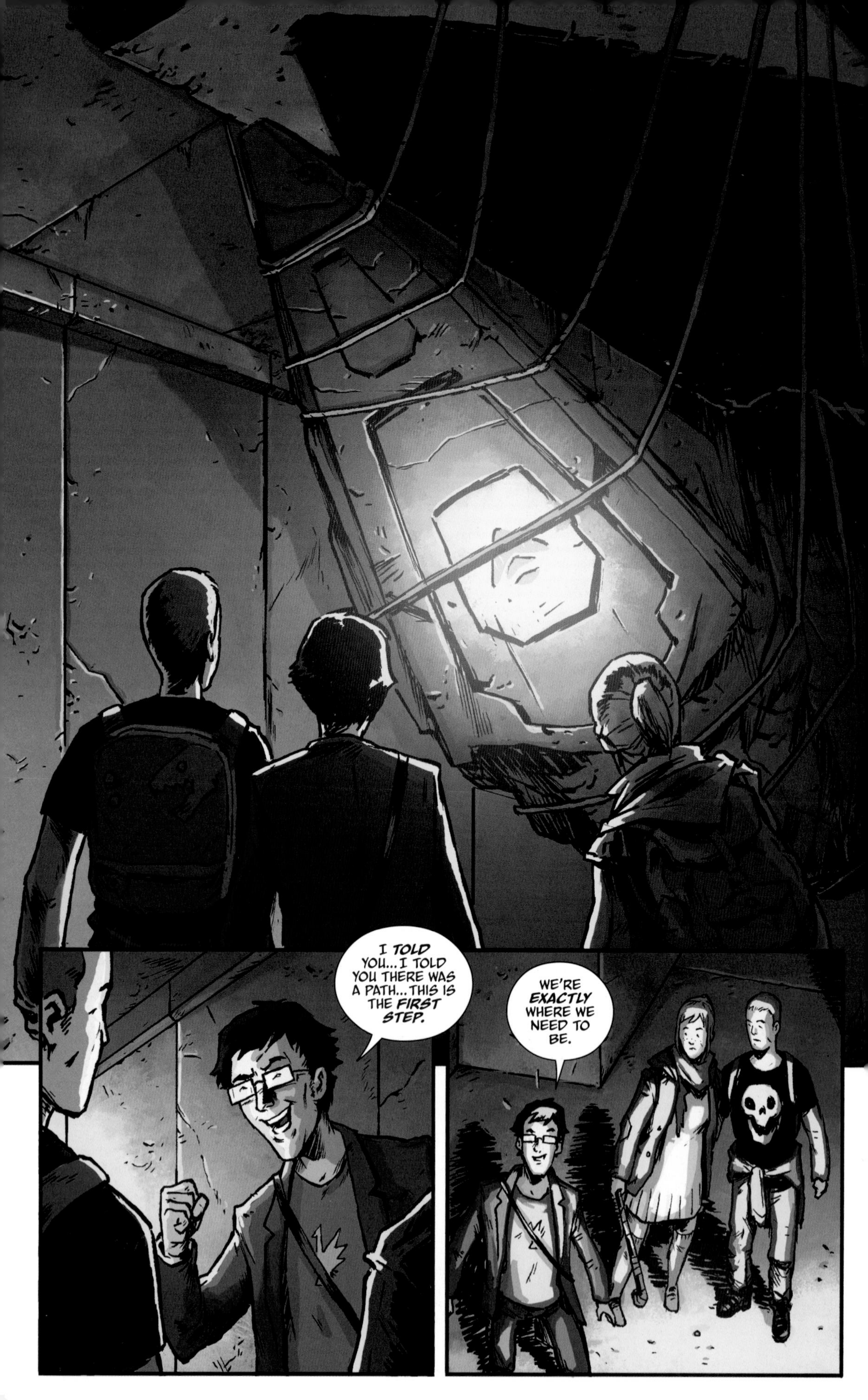
I TOLD YOU... I TOLD YOU THERE WAS A PATH... THIS IS THE FIRST STEP.
WE'RE EXACTLY WHERE WE NEED TO BE.

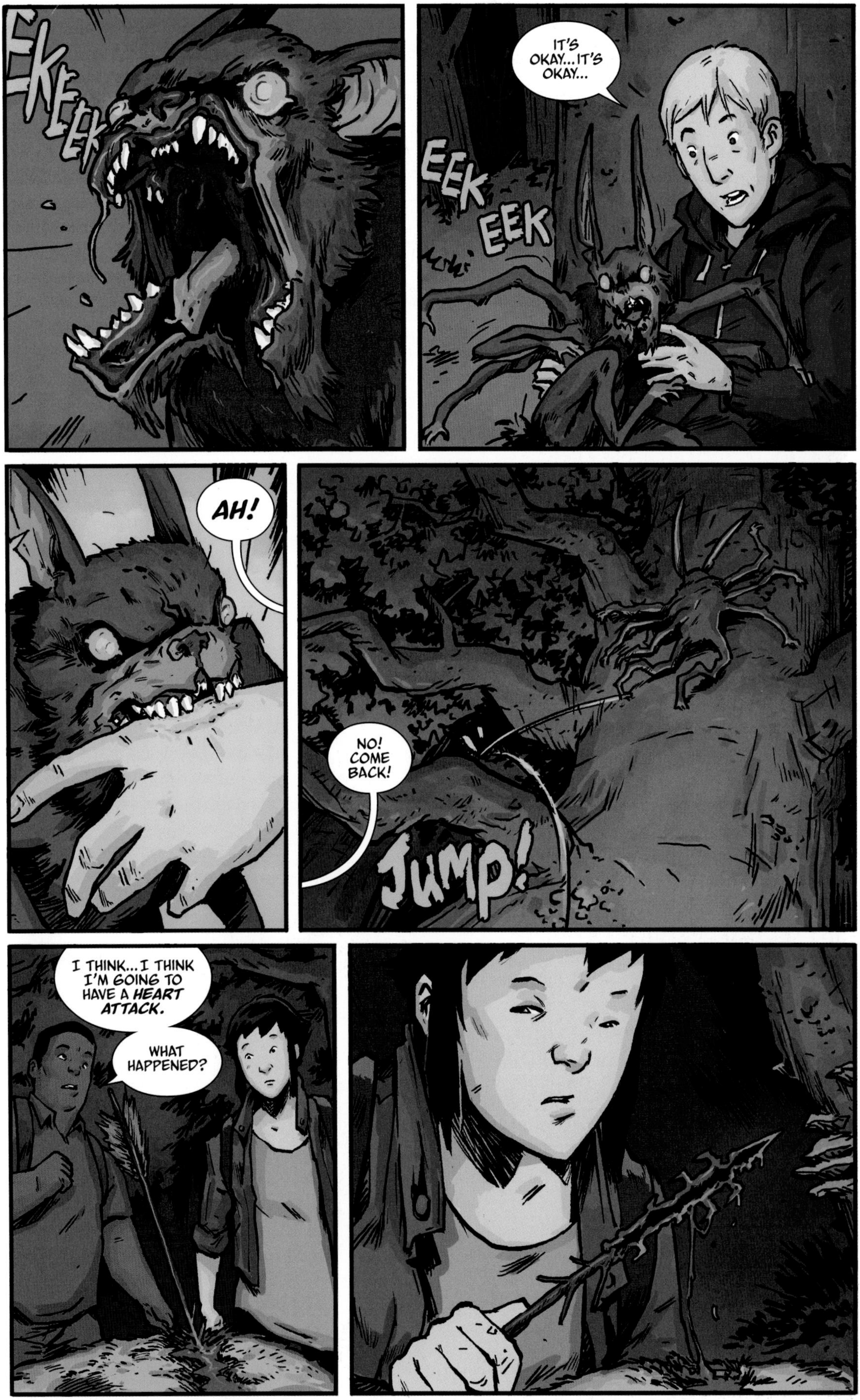
EEKEEEK
IT'S OKAY...IT'S OKAY...
EEK
EEK
AH!
NO! COME BACK!
JUMP!
I THINK...I THINK I'M GOING TO HAVE A *HEART* *ATTACK.*
WHAT HAPPENED?

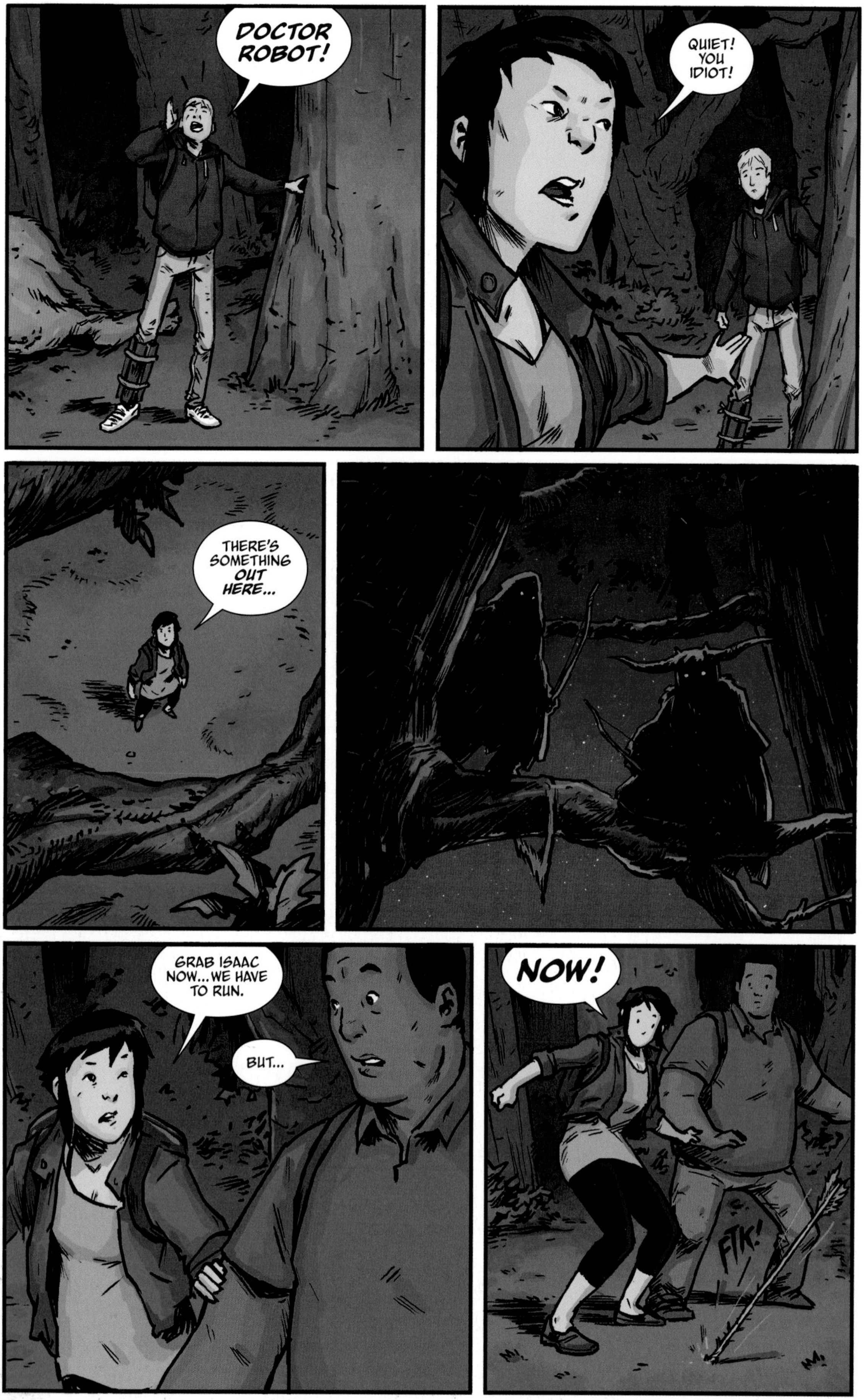
DOCTOR ROBOT!
QUIET! YOU IDIOT!
THERE'S SOMETHING OUT HERE...
GRAB ISAAC NOW...WE HAVE TO RUN.
BUT...
NOW!
FTK!

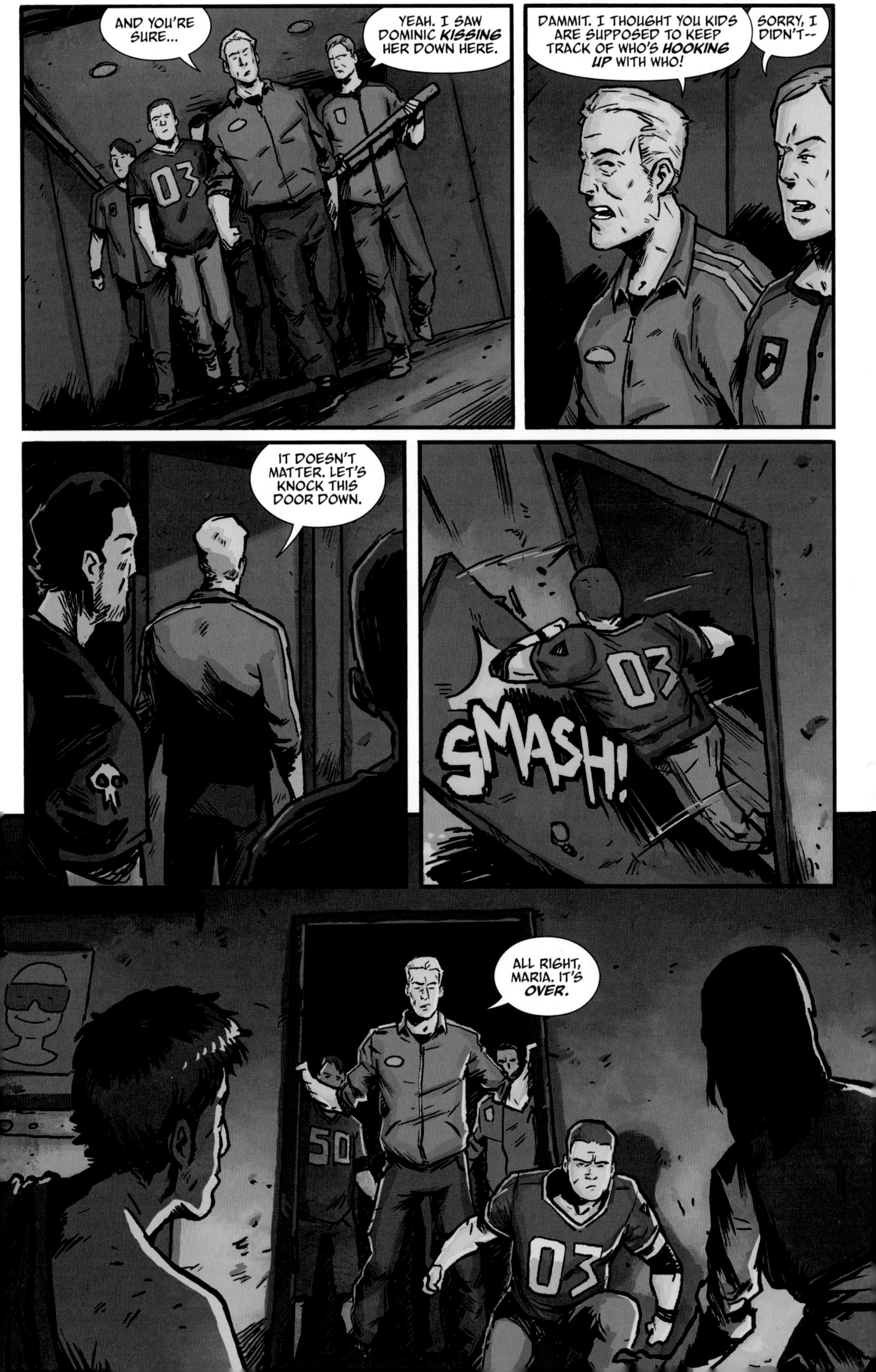
AND YOU'RE SURE...
YEAH. I SAW DOMINIC KISSING HER DOWN HERE.
DAMMIT. I THOUGHT YOU KIDS ARE SUPPOSED TO KEEP TRACK OF WHO'S HOOKING UP WITH WHO!
SORRY, I DIDN'T--
IT DOESN'T MATTER. LET'S KNOCK THIS DOOR DOWN.
SMASH!
ALL RIGHT, MARIA. IT'S OVER.

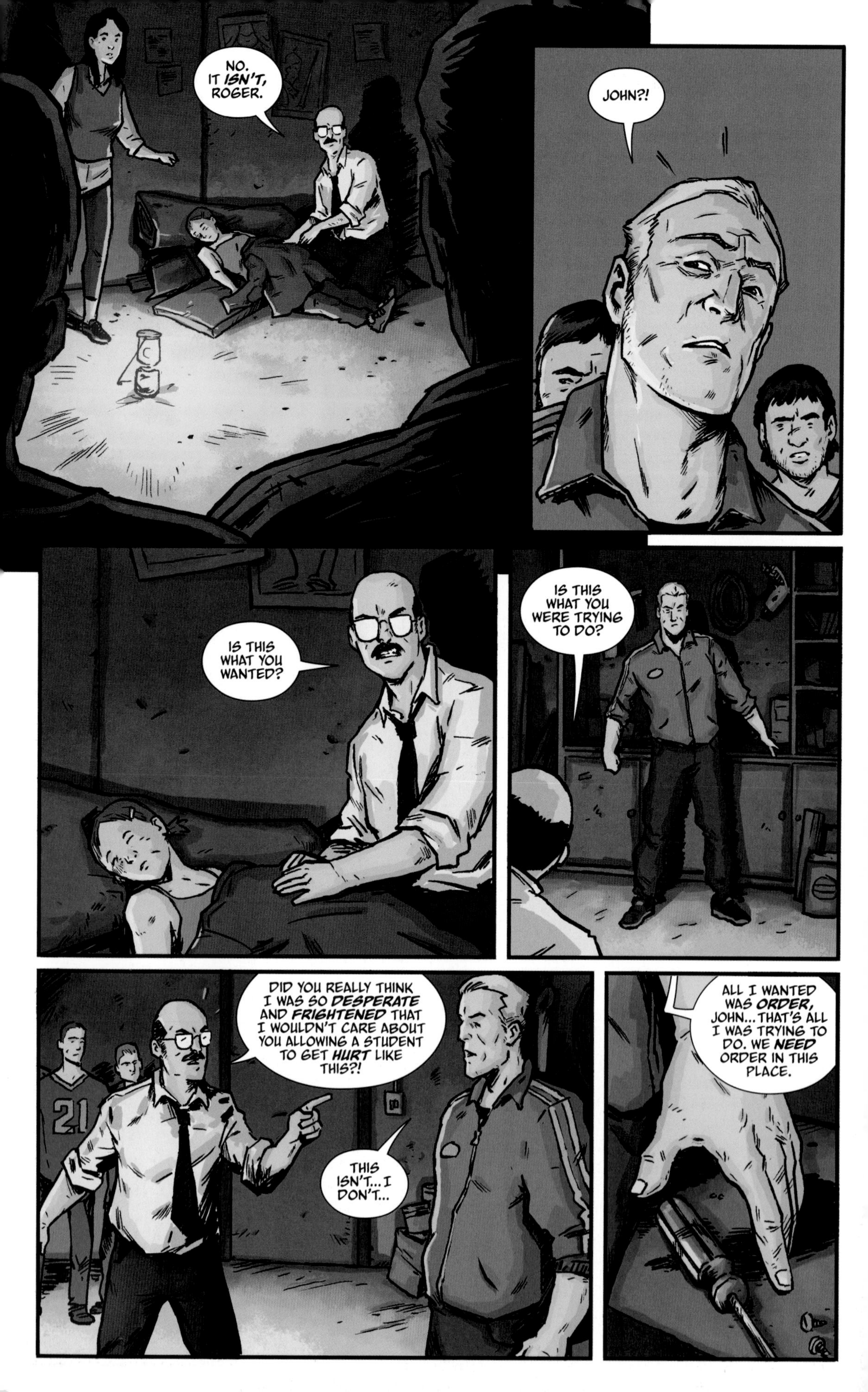
NO. IT ISN'T, ROGER.
JOHN?!
IS THIS WHAT YOU WANTED?
IS THIS WHAT YOU WERE TRYING TO DO?
DID YOU REALLY THINK I WAS SO DESPERATE AND FRIGHTENED THAT I WOULDN'T CARE ABOUT YOU ALLOWING A STUDENT TO GET HURT LIKE THIS?!
THIS ISN'T... I DON'T...
ALL I WANTED WAS ORDER, JOHN... THAT'S ALL I WAS TRYING TO DO. WE NEED ORDER IN THIS PLACE.
21

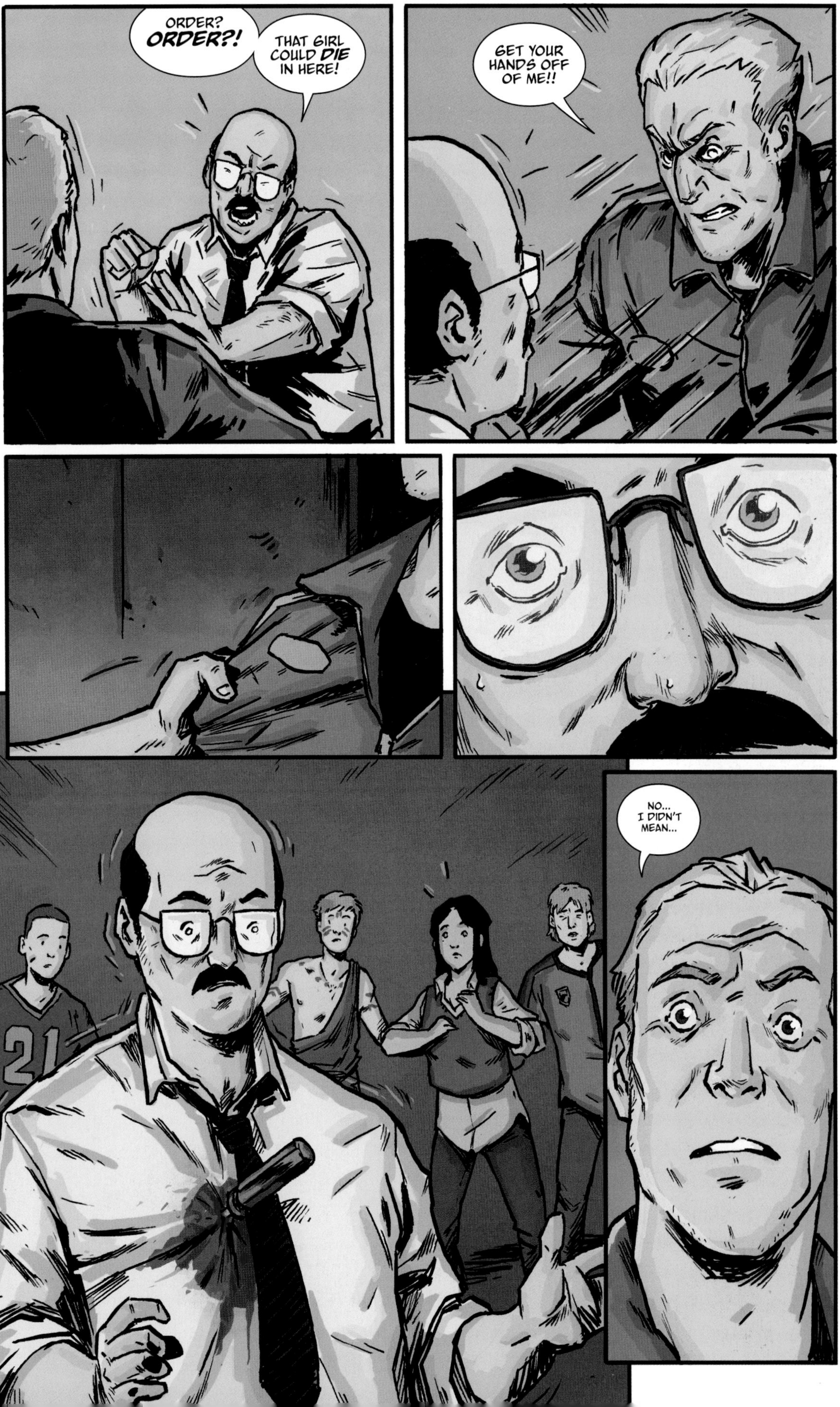
ORDER? ORDER?!
THAT GIRL COULD DIE IN HERE!
GET YOUR HANDS OFF OF ME!!
NO... I DIDN'T MEAN...
21

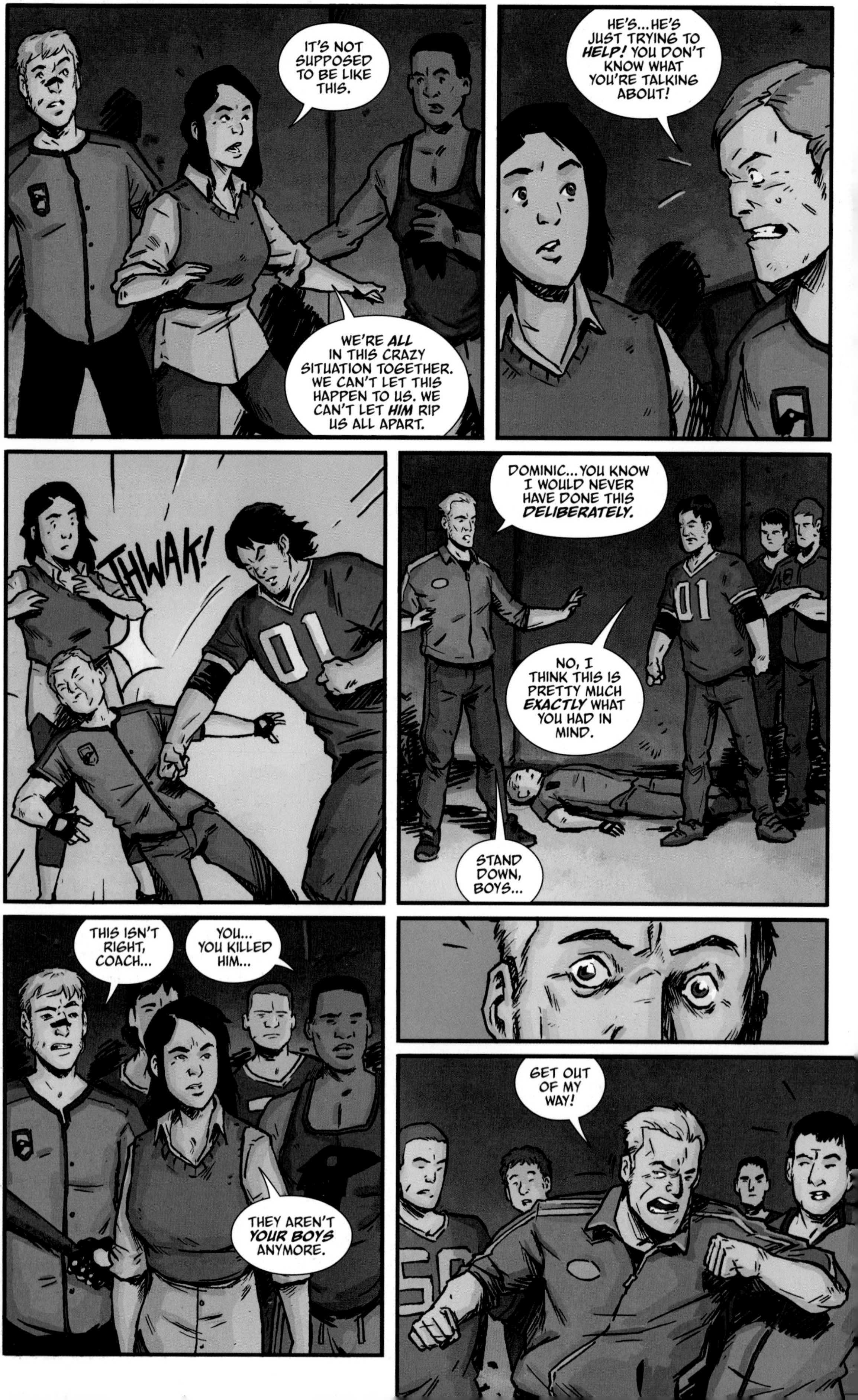
IT'S NOT SUPPOSED TO BE LIKE THIS.
WE'RE ALL IN THIS CRAZY SITUATION TOGETHER. WE CAN'T LET THIS HAPPEN TO US. WE CAN'T LET HIM RIP US ALL APART.
HE'S...HE'S JUST TRYING TO HELP! YOU DON'T KNOW WHAT YOU'RE TALKING ABOUT!
THWAK!
DOMINIC...YOU KNOW I WOULD NEVER HAVE DONE THIS DELIBERATELY.
NO, I THINK THIS IS PRETTY MUCH EXACTLY WHAT YOU HAD IN MIND.
STAND DOWN, BOYS...
THIS ISN'T RIGHT, COACH...
YOU... YOU KILLED HIM...
THEY AREN'T YOUR BOYS ANYMORE.
GET OUT OF MY WAY!

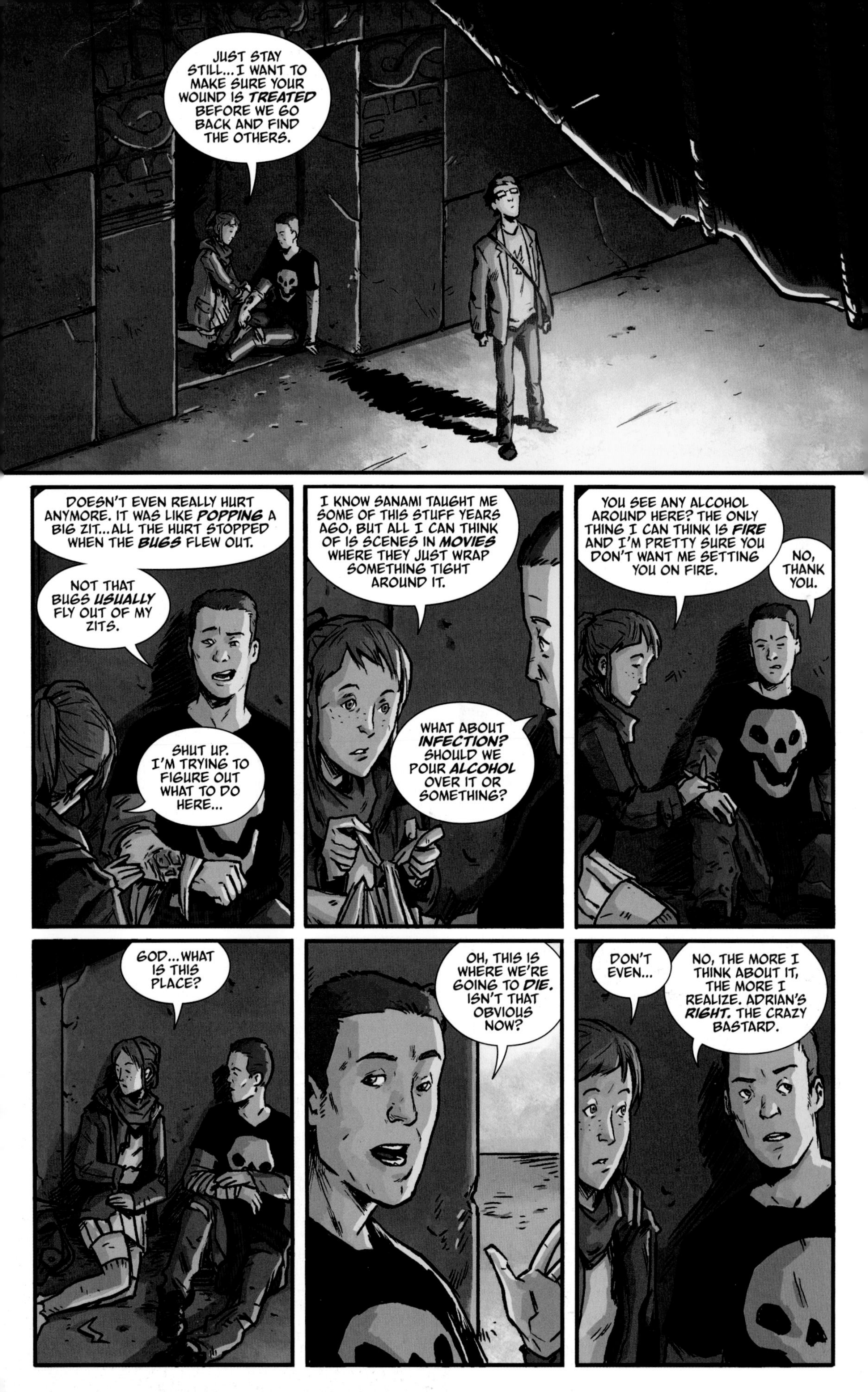
JUST STAY STILL... I WANT TO MAKE SURE YOUR WOUND IS TREATED BEFORE WE GO BACK AND FIND THE OTHERS.
DOESN'T EVEN REALLY HURT ANYMORE. IT WAS LIKE POPPING A BIG ZIT... ALL THE HURT STOPPED WHEN THE BUGS FLEW OUT.
NOT THAT BUGS USUALLY FLY OUT OF MY ZITS.
SHUT UP. I'M TRYING TO FIGURE OUT WHAT TO DO HERE...
I KNOW SANAMI TAUGHT ME SOME OF THIS STUFF YEARS AGO, BUT ALL I CAN THINK OF IS SCENES IN MOVIES WHERE THEY JUST WRAP SOMETHING TIGHT AROUND IT.
WHAT ABOUT INFECTION? SHOULD WE POUR ALCOHOL OVER IT OR SOMETHING?
YOU SEE ANY ALCOHOL AROUND HERE? THE ONLY THING I CAN THINK IS FIRE AND I'M PRETTY SURE YOU DON'T WANT ME SETTING YOU ON FIRE.
NO, THANK YOU.
GOD... WHAT IS THIS PLACE?
OH, THIS IS WHERE WE'RE GOING TO DIE. ISN'T THAT OBVIOUS NOW?
DON'T EVEN...
NO, THE MORE I THINK ABOUT IT, THE MORE I REALIZE. ADRIAN'S RIGHT. THE CRAZY BASTARD.

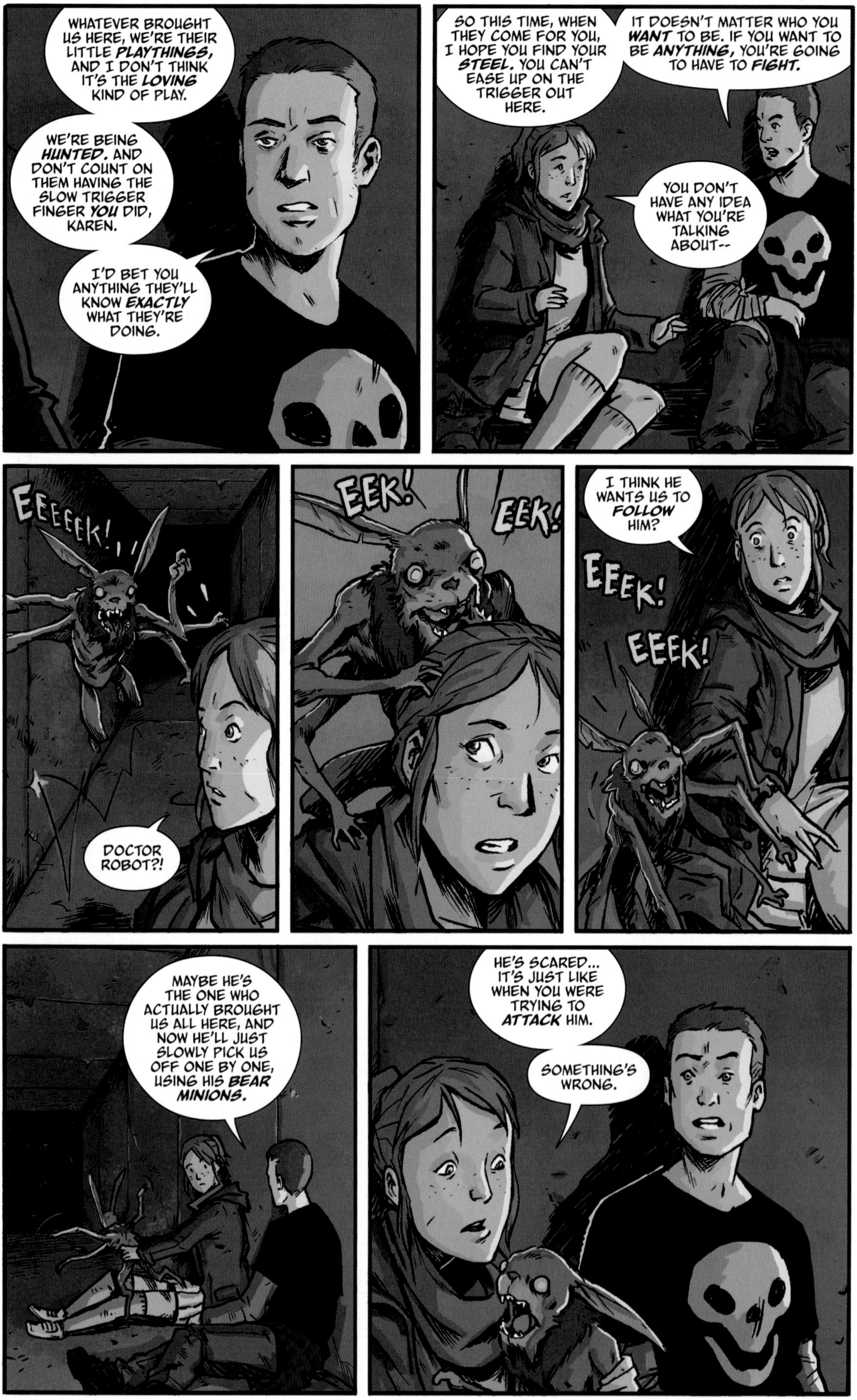
WHATEVER BROUGHT US HERE, WE'RE THEIR LITTLE PLAYTHINGS, AND I DON'T THINK IT'S THE LOVING KIND OF PLAY.
WE'RE BEING HUNTED. AND DON'T COUNT ON THEM HAVING THE SLOW TRIGGER FINGER YOU DID, KAREN.
I'D BET YOU ANYTHING THEY'LL KNOW EXACTLY WHAT THEY'RE DOING.
SO THIS TIME, WHEN THEY COME FOR YOU, I HOPE YOU FIND YOUR STEEL. YOU CAN'T EASE UP ON THE TRIGGER OUT HERE.
IT DOESN'T MATTER WHO YOU WANT TO BE. IF YOU WANT TO BE ANYTHING, YOU'RE GOING TO HAVE TO FIGHT.
YOU DON'T HAVE ANY IDEA WHAT YOU'RE TALKING ABOUT--
EEEEEK!
DOCTOR ROBOT?!
EEK!
EEK!
I THINK HE WANTS US TO FOLLOW HIM?
EEEK!
EEEK!
MAYBE HE'S THE ONE WHO ACTUALLY BROUGHT US ALL HERE, AND NOW HE'LL JUST SLOWLY PICK US OFF ONE BY ONE, USING HIS BEAR MINIONS.
HE'S SCARED... IT'S JUST LIKE WHEN YOU WERE TRYING TO ATTACK HIM.
SOMETHING'S WRONG.

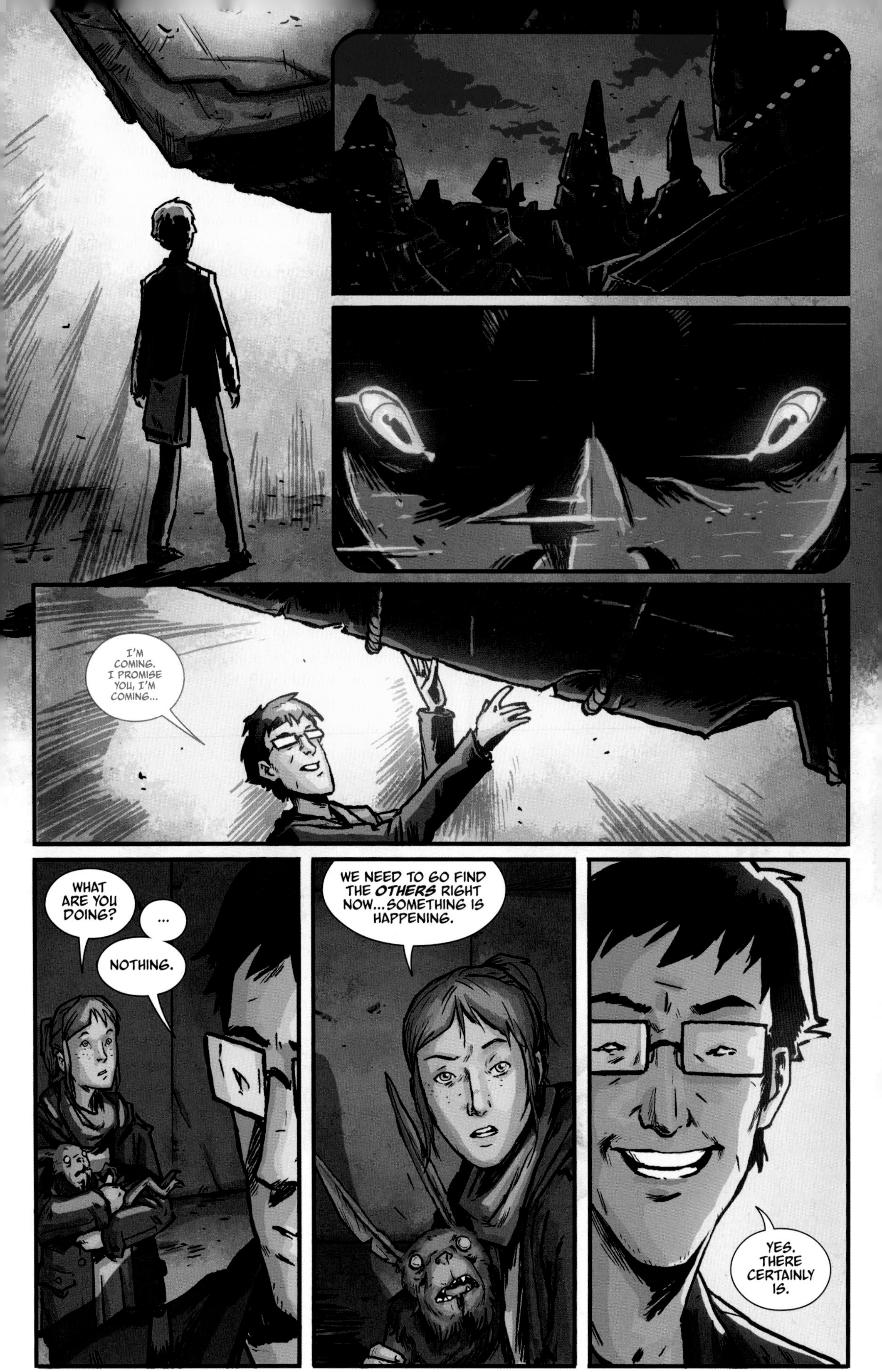
I'M COMING. I PROMISE YOU, I'M COMING...
WHAT ARE YOU DOING?
...
NOTHING.
WE NEED TO GO FIND THE *OTHERS* RIGHT NOW...SOMETHING IS HAPPENING.
YES. THERE CERTAINLY IS.

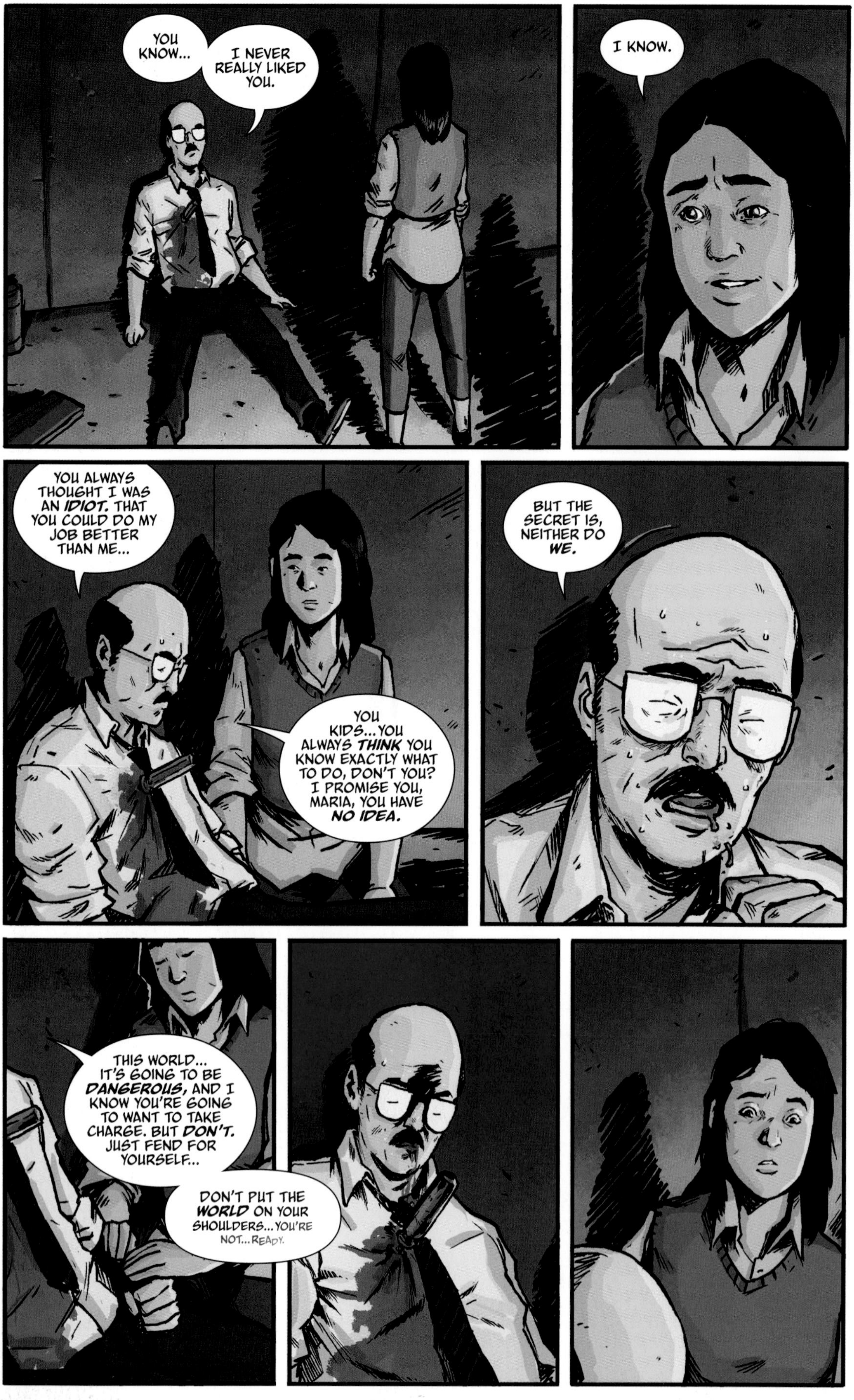
YOU KNOW...
I NEVER REALLY LIKED YOU.
I KNOW.
YOU ALWAYS THOUGHT I WAS AN *IDIOT.* THAT YOU COULD DO MY JOB BETTER THAN ME...
YOU KIDS... YOU ALWAYS *THINK* YOU KNOW EXACTLY WHAT TO DO, DON'T YOU? I PROMISE YOU, MARIA, YOU HAVE *NO IDEA.*
BUT THE SECRET IS, NEITHER DO *WE.*
THIS WORLD... IT'S GOING TO BE *DANGEROUS,* AND I KNOW YOU'RE GOING TO WANT TO TAKE CHARGE. BUT *DON'T.* JUST FEND FOR YOURSELF...
DON'T PUT THE *WORLD* ON YOUR SHOULDERS... YOU'RE NOT... READY.

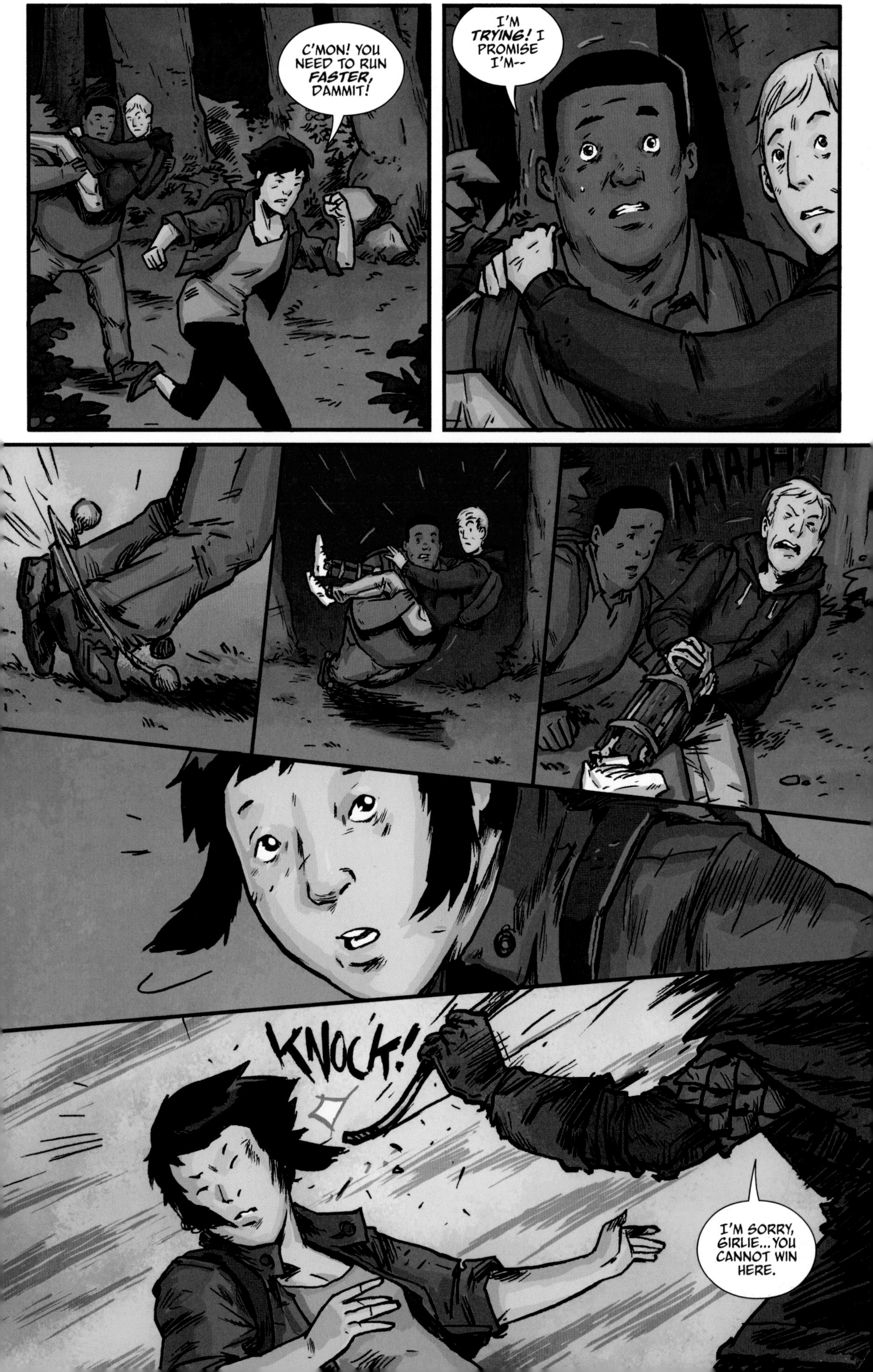
C'MON! YOU NEED TO RUN FASTER, DAMMIT!
I'M TRYING! I PROMISE I'M--
AAAAHH!
KNOCK!
I'M SORRY, GIRLIE... YOU CANNOT WIN HERE.

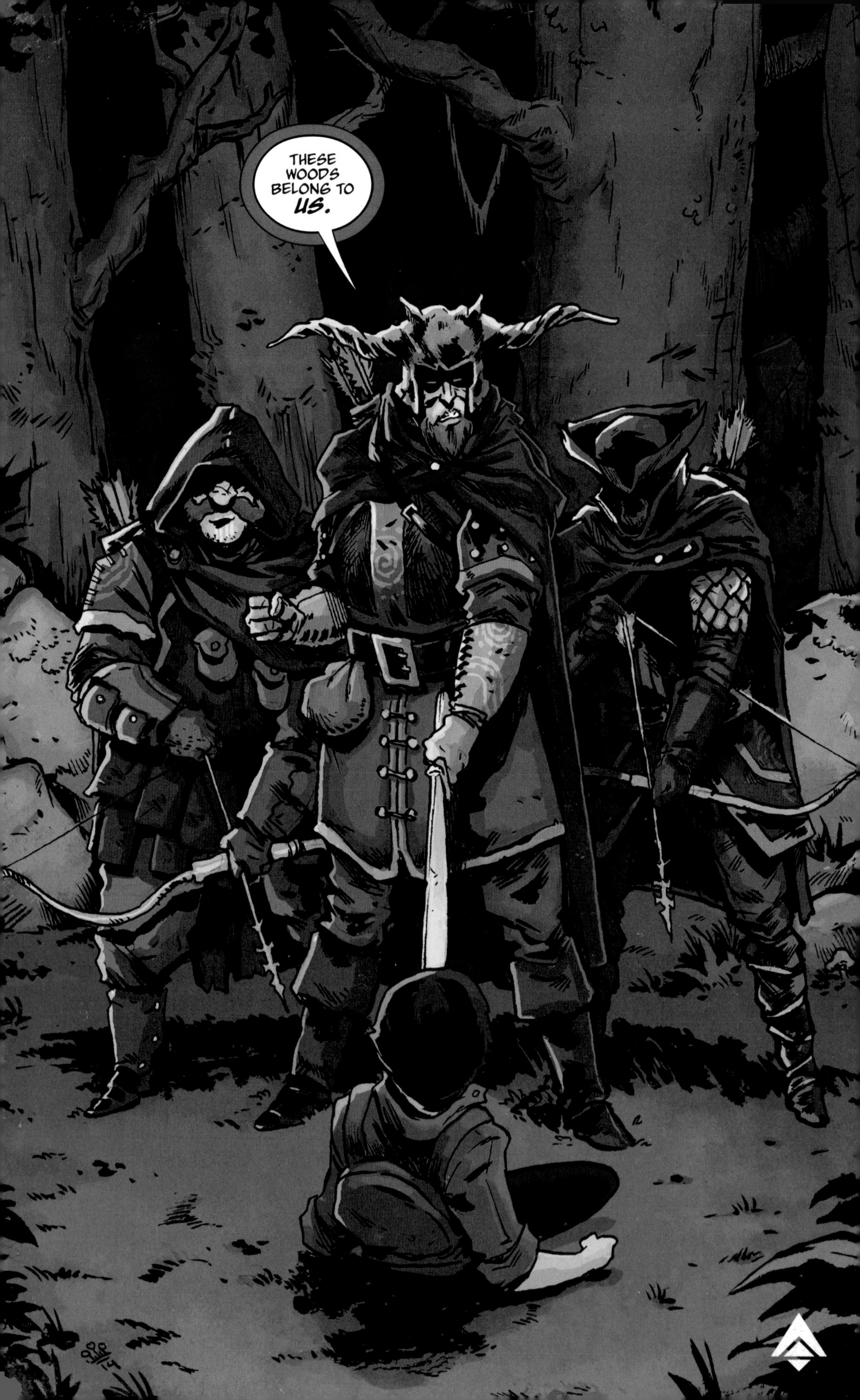
THESE WOODS BELONG TO US.

ISSUE FOUR COVER **RAMÓN K. PÉREZ**

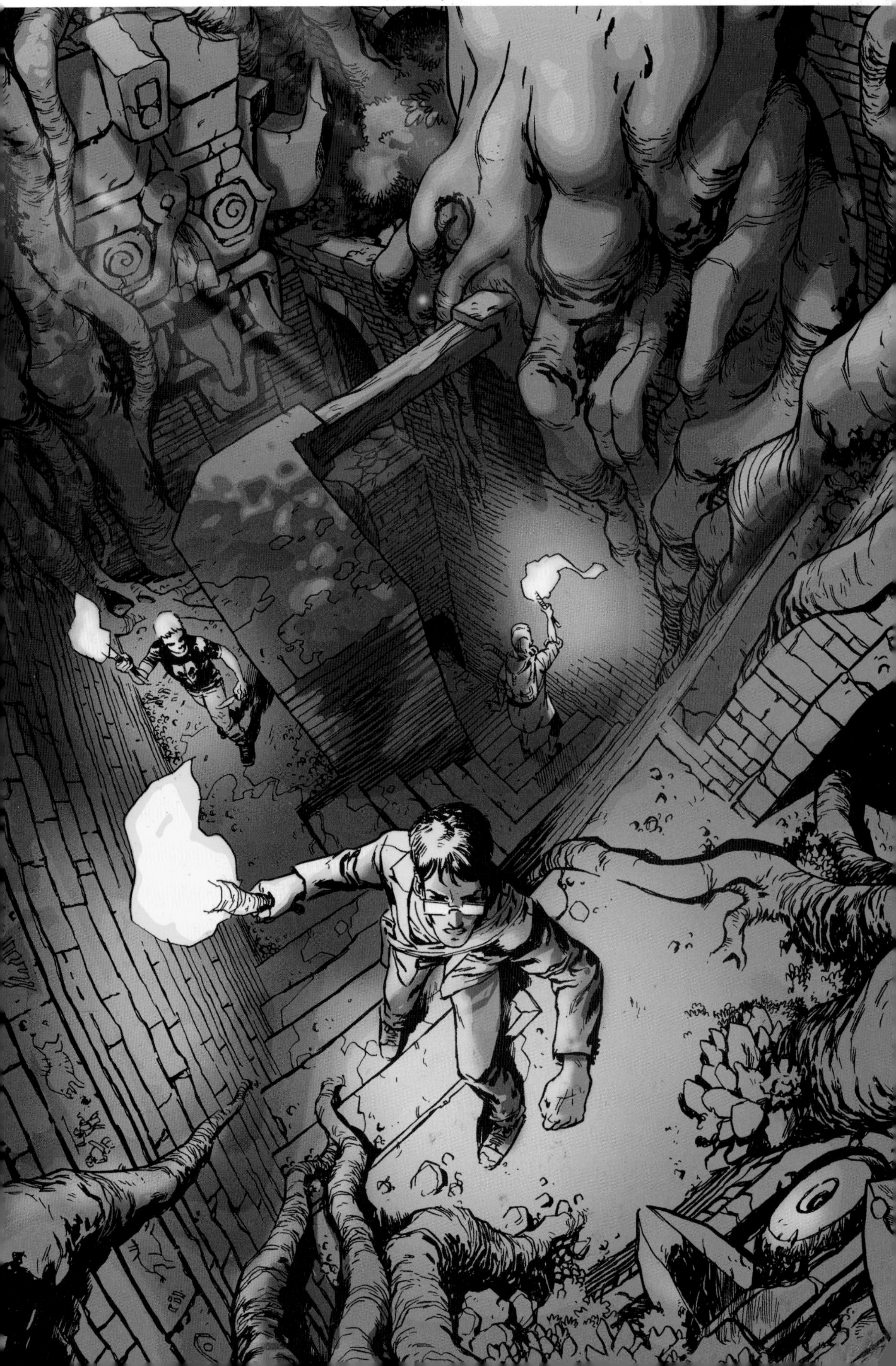

ISSUE ONE VARIANT COVER **MATTHEW WOODSON**

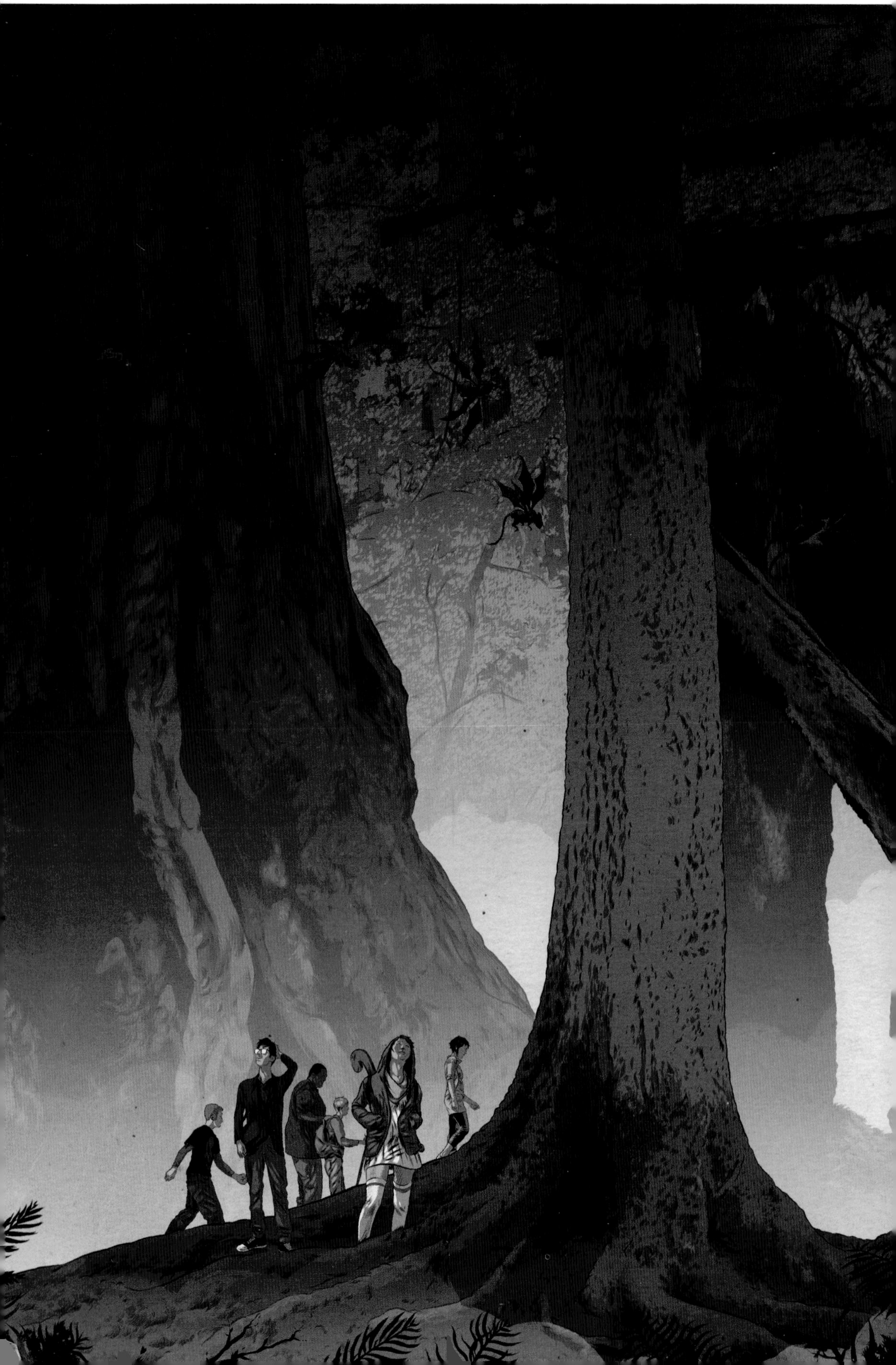

ISSUE ONE VARIANT COVER **PAUL DUFFIELD**

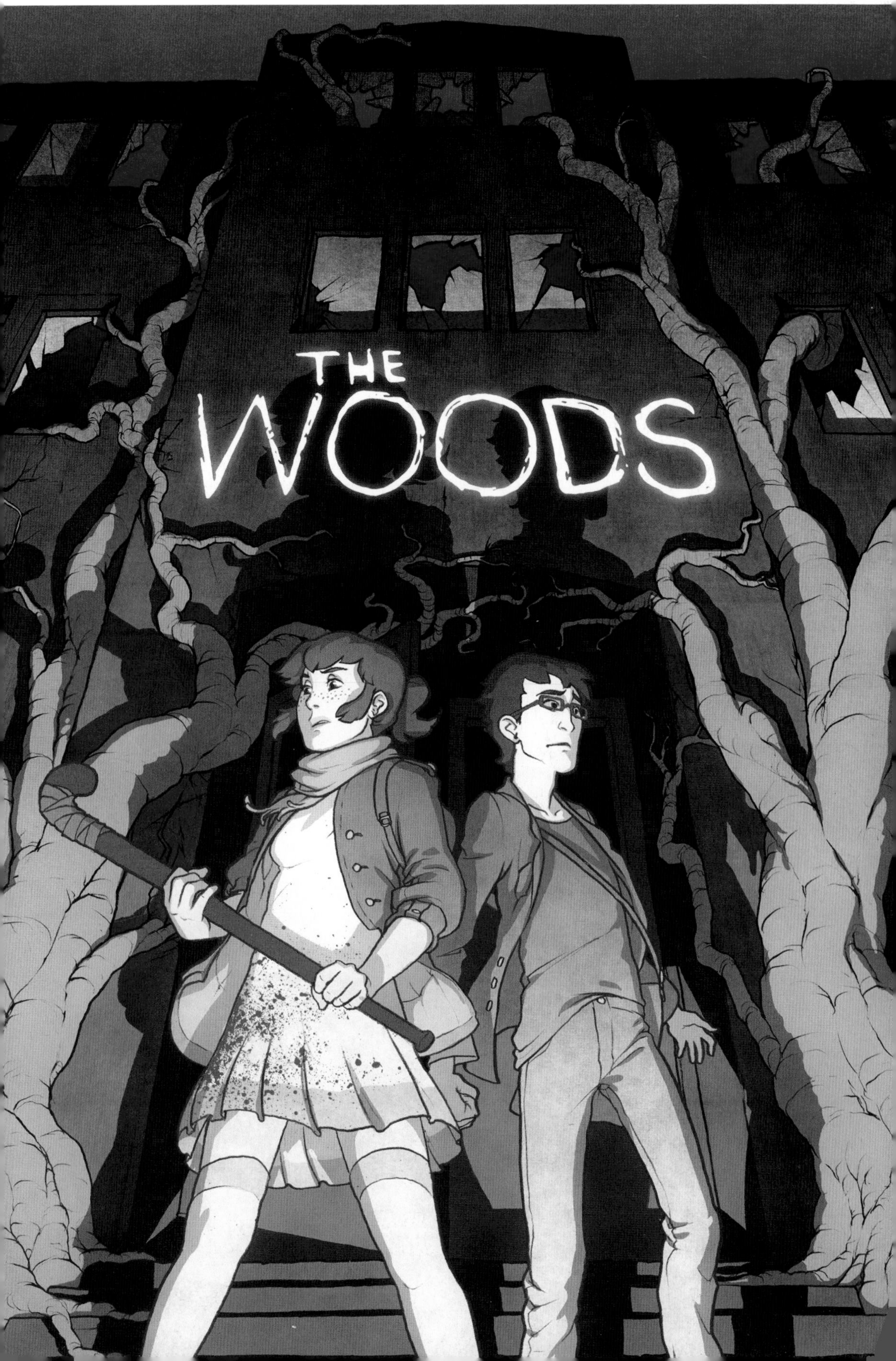
THE WOODS

ISSUE ONE C2E2 EXCLUSIVE COVER **TYLER JENKINS**

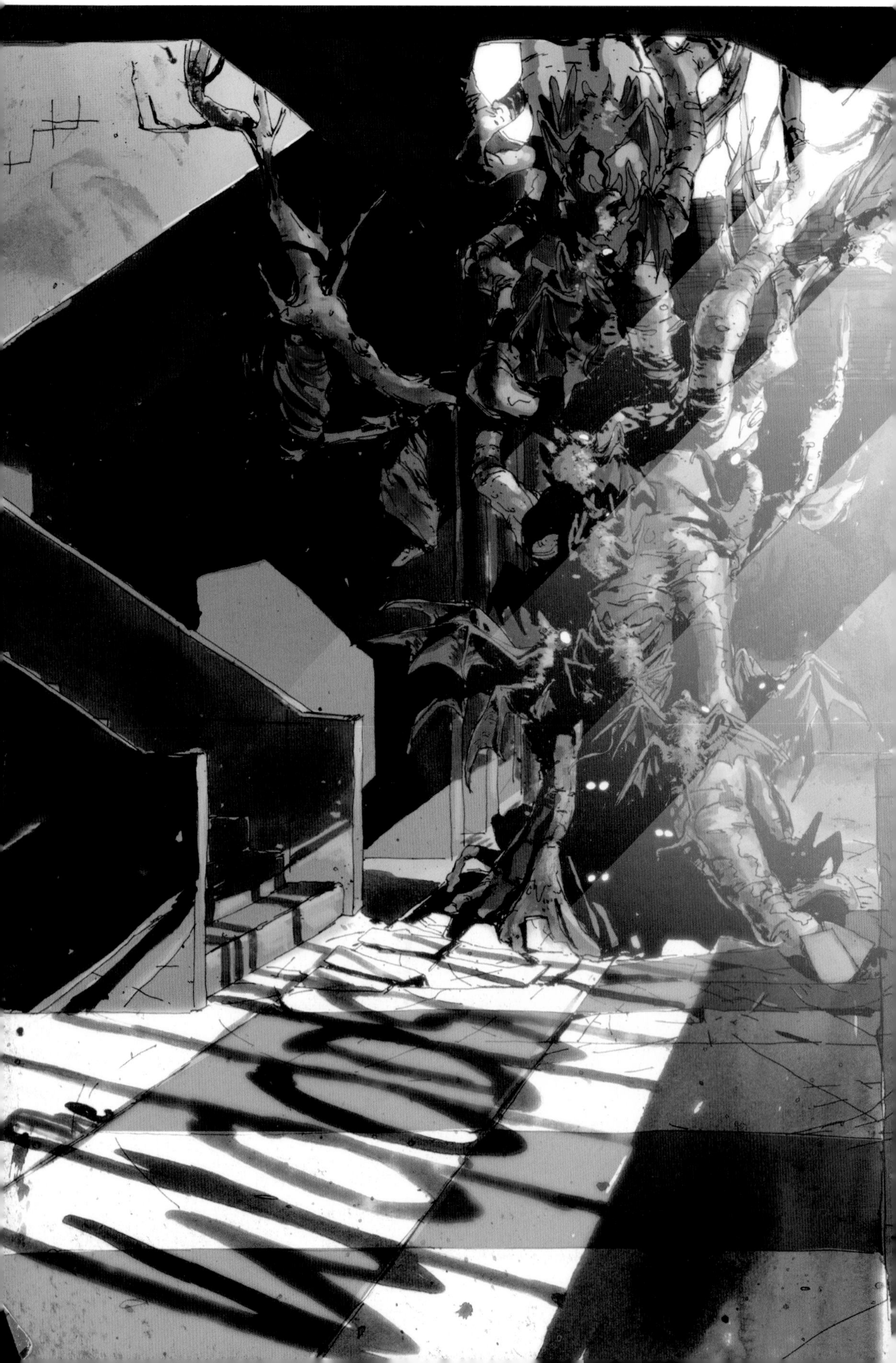

ISSUE ONE SDCC EXCLUSIVE COVER **JEFF STOKELY**

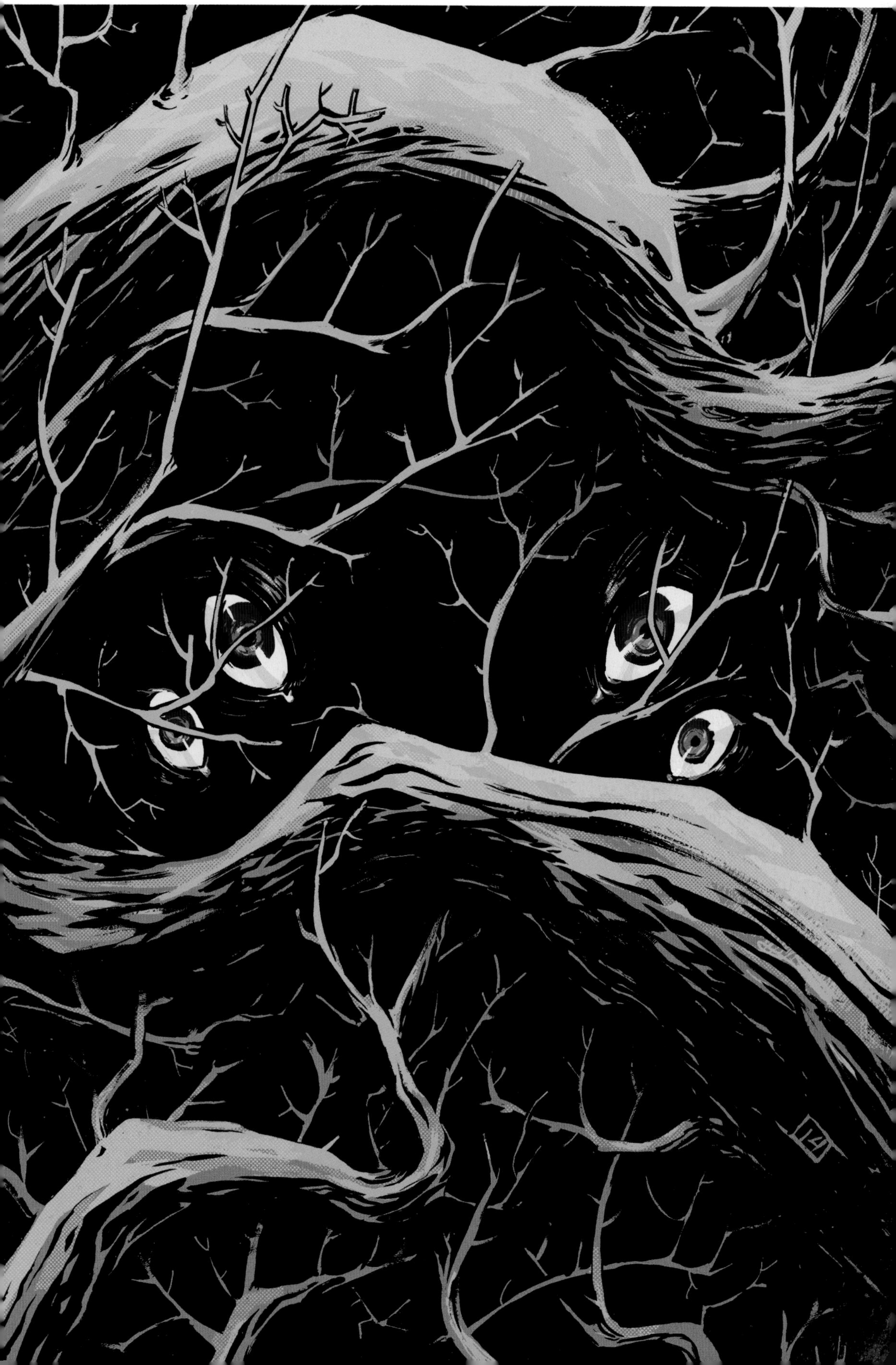

ISSUE ONE CARDS, COMICS & COLLECTIBLES EXCLUSIVE COVER **CRAIG ROUSSEAU**

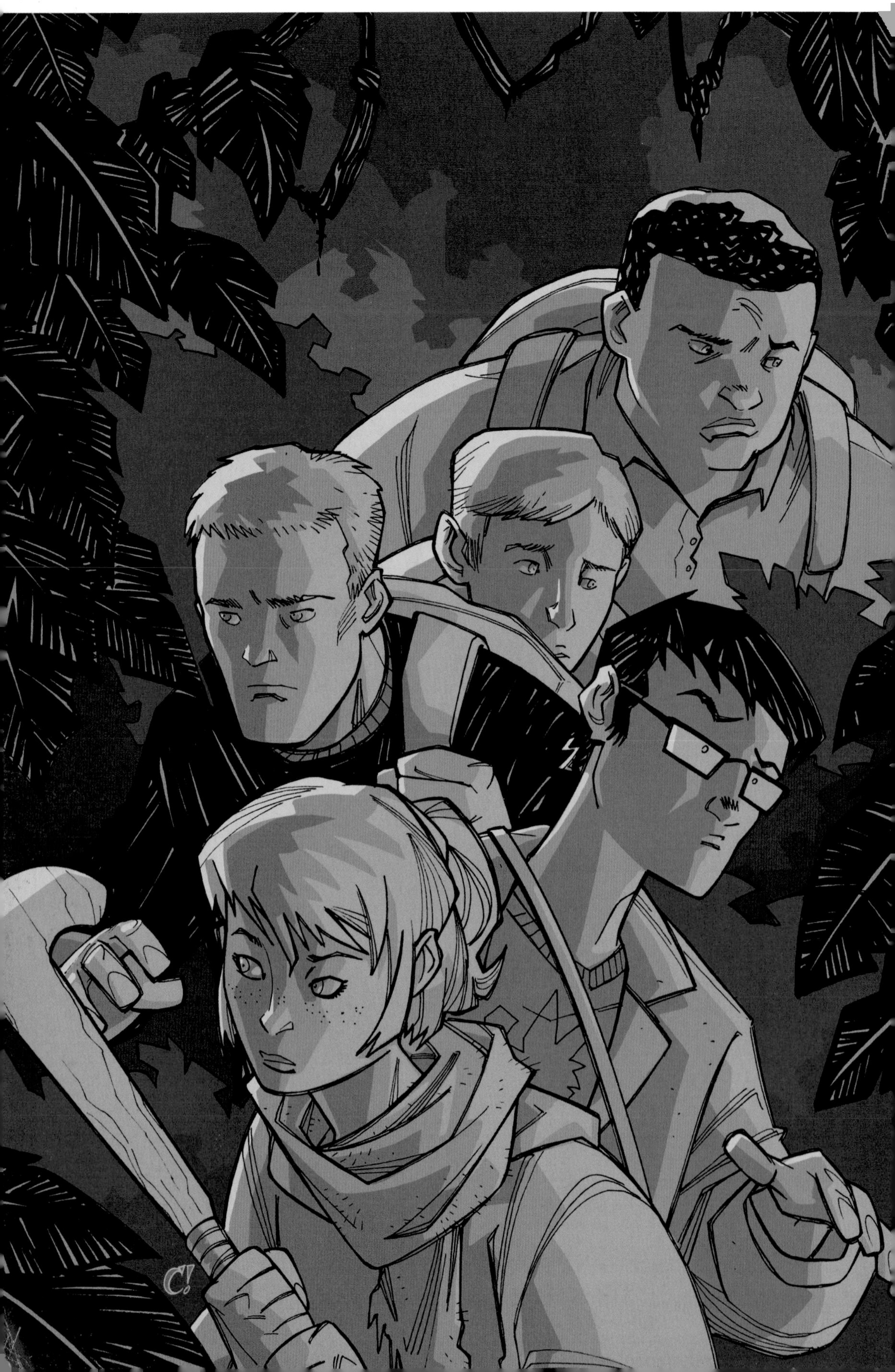

UNLOCKED RETAILER VARIANT COVER **JOE EISMA** WITH COLORS BY **CHRIS BLYTHE**

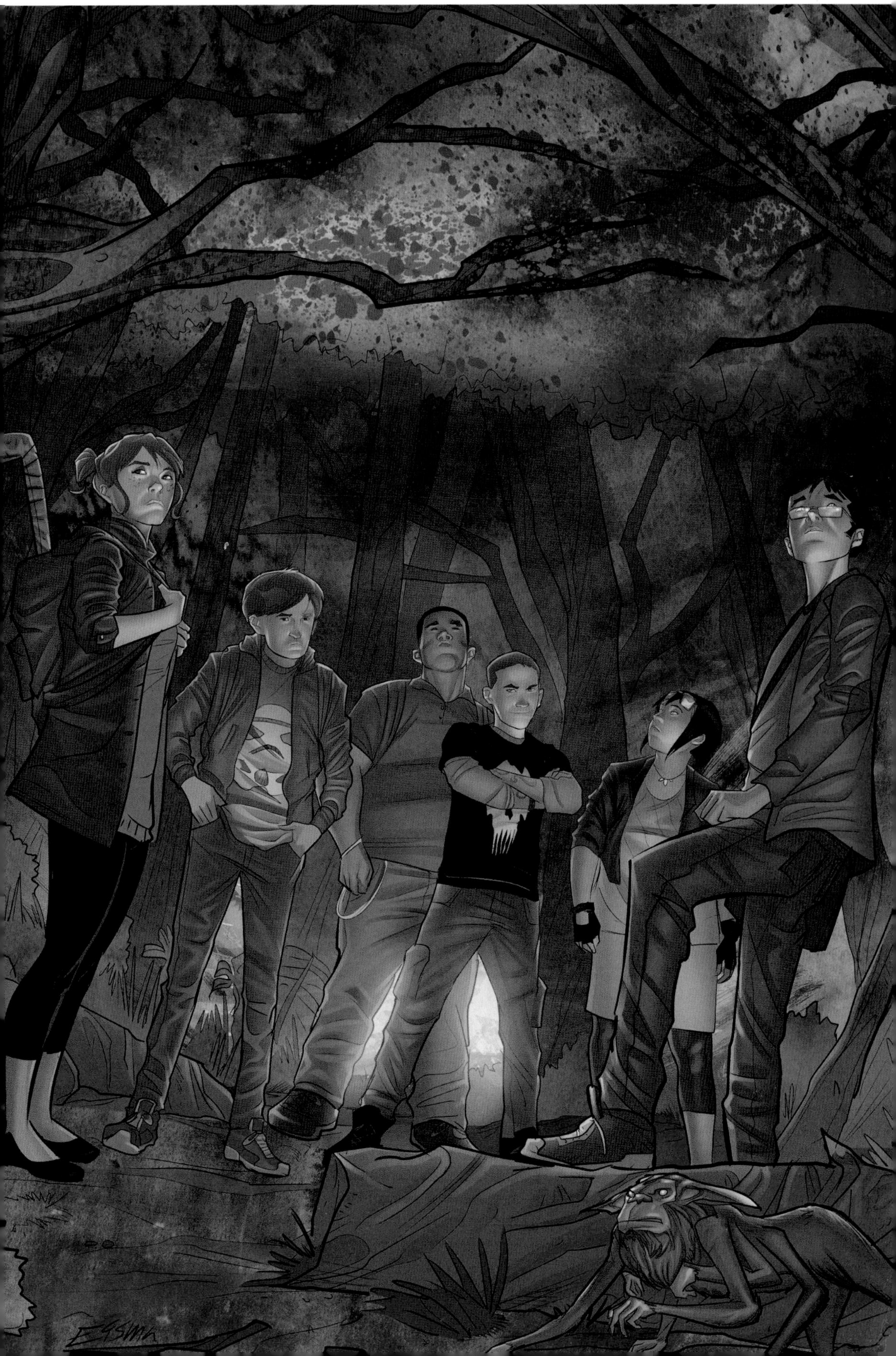

ISSUE TWO VARIANT COVER **MICHAEL DIALYNAS**

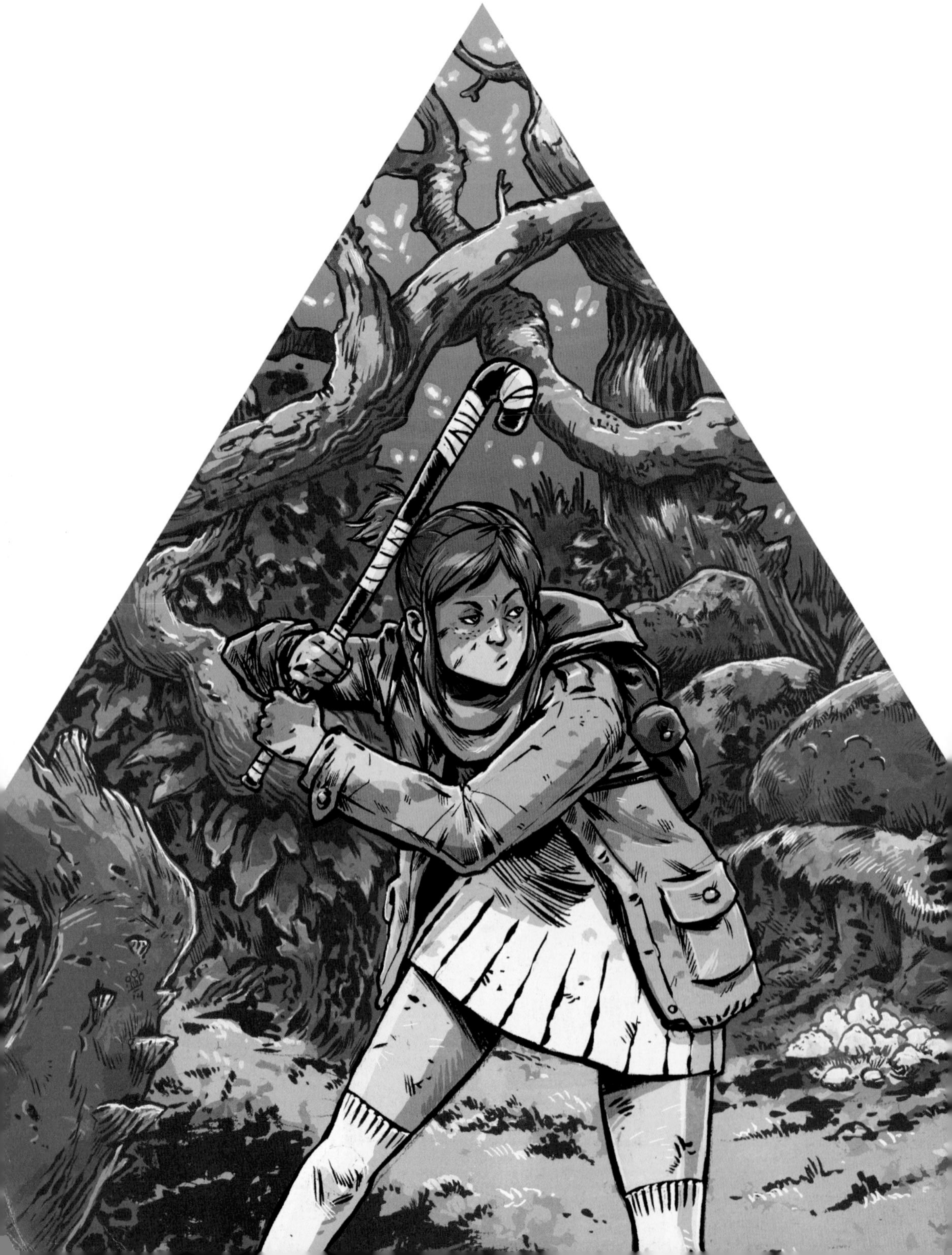

ISSUE THREE VARIANT COVER **MICHAEL DIALYNAS**

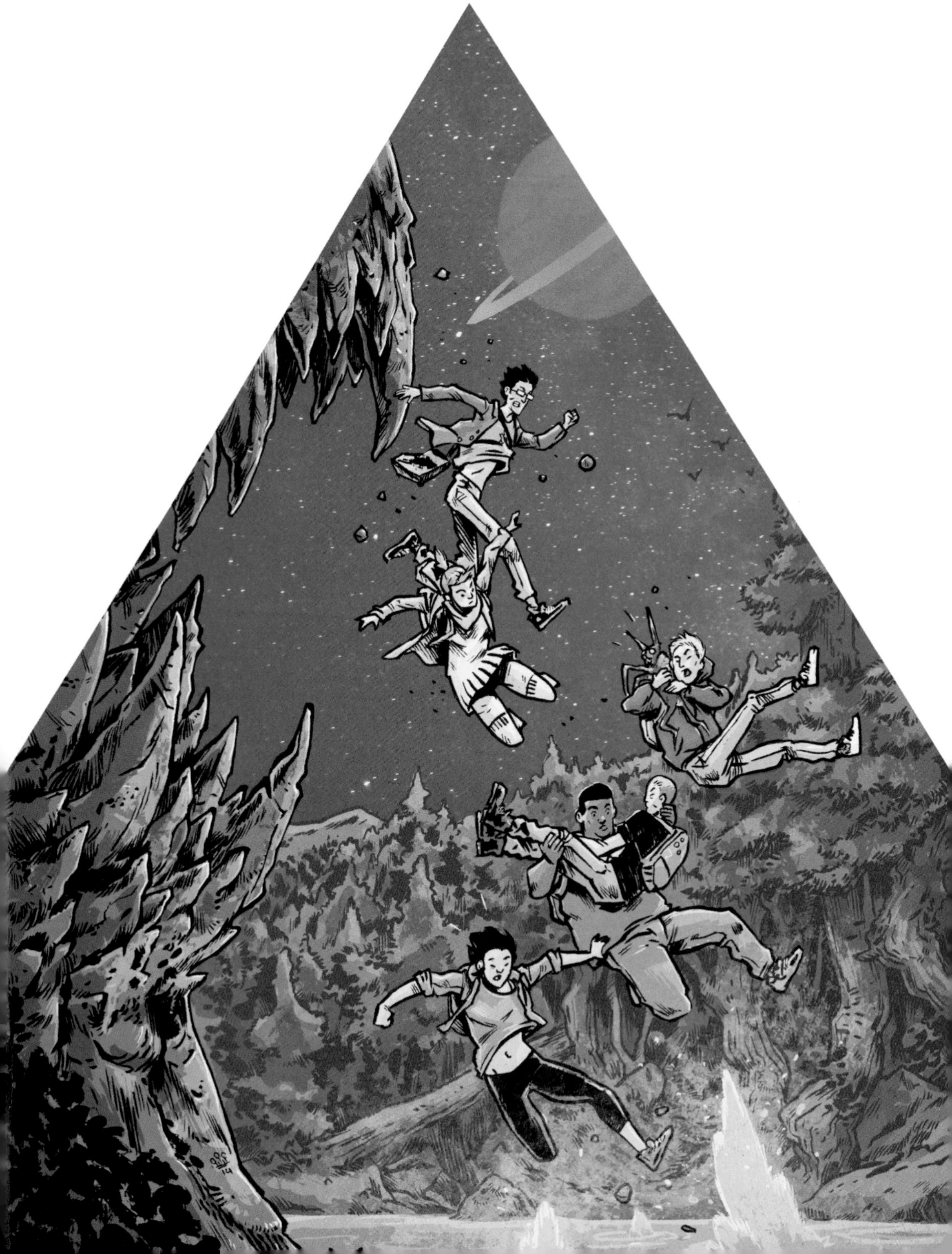

ISSUE FOUR VARIANT COVER **MICHAEL DIALYNAS**

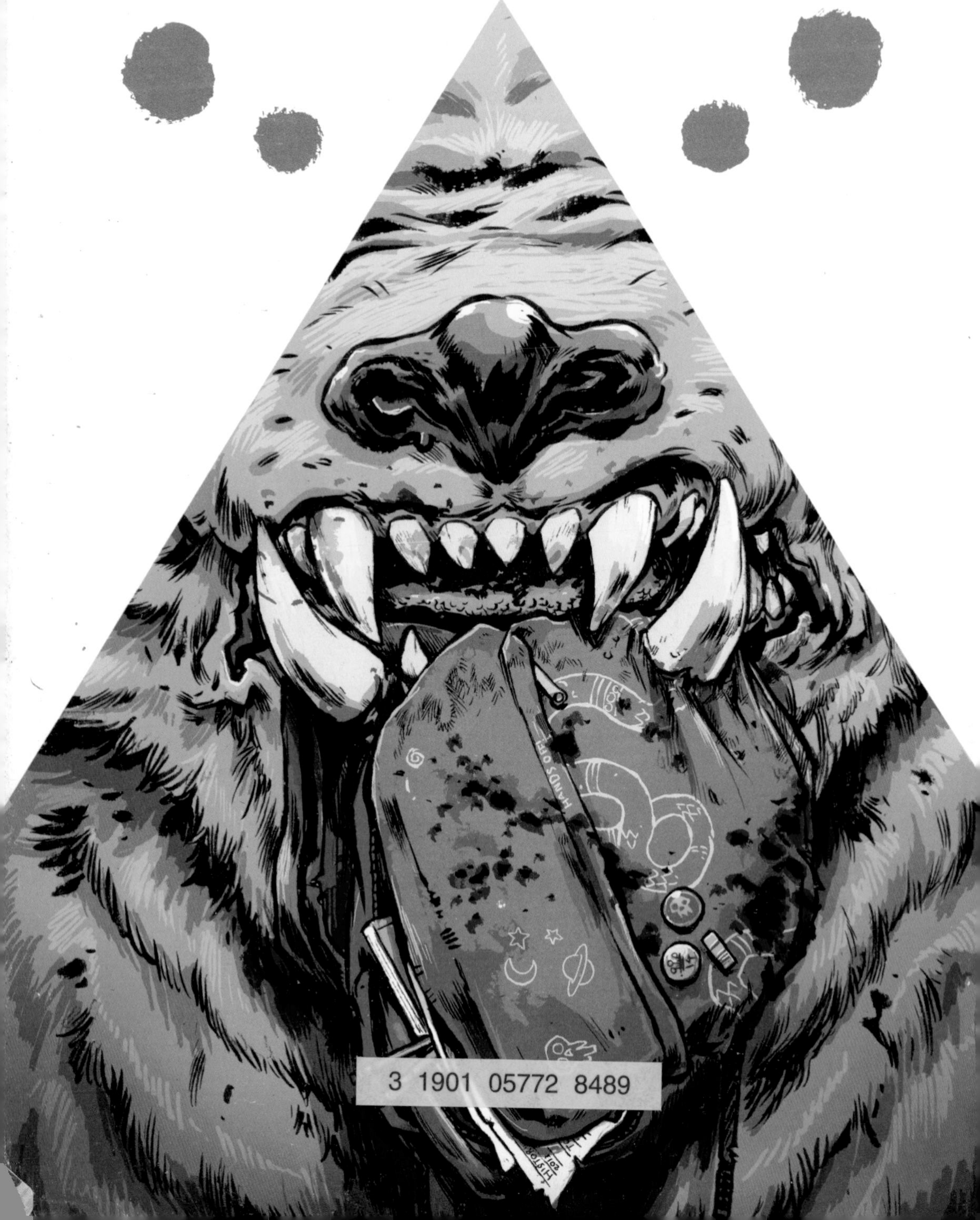
HANDS OFF